New Perspectives on Law, Culture, and Society
Robert W. Gordon and Margaret Jane Radin,
Series Editors

Failed Revolutions

Social Reform and the Limits of Legal Imagination

Richard Delgado
and Jean Stefancic

Westview Press

BOULDER • SAN FRANCISCO • OXFORD

New Perspectives on Law, Culture, and Society

Published in 1994 in the United States of America by Westview Press, Inc., 5500 Central Avenue, Boulder, Colorado 80301-2877, and in the United Kingdom by Westview Press, 36 Lonsdale Road, Summertown, Oxford OX2 7EW

Library of Congress Cataloging-in-Publication Data
Delgado, Richard.
    Failed revolutions : social reform and the limits of legal
imagination / Richard Delgado and Jean Stefancic.
        p.   cm. — (New perspectives on law, culture, and society)
    Includes bibliographical references and index.
    ISBN 0-8133-1806-8 (cloth) — ISBN 0-8133-1807-6 (pbk.)
    1. Social movements—United States.   2. Sociological
jurisprudence.   3. Law reform—Social aspects—United States.
4. Radicalism—United States.   I. Stefancic, Jean.   II. Title.
HN65.D37   1994
303.48'4—dc20   94-11403
                                                                                    CIP

Printed and bound in the United States of America

The paper used in this publication meets the requirements
of the American National Standard for Permanence of Paper
for Printed Library Materials Z39.48-1984.

10   9   8   7   6   5   4   3   2   1

This book is dedicated to the many gallant activists, lawyers and nonlawyers alike, who have struggled over the years against great odds to bring about a more just society.

Some men see things as they are and say, why;
I dream things that never were and say, why not.

—*Robert F. Kennedy*

Contents

Acknowledgments

This book grew out of continuing conversations between us and many others on social reform and law. For suggestions, critique, and encouragement we thank our colleagues Derrick Bell, Robert Berring, Harriet Cummings, John Denvir, Andrea Dworkin, David Getches, Robert Gordon, Laura Lederer, Catharine MacKinnon, Robert Nagel, Robert Post, john powell, George Priest, Margaret Radin, Pierre Schlag, Charles Wilkinson, and Sharon Zukin.

Though writing a book is a solitary venture, thinking, organizing, sifting, and discarding have a communal, or interactive, dimension. They cannot occur in a vacuum. We owe large debts to each of our colleagues and undoubtedly many others who enriched our thinking about law's role in social change. In particular, we presented parts of this book at conferences, workshops, and colloquia at the University of Chicago, Stanford, Vanderbilt, Washington and Lee, Cornell, University of Colorado, and University of San Francisco law schools and at Michigan State University, CUNY-Brooklyn College, Grinnell College, and the Villa Serbelloni. We are grateful to those in attendance for their comments and criticisms.

For research assistance we thank Charles Church, Devona Futch, Liz Griffin, Bonnie Grover, Alenka Han, Susan Raitt, Kelly Robinson, Erich Schwiesow, Karl Stith, and Patricia Templar. We also thank Marjorie Brunner, Kimberly Clay, Anne Guthrie, Cynthia Shafer, and Kay Wilkie for preparing many drafts expertly and with patience and unfailing good humor. We are grateful to the University of Colorado Law School and the University of San Francisco Law School for providing encouragement and material support. Special thanks go to our editor, Spencer Carr, for offering just the right balance of encouragement and critique.

The following journals graciously granted permission to adapt material that appeared in their reviews: *Cornell Law Review, Texas Law Review, Stanford Law Review, University of Pennsylvania Law Review, University of Colorado Law Review, Ohio State Law Journal, Vanderbilt Law Review,* and *William and Mary Law Review.*

And finally, we acknowledge with special gratitude the Rockefeller Foundation Bellagio Study and Conference Center for providing an idyllic setting for the completion of our project.

Richard Delgado
Jean Stefancic

Introduction

We want change—or so we tell ourselves. We are troubled when we see poverty and homelessness. We are disturbed when African-American despair continues, and even deepens, two decades after the civil rights revolution of the 1960s. The environmental crisis worsens every day. People of different backgrounds, speaking in accents that sound strange and foreign to our ears, crowd our sidewalks. The sights and smells of our cities oppress. Crime increases. Our national culture, the consensus that bound us together, seems to be coming apart.

We sense that we are in trouble. We have endless discussions on television, radio, and in the national press about the need for new policies for the cities, for the environment, for education, for redirecting military spending. We try to imagine what would be better. We create task forces and national commissions, and we propose legislation.

Yet these earnest and well-meaning efforts to change things have a way of going for naught. A court or governmental agency disappoints, fails to carry through. Expected allies steal away. Beneficiaries turn out to be less grateful, more difficult to work with. The problem proves more intractable than we had thought. Distracted perhaps by a new and even more pressing crisis, we turn our attention elsewhere, leaving a legacy of half-filled promises and empty programs in our wake.

How and why these things happen is the subject of this book. We write for the reader who wishes things were better—indeed, who may have given time or energy to that end—but is baffled by the slow pace of social change. We write for the reader who is troubled by our time's being one of particular stagnation, when most of the serious business of past reform movements seems to be at a standstill. We write for the reader who struggles to understand why momentum appears to be as often backward as forward—why most revolutions, in the words of our title, fail.

The two of us are, respectively, a law professor and a legal writer–information specialist. In our private lives, both of us have immersed ourselves in reform movements whose unfinished states we find deplorable and puzzling. Because our common area of expertise is the law, many of the examples that follow are drawn from that area. Yet we believe—fear, really—that our conclusions are generalizable, that many of the same limitations and blockages that impede legal actors afflict us all. (See, for example, Chapters 1, 6, and 7 dealing with the problems of social scientists or society at large in recognizing the need for change.)

Most books about reform treat its failures and shortcomings as instances of a defect of *will*. Typically the writer deplores the lack of success of a favorite movement and exhorts his or her audience to do better in the future. But as the reader of this book will see, many of our failures stem from defects of *imagination*. We fail to see far enough into the source of our predicament. Or, if someone points out its full dimensions to us, we fail to listen and hear. We overlook or interpret away evidence that reform is in order. Or we settle on the tamest version of it. Our book is about these and other barriers that limit the imaginations of legal scholars, judges, and society at large with respect to change. It is about the many means, most of them unconscious, by which we suppress, marginalize, and derail dissident voices calling for reform. It is about the array of preconceptions, meanings, and habits of mind that limit and frame the horizon of our possibilities.

Why does the marketplace of ideas fail to remedy deeply inscribed social ills like racism and sexism? How do judges, including our greatest jurists, continue to hand down decisions that a later time finds shocking and regressive? How do lawyers and legal scholars replicate and rehearse old arguments, seldom breaking free to new planes of legal thought and innovation? Why do maverick thinkers find themselves without a community, and how are outsiders marginalized, their voices tamed and silenced?

Why do ostensibly fair-minded social scientists and observers have difficulty seeing evidence for social reform? How do moderate saviors inhibit reform movements? How do objective rules and practices favor the more powerful? How does the very language the Supreme Court uses frustrate that institution's role as champion of the weak and powerless?

Each chapter that follows shares with the reader something we have learned by studying cases of failure. Each describes one or more mechanisms we deploy, sometimes unconsciously, to block our own well-intentioned efforts to transform ourselves and our world.

We believe that underlying most of these resistances are two quite natural responses. The first is fear of extinction, of change that is too far-reaching. This reaction causes us to approach the brink of a reform, then to pull back. We know that our individual selves are, to a great extent, continuous with and dependent on our social world. The prospect of that world's radical reform disconcerts. We think: If my world changed too dramatically, it might change me. I would be different; I could lose control over the small area I now control. Prediction would be difficult. Life would not be the same. The fear of reform is like the fear of destruction. The mind veers away, as it does at the thought of our own deaths.

This first impulse explains our ambivalence toward radical change—toward rethinking our relation to the natural world, for example, or eliminating most restraints on worker migration, as the European Community has done. A second reaction comes into play once we decide to move in a certain direction, for example toward school desegregation or air quality control. This we call the "once done" fallacy—the belief that a problem once addressed is solved, and that once solved is solved forever. What seriously committed environmentalist, for example, has not wondered about the short attention span of many of his or her fellow activists? What civil rights worker has not shaken his or her head over the way in which the American public seems to have placed the problems of minorities on the back burner?

These two failings are rooted in the human condition. Although we want change, we also fear it as an annihilation. And when we do get past this barrier, there are others—multiple demands on our time and attention—that cause us to abandon the projects we previously undertook with such hope and energy. Little wonder, then, that the pace of social reform is so halting and slow.

Although we hold no great faith that as a society we will be able to surmount the barriers we identify, the reader will find a few positive suggestions scattered throughout the chapters and summarized in the concluding section. Ultimately, only a change in consciousness—in the way we look upon self, risk, and reform—can enable us to begin tackling the many problems that beset us. That change will entail abandoning the engrained patterns and reactions that cause us to become mired in the first place. We are not optimistic that this will happen. Americans have been more successful at solving practical problems, such as settling the country's interior or building a system of railroads, than at embracing new ways of thinking about each other.

* * *

This book is organized as follows. We first lay out and describe internal mechanisms—processes of thought buried so deeply they are almost innate—that suppress the transformative impulse in ourselves and each other. We then deal with responses to reform now under way, including a variety of marginalizing devices that ensure that reformers are seen as partisan and extreme. Next, we describe what happens when their movements gather force. Often, a "savior" arises to place a revolution on a more moderate course. The role of such an agent is transformative and conservative at the same time.

If the proponents of change nevertheless persevere—undaunted by the host of mechanisms we describe—new mechanisms come into play. Powerful social institutions like the Supreme Court deploy rhetorical devices to marginalize and paint reformers as unreasonable or worse. This book, then, is organized temporally and psychologically, treating problems of imagination, then perception, then reception. Readers interested in pursuing a more traditional institutional analysis can easily locate the portions of the book relating to lawyers (Chapters 3 and 8), judges (2 and 9), the legal academy (4 and 5), and society at large (1, 6, and 7). Within each section, they will find treatment of problems of imagination, perception, and reception that afflict the group in relation to social change.

We do not flatter ourselves in presuming that merely identifying a barrier to change will cause it to give way. Indeed, our escape will often seem like little more than release from one intellectual prison to another, slightly larger, one. Yet, the advances we make may be nevertheless very real; they may be all our situations as positioned actors, limited by our own cultural and historical settings, permit. Knowing the causes of cultural and individual resistance can serve a second, more personal, function for reformers. It can equip them with the understanding necessary to persevere even when things look bleakest and victories are longest in coming. If we understand the many ways in which we inscribe and reinscribe power and hierarchy, we may perhaps avoid ensnarement by them in the future.

It is with these hopes in mind that we write this book.

Credits

Chapter 1: Adapted from "Images of the Outsider in American Law and Culture: Can Free Expression Remedy Systemic Social Ills?" 77 *Cornell Law Review* 1258 (1992). Copyright © 1992 by Cornell University. Reprinted by permission.

Chapter 2: Adapted from "Norms and Narratives: Can Judges Avoid Serious Moral Error?" 69 *Texas Law Review* 1929 (1991). Copyright © 1991 by the Texas Law Review Association. Reprinted by permission.

Chapter 3: Adapted from "Why Do We Tell the Same Stories? Law Reform, Critical Librarianship, and the Triple Helix Dilemma," 42 *Stanford Law Review* 207 (1989). Copyright © 1989 by the Board of Trustees of the Leland Stanford Junior University. Reprinted by permission.

Chapter 4: Adapted from "The Imperial Scholar Revisited: How to Marginalize Outsider Writing, Ten Years Later," 140 *University of Pennsylvania Law Review* 1349 (1992). Reprinted by permission.

Chapter 5: Adapted from "The Law Review Symposium Issue: Community of Meaning or Re-inscription of Hierarchy?" 63 *Colorado Law Review* 651 (1992). Reprinted by permission.

Chapter 6: Adapted from "Pornography and Harm to Women: 'No Empirical Evidence'?" 53 *Ohio State Law Journal* 1037 (1992). Reprinted by permission.

Chapter 7: Adapted from "Our Better Natures," 45 *Vanderbilt Law Review* 409 (1991). Copyright © 1991 by Vanderbilt Law Review. Reprinted by permission.

Chapter 8: Adapted from "Shadowboxing: An Essay on Power," 77 *Cornell Law Review* 813 (1992). Copyright © 1992 by Cornell University. Reprinted by permission.

Chapter 9: Adapted from "Scorn," *William and Mary Law Review*, forthcoming, and "Imposition," *William and Mary Law Review*, forthcoming. Reprinted by permission.

PART ONE

On the Difficulty of Imagining a Better Society

If we cannot envision a better world, our efforts to create one will obviously be hampered. Each of the three chapters that follow addresses a difficulty that we face in our imaginative capacities. The first chapter discusses a mechanism that our society relies on to counter error and facilitate reform: the marketplace of ideas. We point out that our vaunted system of free speech is much more effective in resolving small, clearly bounded controversies than in redressing deeply inscribed social ills such as racism and sexism. The second chapter focuses more narrowly on the judiciary. American society often counts on judges to promote, or at least not stand in the way of, social reform. Yet, even the greatest justice may hand down decisions so shocking that readers of a later age wonder how the judge could have written as he did. Drawing on the analysis laid out in the first chapter, we show how this is so. Chapter 3 focuses on the role of lawyers. Many attorneys begin their legal careers hoping to help the downtrodden and combat injustice. Yet the very categories of legal thought contained in widely used research and indexing systems cause the lawyer to rehearse familiar arguments and ask for limited, predictable forms of relief.

Judging, lawyering, and political debate all rely on words and categories. These, in turn, reflect our sense of the world, the way things are. They mirror social arrangements that work for us, enable us to function comfortably. Any new story, any new way of thinking about reality, can easily strike us as outlandish and wrong. It turns out that we are much less receptive to change than we like to think.

1

Images of the Outsider in American Law and Culture: Can Free Expression Remedy Deeply Inscribed Social Ills?

Free speech is said to be a prime instrument of social reform. Yet that faith—indeed conventional First Amendment doctrine generally—is beginning to show signs of strain. Outsider groups and women argue that free speech law inadequately protects them from certain types of harm.[1] Further, on a theoretical level, some scholars are questioning whether free expression can perform the lofty functions of community building and consensus formation that society assigns to it.[2]

We believe that in both situations the source of the difficulty is the same: failure to take account of the ways language and expression work. The results of this failure are more glaring in some areas than others. Much as Newtonian physics enabled us to explain many phenomena of daily life but required modification to address others on a larger scale, First Amendment theory will need revision to deal with issues at its furthest reaches. And just as the new physics ushered in notions of perspective and positionality, First Amendment thinking will need to incorporate these as well.

Conventional First Amendment doctrine is most helpful in connection with small, clearly bounded disputes. Free speech and debate can help resolve controversies such as whether a school disciplinary or local zoning policy is adequate, whether a new sales tax is likely to increase or decrease net revenues, or whether one candidate for political office is better than another. Speech is less able, however, to deal with systemic social ills, such as racism or sexism, that are widespread and deeply woven into the fabric of society. Free speech, in short, is least helpful where we need it most.

Several museums recently have featured displays of racial memorabilia.[3] These collections depict a shocking parade of Sambos, mammies, coons, uncles—bestial, happy-go-lucky, watermelon-eating African-Americans. They show advertising logos and household commodities in the shape of blacks with grotesquely exaggerated facial features. Other images depict primitive, terrifying, larger-than-life black men in threatening garb and postures, often with apparent designs on white women. In a similar vein, films depict minstrel shows and sequences of blacks so incompetent, shuffling, and dim-witted that it is hard to see how they survived to adulthood.

Seeing these haunting images today, one is tempted to ask, How could their creators—cartoonists, writers, filmmakers, and graphic designers (individuals, certainly, of higher-than-average education)—create such appalling images?[4] And why did no one protest? The collections mentioned feature African-Americans, but the two of us, motivated by curiosity, examined the history of ethnic depiction for each of the four main minority subgroups of color in the United States—Mexicans, African-Americans, Asian-Americans, and Native Americans. In each case we found the same sad story: Each group is depicted, in virtually every epoch, in terms that can only be described as demeaning or worse. In addition, we found striking parallels among the stigma-pictures that society disseminated of the four groups. The stock characters may have different names and appear at different times, but they bear remarkable likenesses and seem to serve similar purposes for the majority culture.

In this chapter, we will discuss these ethnic depictions and offer our answer to the "How could they" question. In brief, we hold that those who composed and disseminated these images simply did not see them as grotesque. Their consciences were clear; their blithe creations did not trouble them. It is only today, decades later, that these images strike us as indefensible and shocking. Our vaunted system of free expression, with its marketplace of ideas, cannot correct serious systemic ills such as racism or sexism *simply because we do not see them as such at the time*. No one can formulate an effective contemporaneous message to challenge the vicious depiction; this happens only much later, after consciousness shifts and society adopts a different narrative.[5] Our own era is no different.

We call the belief that we can somehow control our consciousness, despite limitations of time and positionality, the *empathic fallacy*.[6] In literature, the *pathetic fallacy* holds that nature is like us, that it is endowed with feelings, moods, and goals we can understand.[7] The poet, noticing that it is raining—and he is feeling sad—writes that the world weeps with him. The correlate of the pathetic fallacy, which we term the empathic fallacy, is the belief that we can enlarge our sympathies through linguistic means alone. By exposing ourselves to ennobling narratives, we tell ourselves, we can broaden our experience, deepen our empathy, and achieve new levels of sensitivity and fellow-feeling. We can, in short, think, talk, read, and write our way out of bigotry and narrow-mindedness, out of our limitations of experience and perspective. As we illustrate, however, we can do this only to a very limited extent.

Images of the Outsider

A small but excellent literature chronicles the depiction in popular culture of each of the major subgroups of color.[8]

African-Americans

Early in our history slave traders rounded up African villagers and transported them to the New World in chains. En route, many died; those who survived were sold and forced to work in the fields and houses of a colonial nation bent on economic development and expansion. By the eve of the Civil War, over 4 million African-Americans were condemned to live out an American nightmare.[9]

Slave codes regulated behavior, deterring rebellion and forbidding intermarriage. They also prohibited Southern blacks from learning to read and write,[10] thereby denying them access to a world of print replete with arguments about "the rights of man." The dominant image of a black in the popular theater and literature of the late eighteenth century was that of the docile and contented slave,[11] childlike, lazy, illiterate, and dependent on the protection and care of a white master. The first appearance of Sambo, a "comic Negro" stereotype, occurred in a 1781 play called *The Divorce*.[12] This black male character, portrayed by a white in blackface, danced, sang, and acted the buffoon. The black man's potential as a sexual and economic competitor was minimized by portraying him as an object of laughter.

Blackface minstrelsy found new popularity in the 1830s when Thomas D. Rice created Jim Crow, modeled on an elderly crippled black slave who shuffle-danced and sang.[13] It is thought that Rice even borrowed the old man's shabby clothes for a more authentic performance. Rice's *Jump Jim Crow* won him immediate success in the United States and England. By the 1840s minstrel shows were standard fare in American music halls.[14] In these shows, whites in blackface created and disseminated stereotypes of African-Americans as inept urban dandies or happy childlike slaves.[15] Probably more whites—at least in the North—received their understanding of African-American culture from minstrel shows than from firsthand acquaintance with blacks.

Because laws forbade slaves to learn to read or write, slave culture was primarily oral. Thus, it is highly significant that former slaves such as Frederick Douglass and William Wells Brown published accounts of captivity, life on plantations, and escapes to freedom.[16] These early slave narratives, published in the North and circulated among abolitionist societies, presented counterimages to the prevailing myths. The abolitionist movement reached its apogee with the publication of Harriet Beecher Stowe's *Uncle Tom's Cabin*. Though Stowe was successful in presenting the slavemaster as villain, her portrayal of Uncle Tom changed the stereotype of the black slave very little. Previously he had been docile, content, or comic, while in her depiction he became a gentle, long-suffering figure imbued with Christian piety.[17]

After the Civil War, the black image bifurcated. The "good slave" image continued, but it was soon joined by an ominous "shadow" figure. Uncle Tom became romanticized, a black mouthpiece espousing an apologia for the beliefs of the old genteel white Confederacy.[18] Though never overtly sexual, his masculine form reemerged as the avuncular storyteller Uncle Remus, as well as various other uncles.[19] His feminine form evolved into a mammy figure—cook, washerwoman, nanny, and all-around domestic servant—responsible for the comfort of the Southern white household.[20] A fount of practical wisdom with no life of her own, she took an intense interest in the welfare and well-being of the white family she cared for.

During this tumultuous Reconstruction period, the sexuality denied to uncles and mammies found a crude outlet in a new stereotype of the recently freed male Negro as primitive and bestial.[21] The Ku Klux Klan and other raiding parties justified their reign of terror as necessary to control newly freed blacks whom they believed ready to force sex on any white woman they might encounter.[22] This stereotype, appearing in novels with titles like *The Negro as Beast*, was offered to justify the widespread lynching that took 2,500 black lives between 1885 and 1900.[23]

The myth of the unbridled black was given further currency by developments in Western thought and culture during the late nineteenth century: (1) the growth of American imperialism; (2) concerns over absorption of "inferior races"; (3) the white man's burden mentality—the white South bearing the burden in the United States; (4) the manifest destiny belief of the Anglo-Saxons; and (5) the new social science theory concerning genetic inferiority.[24]

Many of these ideas found expression in the powerful, crass, and influential writings of Thomas Dixon. His work represented an effort to satisfy his two goals in life: making money and converting people to his racist beliefs. He believed that whites, both Northern and Southern, were duty bound to protect the Anglo-Saxon heritage, particularly white women who were destined to produce a superior race.[25] In 1905, Dixon wrote *The Clansman*, a tale of two families, one Northern and one Southern, united through marriage.[26] It proved a sensation, particularly in the South. Ten years later, filmmaker D. W. Griffith used the plots of this and another Dixon novel[27] for his epic three-hour film, *The Birth of a Nation*.

The film transformed Dixon's novels into vivid visual images, featuring uncles, mammies, buffoons, an interfering mulatto mistress, and a chase scene in which a black man with animal-like traits pursues a young white woman until she leaps to her death from a pedestal-like perch at the edge of a cliff. The film played to audiences throughout the country. Recent white immigrants from eastern and southern Europe saw the film in movie houses in northern urban centers, where it played for almost a year. In the South it played for fifteen years. A special screening was held at the White House for Dixon's former classmate, President Woodrow Wilson; his guests; and the entire Supreme Court. Wilson later described the film as "like writing history with lightning."[28]

Blacks could do little to confront the film's overwhelming popularity. The National Association for the Advancement of Colored People (NAACP) spoke out against it, but its momentum was unstoppable. Though decrying the film's racism, film critics, many of them liberal, praised its technical and artistic merits.[29]

In contrast, efforts to present the story of Reconstruction from a black point of view were unsuccessful. Novelist Albion Tourgee, a white superior court judge and activist, used black characters who spoke in their own voices to show the freed man as a person who worked hard and attempted to succeed but was victimized by the Ku Klux Klan.[30] Tourgee believed the answer to racism lay in portraying blacks as normal, like everyone else. His novel *Bricks Without Straw* attracted a devoted but small audience; the South's treatment of blacks no longer interested many Northerners, and few Southerners were willing to listen. Black writers suffered a similar fate. Charles Chesnutt, author of *The Conjure Woman*, was included in a list of the foremost storytellers of the time, yet his publisher refused to release his next novel because the previous two about racial themes had sold poorly.[31] As two writers pointed out, "[M]essages only reach those people who are willing to listen. Only when a later audience became receptive ... could [their] tales be ... appreciated."[32]

Although blacks had gained formal legal equality, in 1896 the Supreme Court upheld segregation in *Plessy v. Ferguson*.[33] Lynchings continued; racist stereotypes prevailed. Blacks had little access to the press or the film industry and could do little to change the racism that both industries promulgated. Nevertheless, blacks joined the army in droves during World War I. Segregation in the ranks was rigidly enforced and many blacks returned angry and disheartened. After the war, unrest in the country led to at least twenty-five urban race riots,[34] many in the previously peaceful North.[35] Repressive images immediately increased and prevailed for a little over a decade.

As the disruption abated a few writers, such as Eugene O'Neill and Sinclair Lewis, portrayed blacks and their plight sympathetically. Black writers and artists in New York created the Harlem Renaissance.[36] Blacks' image metamorphosed yet again. Whites, excited and enthusiastic over this new artistic rapprochement with blacks, quickly praised them and their work for elements of the exoticism and primitivism popularized by Paul Gauguin in his South Pacific art. Echoing early images, white society began to regard African-Americans as musically talented, rhythmical, passionate, and entertaining.[37] Although these new characterizations were somewhat more positive, they nevertheless retained elements of condescension.[38] The majority-race critics, intellectuals, and artists who were entranced by the Renaissance may have intended no harm, yet they perpetuated views of African-Americans as the exotic other.[39]

When the United States entered World War II, black soldiers and workers were needed for the war effort; the more virulent forms of racism were held in abeyance.[40] However, when the war ended and the soldiers returned, racial hostilities again sharpened. Having experienced a somewhat less racist environment during the war, black soldiers and workers were not prepared to return to lives of menial work and subservience to whites. For many, expectations of improvement were fed by war propaganda that depicted the United States as fighting for freedom.[41] Activism sprang up; the Civil Rights movement began, and once again the dominant image of blacks took on new forms: the cocky, street-smart black who knows his rights; the opportunistic community leader and militant; the safe, comforting, cardigan-wearing black of TV sitcoms; and the Black Bomber of superstud films, all mutations of, and permutations of, old familiar forms.[42]

Native Americans

The experience of other groups parallels that of blacks. When the colonists arrived in Virginia and Massachusetts in the seventeenth century, they brought with them images of the Indian created in England and Europe. Early explorers described native peoples of the new world as innocent, ingenuous, friendly, and naked.[43] At first, relations between the two groups were cordial. Later, however, more settlers arrived, bringing with them English concepts of property—land transfer, titles, deeds—that were foreign to Indian thought. Indians who did not cooperate with the settlers' plans were forced off their lands. Eventually hostilities broke out,[44] resulting in a conflict that lasted for more than two centuries.

Early writings about Native Americans reflected two romanticized images: the Indian princess, incarnated most notably in Pocahontas;[45] and the man Friday[46] found in *Robinson Crusoe*, the troublesome servant Caliban,[47] the faithful and loyal Chingachgook,[48] and in the twentieth century the buffoon and sidekick Tonto.[49] The first instance of the "captivity narrative" appeared in Massachusetts in 1682 with Mary Rowlandson's *Captivity and Restoration*.[50] Early fiction portrayed Indians as looters, burners, and killers, but not rapists[51]—New Englanders knew that Indians rarely committed rape.[52] But the erotic elements of Rowlandson's story, although mild and subordinated to her religious message,[53] made it the prototype for later captivity tales that emphasized sexual aggression directed toward Simon-pure captives.[54]

Other writers followed suit, but without Rowlandson's delicacy, portraying Indians as animal-like and subhuman,[55] a characterization whose roots go back to Paracelsus (1493–1541), who proposed that Indians were not among the sons of Adam.[56] Shakespeare explored this theme when he wrote *The Tempest* and created a servant for Prospero—Caliban—whose name was an anagram of the newly coined word "cannibal."[57] Cotton Mather and other Puritan writers called Indians wolves, lions, sorcerers, and demons possessed by Satan.[58] By the nineteenth century, Indians had become savage, barbarous, and half-civilized.[59] In early movies restless natives and jungle beasts were practically interchangeable elements.[60] No wonder, then, that Indians, with little protest from the dominant society, were removed to reservations, just as wild and rare beasts were confined to animal preserves.

Later movies of the "cowboys and Indians" genre built on these images when they featured war dances, exotic dress, drunkenness, surprise attacks, scalping, raiding, raping, tomahawks, tom-toms, and torture.[61] D. W. Griffith, creator of *The Birth of a Nation*, incorporated these elements and more in *The Battle of Elderbush Gulch* (1913). In the movie, a white woman, trapped in a cabin surrounded by Indians, awaits her fate, not knowing whether the Indian attackers will kill her or whether one of her white defenders will shoot her before letting the Indians take her alive.[62] By 1911, portrayal of Indians in film had become so demeaning that representatives of four western tribes protested to President William Howard Taft and to Congress.[63] But little change occurred until World War II, when Hollywood transferred the enemy role to the Japanese and Germans. Many of the early Indian movies are still shown on television, feeding the psyches of new generations of children with the familiar stereotypes.[64]

Shortly after the end of the war, Hollywood released *Broken Arrow* (1950), the first movie ever to feature an Indian, Cochise of the Apaches, as hero. Though artistically and historically flawed, it was widely praised. Other "noble savage" films changed the stereotype, but in the opposite direction, portraying Native Americans with exaggerated nobleness[65]—a striking parallel to the adulating treatment whites gave black writers during the Harlem Renaissance.

In 1969, N. Scott Momaday, a Kiowa-Cherokee writer, won the Pulitzer Prize for his novel *House Made of Dawn*. In 1972, PBS aired a BBC production of *The Last of the Mohicans*.[66] In each of these works, the audience was struck by the intelligence of the Native American voice—a far cry from the earlier steady diet (still heard today) of chiefs saying "ugh," braves shrieking war whoops, and Tonto saying "me gettum." However, in earlier times, some whites appreciated Indian diction: Thomas Jefferson wished Congress could speak half as well as orators of Indian nations.[67] William Penn praised the Lenni Lenape language of the Delaware for its subtlety.[68] Yet, speech of the Indians—as well as that of African-Americans, Mexican-Americans, and Asian-Americans—has been mangled, blunted, and rendered inarticulate by whites who then became entitled to speak for them. Like the other groups of color, Native Americans have been disempowered by the very element that, they are told, will save them.[69]

Asian-Americans

With Asian-Americans, we find the same pattern: The dominant depiction in popular culture is negative (although rarely seen as such at the time), *and* the stereotype shifts to accommodate society's changing needs.

In the middle of the nineteenth century, Chinese were welcomed to the United States for their labor: They were needed to operate mines, build railroads, and carry out other physical tasks necessary to the country's development.[70] However, the industrious immigrants soon began to surpass white American workers. They opened small businesses and succeeded in making profitable the mines that others had abandoned.[71] Not surprisingly, Chinese became scapegoats for the 1870s depression. Unionists and writers exaggerated negative traits associated with them—opium smoking, gambling—and succeeded in having anti-Chinese legislation enacted.[72] By 1882 public sentiment had been mobilized sufficiently so that Congress was able to pass the Chinese Exclusion Act, which reduced the number of Chinese in the United States from 105,000 in 1880 to 65,000 in 1908.[73]

During this period, Japan's international position was on the rise, yet U.S. writers and politicians depicted all Asians as inferior, unassimilable, willing to work inhuman hours at low wages, and loyal to foreign despots.[74] When Japan defeated China and then Russia, it began to replace China as the "yellow peril."[75] By 1924, all Asians were barred, an exclusion the Supreme Court had upheld for the Chinese in 1889.[76] During a period of increasing tensions between the two countries, the film industry portrayed Japanese and other Asians—during this period few distinctions were made—in unremittingly negative terms. As with African-Americans and Native Americans, Asian men were depicted as cunning, savage, and as potential rapists interested in defiling white women.[77] (In sharp contrast, white male actors were seen as having legitimate access to Asian women.)

As militancy grew, films began to appear that devalued Asian life.[78] *They* didn't value life, the narratives of the day said. Why should we value theirs? During earlier periods, when racism against Asians was relatively quiescent, writers and filmmakers employed the stock character of the Charlie Chan[79]—the hapless, pidgin-talking Asian, in many respects the functional equivalent of the Sambo or uncle. But as anti-Japanese sentiment increased, movies began depicting even domestic Asians as devious and untrustworthy.[80] Anti-Asian films were profitable; Hollywood would often assign a Japanese actor to play a Chinese villain and vice versa.[81]

Continuing this pattern, W. R. Hearst sponsored *Patria,* an anti-Asian film serial that first appeared in 1919 and continued for several years; it depicted Asians as a yellow menace. At one point, Woodrow Wilson became disturbed by the virulence of Hearst's production and wrote a letter asking him to soften it. Hearst responded by changing the series so that it became dominantly anti-Mexican.[82] In the period immediately preceding and during World War II, anti-Japanese images continued to proliferate.[83] A stock character was the master Oriental criminal, often played by Anglo actors in makeup.[84] By this time, films and novels were distinguishing between Chinese (who were good) and Japanese (who were bad).[85] After Pearl Harbor, intense anti-Japanese propaganda resulted in federal action to intern 110,000 Japanese-Americans, many of whom had lived in the United States all their lives.[86] Many lost farms, houses, and other property.[87] It later came to light that much of the evidence of sabotage and fifth column activities had been fabricated.[88]

Following World War II, depictions of blacks and Indians were upgraded to some extent, but those of Asians only a little. Many of James Bond's villains, for example, have been Asian. In recent days, Japan has once again become a serious economic rival of the United States, producing automobiles, computers, and other products at a price and quality American industry has proven unable to match. Predictably, a further wave of anti-Asian sentiment and stereotyping has reemerged.[89]

Mexican-Americans

Images of Mexican-Americans ("Chicanos") fall into three or four well-delineated stereotypes which change according to society's needs: the greaser, the conniving and treacherous *bandido,* the happy-go-lucky and

shiftless lover of song, food, and dance, and the tragic, silent "Spanish"—
the tall, dark, and handsome type found in romantic fiction.[90] As they do
with blacks, Asians, and Indians, most Americans have relatively few in-
terpersonal contacts with Mexican-Americans; therefore, these images become the individual's only reality. And when such contact actually takes
place, the average person tends to place the Mexican-American in one of
the ready-made categories. Stereotyping thus denies members of both
groups the opportunity to interact with each other on anything like a complex, nuanced, human level.[91]

During and just after the conquest, when the United States was seizing,
then settling, large tracts of Mexican territory in the Southwest, Western
fiction depicted Anglos bravely displacing shifty, brutal, treacherous Mexicans.[92] After the war with Mexico (1846–1848) ended and control of the
Southwest passed to American hands, a subtle shift occurred. Anglos living and settling in the new regions were portrayed as independent, thrifty,
industrious, mechanically resourceful, and interested in progress; Mexicans, as traditional, sedate, and lacking in mechanical resourcefulness and
ambition.[93] Writers both on and off the scene created the same images of
indolent, pious Mexicans—ignoring the enterprising farmers and ranch-
ers who, for two centuries, withstood or negotiated with Apaches and Co-
manches and built a sturdy society with irrigation, land tenure, and mining codes.[94]

In the late conquest period, depiction of this group bifurcated. As happened during a different period with African-Americans, majority-race
writers created two images of the Mexican: the "good" (loyal) Mexican
peon or sidekick, and the "bad" fighter-greaser Mexican who did not
know his place. The first was faithful and domestic; the second, treacherous and evil. As with other groups, the second image had sexual overtones: The greaser coveted Anglo women and would seduce or rape them
if given the opportunity.[95] Children's books of this time, like the best-sell-
ing Buffalo Bill series, were full of Mexican stereotypes used to reinforce
moral messages to the young: *They* are like this, *we* like that.[96] The series
ended in 1912.

The first thirty years of this century saw heavy immigration of mainly
poor Mexican workers. The first Bracero programs (official temporary im-
portation of field hands) appeared.[97] Increasing numbers of whites-only
signs and segregated housing and schools appeared, aimed now at Mexicans in addition to blacks.[98] Since there now was an increased risk of interaction and intermarriage, novels and newspapers reinforced the notion of
the immigrants' baseness, simplicity, and inability to assimilate.[99]

The movies of this period depicted Latins as buffoons, sluts, and con-
nivers;[100] even some of the titles were disparaging: for example, *The Greaser's Gauntlet*.[101] Films featured brown-skinned desperadoes stealing

horses or gold, lusting after pure Anglo women, and shooting noble Saxon heroes in the back.[102] Animated cartoons and short subjects, still shown on television, featured tequila-drinking Mexicans, bullfighters, Speedy Gonzalez and Slowpoke Rodriguez, and clowns—as well as light-skinned, upper-class Castilian caballeras, wearing elaborate dresses and carrying castanets.[103]

World War II brought a need for factory and agricultural workers and a new flood of immigrants.[104] Images softened to include "normal," or even noble, Mexicans, like the general of Marlon Brando's *Viva Zapata*. Perhaps realizing it had overstepped, Hollywood diminished the virulence of its anti-Mexican imagery. Yet the Western genre, with Mexican villains and bandits, continues; the immigrant speaking gibberish still makes an appearance. Even the most favorable novel and film of the postwar period, *The Milagro Beanfield War*, ends in stereotypes.[105]

A few writers found their own culture alienating and sought relief in a more serene Southwest culture. As with the Harlem Renaissance, these creative artists tended to be more generous to Mexicans, but nevertheless retained the Anglo hero as the central figure or Samaritan who uplifts the Mexican from his or her traditional ignorance.

How Could They? Lessons from the History of Racial Depiction

The depiction of ethnic groups of color is littered with negative images, although the content of those images changes over time. In some periods, society needed to suppress a group, as with blacks during Reconstruction, and coined an image to suit that purpose—that of primitive, powerful, larger-than-life blacks, terrifying and barely under control. At other times, for example during slavery, society needed reassurance that blacks were docile, cheerful, and content with their lot. Images of sullen, rebellious blacks dissatisfied with their condition would have made white society uneasy. Accordingly, images of simple, happy blacks, content to do the master's work, were disseminated.

Other racial groups, at various times and in response to different social needs, were depicted as Charlie Chans; hapless, lazy Mexicans interested only in singing and dancing; conniving Indians or greasers; devious or superindustrious Asians willing to work inordinate hours; and so on—all depending on what society needed: immigration or the opposite, cheap or excess labor, suppression, indifference, guilt assuagement.

In every era, ethnic imagery comes bearing an enormous amount of social weight.[106] Efforts like Indian relocation, Bracero programs, and Japanese internment happen ineluctably and in a way that seems natural, permissible, and "right." Our First Amendment and system of free expression keep the needs of the control group, the creative community, the mass of people, and the subjugated groups themselves all nicely in balance. Nevertheless, we believe that we are in control, that we can use speech, jiujitsu fashion, on behalf of oppressed peoples.[107] We tell ourselves that speech can serve as a tool of destabilization. It is virtually a prime tenet of liberal jurisprudence that by talk, dialog, exhortation, and so on, we can present each other with passionate, appealing messages that will counter the evil ones of racism and sexism and thereby advance society to greater levels of fairness and humanity.[108]

Consider, for example, the current debate about campus speech codes. In response to a rising tide of racist incidents, many campuses have enacted rules that forbid certain types of face-to-face insult.[109] These codes invariably draw fire from free speech absolutists and many campus administrators on the ground that they would interfere with free speech. Campuses, they argue, ought to be "bastions of free speech." Racism and prejudice are matters of ignorance and fear, for which the appropriate remedy is more speech. Suppression merely drives racism underground, where it will fester and emerge in even more hateful forms. Speech is the best corrective for error; regulation risks the specter of censorship and state control.[110] Efforts to regulate pornography, Klan marches, and other types of race-baiting often meet similar responses.

But modernist and postmodernist insights about language and the social construction of reality show that reliance on countervailing speech that will, in theory, wrestle with bad or vicious speech is often misplaced. This is so for two interrelated reasons: The argument rests, first, on simplistic and erroneous notions of narrativity and change, and, second, on a misunderstanding of the relation between the subject, or self, and new narratives.

The First Reason—Time Warp: Why We Can Only Condemn the Old Narrative

As we have seen, the racism of other times and places stands out, strikes us as glaringly and appallingly wrong. But this realization dawns only decades or centuries later; we acquiesce in today's version with little realization that it is wrong, that a later generation will ask "How could they?" about *us*. We only condemn the racism of another place (South Africa) or time. But that of our own place and time strikes us, if at all, as unexceptionable, trivial, well within literary license. Every form of creative work (we tell ourselves) relies on stock characters. What's so wrong with a novel that employs a black who ..., or a Mexican who ... ? Besides, the argument goes, those groups are disproportionately employed as domestics, are responsible for a high proportion of our crime, are they not? And some actually talk this way; why, just last week, I overheard …

This time-warp aspect of racism makes speech an ineffective tool to counter it. Racism is woven into the warp and woof of the way we see and organize the world.[111] It is one of the many preconceptions we bring to experience, use to construct and make sense of our social world.[112] Racism forms part of the dominant narrative, the group of received understandings and basic principles that form the baseline from which we reason. How could these be in question? The dominant narrative changes very slowly, resisting alteration. We interpret new stories in light of the old. Ones that deviate too markedly from our pre-existing stock are dismissed as extreme, coercive, political, and wrong. The only stories about race we are prepared to condemn, then, are the old ones giving voice to the racism of an earlier age, ones that society has already begun to reject. We can condemn Justice Brown for writing as he did in *Plessy v. Ferguson,* but not university administrators who refuse remedies for campus racism, failing to notice the remarkable parallels between the two.[113]

The Second Reason: Our Narratives, Our Selves

Racial change is slow, then, because the story of race is part of the master narrative we use to interpret experience. This narrative teaches that race matters, that people are different, with the differences lying always in a predictable direction. It holds that certain cultures, unfortunately, have less ambition than others, that the majority group is largely innocent of racial wrongdoing, that the current distribution of comfort and well-being is roughly what merit and fairness dictate. Within that general framework, only certain matters are open for discussion: How different? In what ways? With how many exceptions? And what measures should we take to deal with this unfortunate situation and at what cost to whites? This is so because the narrative leaves only certain things intelligible; other arguments and texts would seem incoherent.

A second and related insight focuses not on the role of narratives in confining change to manageable proportions but on the relationship between our selves and those narratives. The reigning First Amendment metaphor—the marketplace of ideas—implies a separation between subjects who do the choosing and the ideas or messages that vie for their attention. Subjects are "in here," the messages "out there." The preexisting subjects choose the idea that seems most valid and true—somewhat in the manner of a diner deciding what to eat at a buffet.

But we are beginning to realize that this mechanistic view of an autonomous subject choosing among separate, external ideas is simplistic. In an important sense, we *are* our current store of narratives, and they us. We subscribe to a stock of explanatory scripts, plots, narratives, and understandings that enable us to make sense of—to construct—our social world. Because we then live in that world, it begins to shape and determine *us*, who we are, what we see, how we select, reject, interpret, and order subsequent reality.[114]

Our ability to escape the confines of our own preconceptions is thus quite limited. The contrary belief—that through speech and remonstrance alone we can endlessly reform ourselves and each other—we call the *empathic fallacy*. It and its companion, the *pathetic fallacy*, are both based on *hubris*, the belief that we can be more than we are. The empathic fallacy holds that through speech and remonstrance we can surmount our limitations of time, place, and culture, can transcend our own situatedness. But our examination of the cultural record, as well as postmodern understandings of language and personhood, both point to the same conclusion: The notion of ideas competing with each other, with truth and goodness emerging victorious from the competition, has proven seriously deficient when applied to evils, like racism, that are deeply inscribed in the culture.[115] We have constructed the social world so that racism seems normal, part of the status quo, in need of little correction. It is not until much later that what we believed begins to seem incredibly, monstrously wrong. How could we have believed *that*?

True, every few decades occasional geniuses will rise up and offer a work that recognizes and denounces the racism of the day. Unfortunately, they are ignored—they have no audience. Witness, for example, the recent "discovery" of long-forgotten black writers such as Charles Chesnutt, Zora Neale Hurston, and the authors of the slave narratives.[116] Consider that Nadine Gordimer won the Nobel Prize after nearly forty years of writing about the evils of apartheid; Harriet Beecher Stowe's book sold well only after years of abolitionist sentiment and agitation had sensitized her public to the possibility that slavery was wrong. One should, of course, speak out against social evils. But we should not accord speech greater efficacy than it has.

The Nature of the Evil

Another way of approaching speech's role in correcting racism is by examining not language but the referent: race. This examination shows that racism contains features that render it relatively unamenable to redress through words. Racism, even when blatant, resists efforts to rally others against it. Further, talking often makes matters worse.

How Much Racism Exists? The Difference Perspective Makes. Much racism is not seen as such at the time of its commission. But the extent of even the blatant variety is often underappreciated by whites. The reason is simple:

Few acts of clear-cut racism take place within their view.[117] Racism is often covert; the vignettes tend to be played out behind the scenes when no one else is watching. A merchant who harasses even well-behaved black teenage shoppers will probably not do so if other whites are watching. A white apartment owner will probably not deny a superbly qualified black applicant an apartment if a friend or observer is present.

As a result of its covert nature, many persons of the majority race, even those of good will, consistently underestimate the extent of racism in society.[118] Persons of color, who are on the receiving end of it, generally report much more racism than do whites and naturally place greater priority on remedying it.[119] This puzzles some whites, who wonder whether blacks are exaggerating or trying to guilt-trip them to gain an unfair advantage.[120] The problem is perspective: Imagine that one's body were somehow magnetically charged. One would go through life astonished at how many metal filings there are in the world and how much we need a clean-up operation. Those not caught in this Kafkaesque predicament would naturally fail to appreciate the situation's urgency.[121]

The Subtle Nuances. Racism's victims become sensitized to its subtle nuances and code words—the body language, averted gazes, exasperated looks, terms such as "you people," "innocent whites," "highly qualified black," "articulate," and so on—that, whether intended or not, convey racially charged meanings.[122] Like an Aleut accustomed to reading the sky for signs of snow, or a small household pet skilled at recognizing a clumsy footfall, racism's perpetual victims are alert to the various guises racism and racial signalling take. Sympathizers of majority hue often must labor to acquire the knowledge that for minorities comes all too easily.

On Not Seeing What One Chooses Not to See. Some refuse to see racism in acts that trigger suspicion in the mind of any person of color.[123] A well-qualified black applicant fails to get the job. Perhaps (we say) it was his attire, his age, or the way he held himself that caused his rejection. Perhaps he seemed too diffident or too anxious to get the job. Perhaps he had traits, such as voice intonations, that might irritate the firm's customers. Choosing to believe in a race-free world reduces guilt and the need for corrective action. Racism is often a matter of interpretation; when an interpretation renders one uncomfortable and another does not, which will a person often make?

Unlearning the Lessons of the Past. Finally, members of the majority race forget how to see and condemn racism. We generalize the wrong lesson from the past, namely that racism has virtually disappeared. We notice, for example, that today there are fewer Sambos than in the past. We thus conclude that those writers from the past must have been acting against conscience, that is, were malevolent and realized that what they were doing was wrong (as we realize it today), but went ahead and did it anyway. Yet, we think, "I do not act against conscience and neither do my friends."

In fact, those earlier writers were acting blithely, not against conscience, any more than we do today in maintaining our own versions of racism and racist imagery. The Willie Horton commercial struck many as falling within the bounds of fair play, perhaps only slightly exaggerated—at any rate the sort of thing one must expect in the rough-and-tumble world of politics. Besides, we say to ourselves, do not blacks in fact commit a high percentage of violent crime; did I not read that ...?

How the System of Free Expression
Sometimes Makes Matters Worse

Speech and free expression are not only poorly adapted to remedy racism, they often make matters worse; far from being stalwart friends, they can impede the cause of racial reform. They encourage writers, filmmakers, and other creative people to feel amoral, nonresponsible in what they do. Because there is a marketplace of ideas, the rationalization goes, another filmmaker is free to make an antiracist movie that will cancel out any minor stereotyping in the one I am making. My movie may have other redeeming qualities. Besides, it is good entertainment—everyone in the industry uses stock characters like the black maid or the bumbling Asian tourist. How can one create a film without stock characters?

Further, when insurgent groups attempt to use speech as an instrument of reform, courts almost invariably construe First Amendment doctrine against them. Civil rights activists in the 1960s made the greatest strides when they acted in defiance of the First Amendment as then understood.[124] They marched, were arrested and convicted; sat in, were arrested and convicted; distributed leaflets, were arrested and convicted. Many years later, after much gallant lawyering and the expenditure of untold hours of effort, the conviction might be reversed on appeal if the original action had been sufficiently prayerful, mannerly, and not too interlaced with an action component. The experience of the civil rights movement does not bear out the usual assumption that the First Amendment is of great value for racial reformers. *Speech* may have been of some small value at different times; free speech generally not.

Current First Amendment law is similarly skewed. Examination of the many "exceptions" to First Amendment protection discloses that most favor the interests of the powerful. If one says something disparaging of a wealthy and well-regarded individual, one discovers that one's words were not free after all; the wealthy individual has a type of property interest in his or her community image, damage to which is compensable even though words were the sole instrument of the harm.[125] Similarly, if one infringes the copyright or trademark of a well-known writer or industrialist, again it turns out that one's action is punishable.[126] Further, if one disseminates an official secret valuable to a powerful branch of the military or defense contractor, that speech is punishable.[127] If one speaks disrespectfully to a judge, police officer, teacher, military official, or other powerful authority figure, again one discovers that one's words were not free;[128] and so with words used to defraud,[129] form a conspiracy,[130] breach the peace,[131] or untruthful words given under oath during a civil or criminal proceeding.[132]

Yet the suggestion that we create a new exception to protect the lowly and vulnerable—isolated, young black undergraduates attending dominantly white campuses—is often met with consternation. The First Amendment must be a seamless web, it is said. Minorities, if they knew their own self-interest, should appreciate this even more than others.[133] The one-sidedness of free-speech doctrine makes the First Amendment much more valuable to the majority than to the minority.

The system of free expression also has a powerful after-the-fact apologetic function. Elite groups use the supposed existence of a marketplace of ideas to justify their own superior position.[134] Imagine a society in which all As were rich and happy, all Bs were moderately comfortable, and all Cs were poor, stigmatized, and reviled. Imagine also that this society scrupulously believes in a free marketplace of ideas. Might not the As benefit greatly from such a system? On looking about them and observing the inequality in the distribution of wealth, longevity, happiness, and safety between themselves and the others, they might feel guilt. Perhaps their own superior position is undeserved or at least requires explanation. But the existence of an ostensibly free marketplace of ideas renders that effort unnecessary. Rationalization is easy: Our ideas, our culture competed with their more easygoing ones and won. It was a fair fight. It is up to them to change, not us.

A free market of racial depiction resists change for two final reasons. First, the dominant pictures, images, narratives, plots, roles, and stories ascribed to and constituting the public perception of minorities are always dominantly negative. Through an unfortunate psychological mechanism, incessant bombardment by negative images inscribes those images on the souls and minds of minority persons. Minorities internalize the stories they read, see, and hear every day. Persons of color can easily become demoralized, blame themselves, not speak up vigorously.[135] The expense of speech also precludes the stigmatized from participating effectively in the marketplace of ideas.[136] They are often poor—indeed, one theory of racism holds that maintenance of economic inequality is its prime function[137]—and hence unlikely to command the means to bring countervailing messages to the eyes and ears of others.

Second, even when minorities do speak they have little credibility. Who would credit a speaker or writer one associates with buffoonery, menial work, intellectual inadequacy, laziness, lasciviousness, demanding resources beyond his or her deserved share?

Our very imagery of the outsider shows that, contrary to the usual view, society does not really want them to speak out effectively on their own behalf, in fact cannot visualize them doing so. Ask yourself: How do outsiders speak in the dominant narratives? Poorly, inarticulately, with broken syntax, short sentences, grunts, and unsophisticated ideas. Try to recall a single popular narrative of an eloquent, self-assured black (for example) orator or speaker. In the real world, of course, they exist in profusion. But when we stumble upon them, we are surprised: "What a welcome 'exception'!"

Words, then, can wound. But the fine thing about the current situation is that one gets to enjoy a superior position and feel virtuous at the same time. By supporting the system of free expression no matter what the cost, one is upholding principle. One can belong to impeccably liberal organizations and believe one is doing the right thing, even while taking actions that are demonstrably injurious to the least privileged, most defenseless segments of our society.[138] In time, one's actions will seem wrong, will be condemned as such, but paradigms change slowly. The world one helps to create—a world in which denigrating depiction is good or at least acceptable, in which minorities are clowns, maids, or Willie Hortons, and only rarely fully individuated human beings with sensitivities, talents, personalities, and frailties—will survive into the future. One gets to create culture at outsiders' expense. One gets to sleep well at night, too.

Racism is not a mistake, not a matter of episodic, irrational behavior carried out by vicious-willed individuals, not a throwback to a long-gone era. It is ritual assertion of supremacy performed largely unconsciously. Racism seems right, customary, and inoffensive to those engaged in it, while bringing psychic and pecuniary advantages. The notion that more speech, more talking, more preaching, and more lecturing can counter this system of oppression is appealing, lofty, romantic—and wrong.

What Should Be Done? If Not Speech, Then What?

What can be done? One possibility we must take seriously is that *nothing* can be done—that race and perhaps sex-based subjugation is so deeply embedded in our society, so useful for the powerful, that nothing can dislodge it. No less gallant a warrior than Derrick Bell has recently expounded his view of "racial realism": Things will never get better; powerful forces maintain the current system of white-over-black supremacy. Just as the Legal Realists of the early years of this century urged society to cast aside comforting myths about the uniformity, predictability, and "scientific" nature of legal reasoning, legal scholars must do something similar today with respect to race.[139] Reformers must labor for what they believe right with no certainty that their programs will ever prove successful. Holding out the hope that reform will one day bear fruit is unnecessary, unwise, and calculated only to induce despair, burnout, and paralysis.

We agree with much of what Bell says. Yet we offer—as a result of our own research and analysis—four suggestions for a program of racial reform. We do this while underscoring the limitations of our own prescriptions, including the near-impossibility of getting society to take seriously something whose urgency it seems constitutionally unable to appreciate. First, we should act decisively in cases of racism that we do see, treating them as proxies for the ones we know remain unseen. Second, past mistreatment will generally prove a more reliable basis for remedial action (such as affirmative action or reparations) than future or current considerations.[140] The racism of the past is the only kind that we recognize, the only kind we condemn.[141] Third, whenever possible we should employ and empower minority speakers of color and expose ourselves to their messages.[142] Their reality, while not infallible and certainly not the only one, is the one we must heed if we wish to avoid history's judgment.[143] It is likely to be the one society will adopt in thirty years. Scholars should approach with skepticism the writings of those neoconservatives, including some of color, who make a practice of telling society that racism is ended.[144] In the sense we have described, there *is* an "essential" unitary minority viewpoint. The others are wrong.[145]

Finally, we should deepen suspicion of remedies for deep-seated social evils that rely only on speech and exhortation. The First Amendment is an instrument of variable efficacy, more useful in some settings than others. Overextending it provokes the anger of oppressed groups and casts doubt on speech's value in settings where it is, in fact, useful. With deeply inscribed cultural practices that most can neither see as evil nor mobilize to reform, we should forthrightly institute changes in the structure of society that will enable persons of color—particularly the young—to avoid the worst assaults of racism. As with the controversy over campus racism, we should not let a spurious motto that speech be "everywhere free" stand in the way of outlawing speech that is demonstrably harmful, that is compounding the problem.

Because of the way the dominant narrative works, we should prepare for the near certainty that these suggestions will be criticized as unprincipled, unfair to "innocent whites," extreme. Understanding how the dialectic works, and how the scripts and counterscripts work their dismal paralysis, may, perhaps, inspire us to continue even though the path is long and the night dark.

2

Judges' Misjudgments

Are judges free from the fetters described in Chapter 1? We like to think so. Law school teaches a vision of the common law as evolving toward ever-higher reaches of wisdom and flexibility. We have even higher hopes for our public, constitutional jurisprudence. Despite lofty ambitions of justice, however, our system of law has yielded many embarrassingly inhumane decisions.[1] Opinions steeped in what we later see as serious moral error come down all too frequently—at least one per generation. Every casebook has chapters devoted to doctrines or precedents that we are glad to relegate to history. And anyone who reads legal biography knows that even the most eminent Justices—Taney, Holmes, Field, Marshall—have chapters that mar their otherwise outstanding careers.

The concept of "serious moral error" is, of course, impossible to define and perhaps ultimately incoherent. We use the term in three limited senses. A decision embraces serious moral error if (1) it proceeds blithely ignorant of moral complexity; (2) it is broadly or universally condemned by subsequent generations, somewhat akin to being overruled; and (3) its assumptions, for example, about women, are roundly refuted by later experiences. Judges will always hand down decisions that will seem offensive to some. We reserve the term "serious moral error" for those shocking cases that virtually everyone later condemns.

One obvious explanation for these mistakes is judicial inability to identify—imaginatively—with the person whose fate is being decided. Because of the particularized stock of life experiences and understandings judges bring to the bench, these notorious opinions seemed to their authors unexceptionable, natural, "the truth." Only hindsight, benefited by increased empathy and understanding, exposes an opinion as monstrous, anomalous—a moral abomination. We do not view the mistake as merely technical (e.g., failing to reflect carefully on precedent), or as one of prudence (e.g., deciding a case on broader grounds than necessary). Rather, we condemn the judge for a failure of sympathy or nerve.

If a judicial lack of other-awareness rendered these now-embarrassing opinions acceptable at the time, would it have made much difference if the judges had exposed themselves to other points of view? Can such exposure accelerate the process of defining justice? A recent movement in the law, "law and literature," promotes a broadened perspective of our condition through the reading of great works with this ambition in mind. Members of the movement believe that lawyers and judges, by reading and discussing the world's great texts, may gain sympathy through vicarious experience and thereby avoid pitfalls to which they might otherwise succumb.[2] How much of this belief is idealistic wishful thinking?

A precise answer to this question is, of course, unattainable, but it is our premise that some insight into the potential and limits of this approach can be gained by examining it at a greater level of concreteness than is usually employed. Accordingly, we look to a handful of cases that society has judged harshly and seek to identify then-current literature that might have changed the outcome of the cases or the tone of the opinions.

We examine selected constitutional decisions embodying serious moral error (as we have defined it) and juxtapose those decisions with literary texts that contain a narrative or perspective that the authors were not aware of or ignored. In each case, the narrative might plausibly have saved the judge from error—or at least have made writing the wrong decision more difficult.

Although some of the illustrative cases display a blithe, almost mechanical, simplicity (as though the author were completely unaware of the treacherous moral ground on which he trod), more often the opinions betray a hint of moral ambivalence. The tension between what is proclaimed as "law" and subsequent retreats and disclaimers, which often take the form of recitations on the limits of the judicial role, reveals traces of a Pilate-like fear of reprobation. To the discerning reader, the "our hands are tied" disclaimer betrays doubts about the decision's correctness—doubts troubling enough to compel a denial of personal responsibility but not enough so as to change the judge's action.

Could reading a well-written, deeply felt counternarrative save a judge from history's condemnation in cases like the ones we will discuss? We examine this possibility, concluding that the saving potential of most counternarratives is considerably more limited than we would like to believe. As we pointed out in Chapter 1, we are all situated actors whose selves, imaginations, and range of possibilities are constructed by our social setting and experience. We *are*, in a sense, our current narratives. Thus, an unfamiliar narrative invariably generates resistance; despite our best efforts, counterstories are likely to effect (at most) small, incremental changes in the listener or reader. The question of the extent to which one may escape one's cultural milieu is complex and vexing. But we raise an even more disconcerting possibility: Not only does our status as situated actors create in judges and other policymakers a resistance to potentially saving counternarratives, but it limits the very range of counternarratives from which policymakers might draw. To the extent that this is so, literature can save us from minor but not major moral error—from tomorrow's but not next century's judgment.

The "canon" is always narrow because counternarratives, even when they exist and are known, are assimilated and understood in light of the reader's experience. Stories that deviate too much from our own experience strike us as wrong, untrue, coercive, "political"—unworthy of inclusion. Saving narratives thus rarely come to the attention of busy bureaucrats, like judges. And when they do, they reject them for reasons we detail.

Notorious Cases and Saving Narratives: What the Juxtaposition Shows

The nine cases that follow are widely condemned today. Yet each, at the time, seemed to the author of the opinion unexceptional and true. The cases all center around treatment of subordinated groups: blacks, women, indigenous people, Asians, homosexuals, and developmentally handicapped persons. We follow each opinion with a corresponding counternarrative that might have saved its authors from serious moral error. In each case, the judge either was unaware of the narrative or simply ignored it. When society later adopted the counternarrative, condemnation followed.

Dred Scott *and* Plessy v. Ferguson

The two most notorious cases upholding this nation's treatment of blacks, *Dred Scott v. Sandford*[3] and *Plessy v. Ferguson*,[4] are now universally condemned. But at the time of their decision (1856 and 1896, respectively), they were accepted as valid and even inevitable constitutional renderings. In *Dred Scott*, Chief Justice Taney painstakingly explained why blacks could not become citizens. He relied primarily on the long history of the white man's disdain for blacks to show that the writers of the Declaration of Independence and the framers of the Constitution could not have meant to include blacks in their eloquent demands of liberty for all men:

> They had for more than a century before been regarded as beings of an inferior order, and altogether unfit to associate with the white race, either in social or political relations; and so far inferior, that they had no rights which the white man was bound to respect; and that the negro might justly and lawfully be reduced to slavery for his benefit. He was bought and sold, and

treated as an ordinary article of merchandise and traffic, whenever a profit could be made by it. This opinion was at that time fixed and universal in the civilized portion of the white race. It was regarded as an axiom in morals as well as in politics, which no one thought of disputing, or supposed to be open to dispute.[5]

The circularity of the reasoning is apparent: Had they been worthy of citizenship, we could not have treated them so badly. Taney's writing reached near-ironic proportions when he pointed to the high moral character of the founding fathers as further proof that blacks were not meant to be included within the protections they were laying down:

> [T]he men who framed the declaration were great men—high in literary acquirements—high in their sense of honor, and incapable of asserting principles inconsistent with those on which they were acting. They perfectly understood the meaning of the language they used, and how it would be understood by others; and they knew that it would not in any part of the civilized world be supposed to embrace the negro race, which, by common consent, had been excluded from civilized Governments and the family of nations, and doomed to slavery.[6]

With this as his predicate, Taney could justify rejection of blacks' citizenship claims by straightforward strict interpretation: "It is not the province of the court to decide upon the justice or injustice, the policy or impolicy, of these laws. ... The duty of the court is, to interpret the instrument they have framed ... according to its true intent and meaning when it was adopted."[7]

Could the *Dred Scott* majority have been swayed by a saving narrative? In 1856, relatively few slave writings were published, for obvious reasons. But Harriet Beecher Stowe's widely read abolitionist novel *Uncle Tom's Cabin*[8] was published in 1852, and it is likely that the Justices had heard of it. *Narrative of the Life of Frederick Douglass,*[9] published in 1845, was equally well known, and Douglass himself was a well-known scholar and speaker. Could Taney have written his vindication of slavery had he read even the first chapter of Douglass's narrative? In it, Douglass recounted the pain of never having known his mother. He remembered the comfort of her presence on the few occasions her master allowed her, after a day's work in the fields, to walk the twelve miles to see her son. She had to start back almost immediately in order to be back in the field at sunrise and spare herself a whipping.

> For what this separation is done, I do not know, unless it be to hinder the development of the child's affection toward its mother, and to blunt and destroy the natural affection of the mother for the child.[10]

Douglass's feelings about his father-master were as bitter as his feelings for his mother were tender. He said:

> [S]laveholders have ordained, and by law established, that the children of slave women shall in all cases follow the condition of their mothers; and this is done too obviously to administer to their own lusts, and make a gratification of their wicked desires profitable as well as pleasurable.[11]

Could Taney and the majority have remained unaffected after reading Douglass's account of the suffering of an entire race for the sake of another's economic and social comfort? Could they have resisted empathizing with the sensitive child who was forced to arise each morning to a world full of characters more terrible than those the Justices imagined in their worst childhood nightmares?

> I have often been awakened at the dawn of day by the most heart-rending shrieks of an own aunt of mine, whom he used to tie up to a joist, and whip upon her naked back till she was literally covered with blood. ... The louder she screamed, the harder he whipped. ... I never shall forget it whilst I remember any thing.[12]

Could any white reader fail to react with horror and shame? Douglass's narrative was published more than ten years before the decision in *Dred Scott*. But we can guess that the Justices had not bothered to read it or that it did not affect their decision, for six of the eight others agreed with Taney's denial of citizenship for blacks, and the dissents did not have the force to save.[13]

Justice Brown's opinion in *Plessy v. Ferguson* is equally notorious for its disdainful treatment of the black race. Although a justification of public segregation is less outrageous than one of slavery, the tone of Brown's opinion renders it equally offensive. It is blithely patronizing and betrays little knowledge of the wrong perpetrated on blacks. Brown found that the Louisiana statute requiring blacks to ride in a coach "separate but equal to" that ridden in by whites violated neither the Thirteenth nor Fourteenth Amendments because a merely

> legal distinction between the white and colored races—a distinction which is founded in the color of the two races, and which must always exist so long as white men are distinguished from the other race by color—has no tendency to destroy the legal equality of the two races ...[14]

and because the Fourteenth Amendment "could not have been intended ... to enforce social, as distinguished from political, equality."

Brown rejected the idea that "the enforced separation of the two races stamps the colored race with a badge of inferiority" and added: "If this be so, it is not by reason of anything found in the act, but solely because the colored race chooses to put that construction upon it." And finally: "If one race be inferior to the other socially, the Constitution of the United States cannot put them upon the same plane."[15]

Justice Harlan's dissent urged a much more generous interpretation. The Fourteenth Amendment, he said, guarantees "exemption from legal discriminations, implying inferiority in civil society ... and discriminations which are steps toward reducing [blacks] to the condition of a subject race." He went on bluntly to state:

> [E]very one knows that the statute in question had its origin in the purpose, not so much to exclude white persons from railroad cars occupied by blacks, as to exclude colored people from coaches occupied by or assigned to white persons. ... No one would be so wanting in candor as to assert the contrary.

Harlan showed that it was possible for a judge to cut through accepted legal justifications and the make-believe realities on which they are premised to reach the actual intentions and consequences of legislation. He labeled the statute "sinister" and showed uncanny foresight in stating that "the judgement this day rendered will, in time, prove to be quite as pernicious as the decision made by this tribunal in the *Dred Scott* case."[16]

However persuasive the Harlan dissent may seem now, it obviously failed to persuade the majority. Were there other sources of moral persuasion, texts that might have presented the other point of view more effectively? Indeed, many were available. In fact, there was a virtual ferment over issues of social inequality and integration.[17] Leading black newspapers editorialized on the subject.[18] Reformers and religious figures questioned whether separate water fountains, hotels, theaters, railroad cars, waiting rooms, and restaurants could exist in a nation committed to liberty for all. A new generation of black writers, including Frank Webb, Frances E. W. Harper, Sutton Griggs, Charles Chesnutt, and Paul Lawrence Dunbar, were writing about the lives of blacks in a nation that, although ostensibly committed to equality, frustrated and denied their humanity and worth at every turn.[19] In many of these books, the protagonist is an upward-striving, hard-working black who is respectable, educated, and white-collar, but who nevertheless is handicapped and rebuffed on his way to success.[20] To be sure, many of these novelists were not wholehearted egalitarians. Some pressed for social integration only for members of their talented class and were quick to distance themselves from less-educated Negroes—ones who had not yet, in their opinion, earned the right to be treated by whites as equals.[21]

Indian Cases

In the early 1800s a young, expansion-minded government sought to justify subjugation of the Native American race in the interest of progress.[22] Control over the lands and lives of Indians was necessary for the development that our founding fathers foresaw. The 1823 decision in *Johnson v. M'Intosh*[23] gave Chief Justice John Marshall a vehicle for articulating the principles of what was to become an elaborate body of law governing the Indians. Although the Indians had a right to occupy land, they had no power to dispose of it, because ownership lay in the government. The source of U.S. ownership, Marshall explained, lay in rights gained by Great Britain under the "discovery doctrine," a euphemistic name for the tacit agreement of finders-keepers among the exploring European states. Marshall declared that "the rights of the original inhabitants were, in no instance, entirely disregarded; but were necessarily, to a considerable extent, impaired. ... [T]heir rights to complete sovereignty, as independent nations, were necessarily diminished, and their power to dispose of the soil at their own will ... was denied."[24]

Perhaps recognizing the tenuousness of this "necessity," Marshall seemed reluctant, at least on a moral level, to commit himself, as author, to the decision he nevertheless made. His opinion is phrased in terms of inevitability, but its result was necessary only in a purely practical sense to legitimate an established system upon which his government relied. Indeed his opinion is full of signs of the internal conflict Marshall, a renowned jurist, must have felt. He warned that the conquered should not be "wantonly oppressed"[25] but went on to observe that the tribes of Indians "were fierce savages, whose occupation was war."[26] He set out the range of possibilities as follows: "To leave them in possession of their country, was to leave the country a wilderness; to govern them as a distinct people, was impossible, because they were as brave and as high spirited as they were fierce, and were ready to repel by arms every attempt on their independence."[27] Cohabitation with the Indians was impossible because it exposed the settlers to "the perpetual hazard of being massacred."[28] European claims were thus justified by whatever means necessary.

As though sensing his error in *Johnson*, Marshall was more generous to the cause of Indian rights and more skeptical of the role of government nine years later in *Worcester v. Georgia*.[29] Georgia law required non-Indians wishing to reside in Indian territory to secure permission from the governor and to take an oath of allegiance to the state's constitution and laws. Marshall focused on the sovereign status of Indian nations, which was recognized in treaties between Indians and the federal government, in deciding whether Georgia's assertion of jurisdiction over non-Indians residing in Cherokee territory was constitutional. He declared Georgia's requirement void because it conflicted with treaties made between the United States and the Cherokees (describing the latter, by implication, as a sovereign nation).

In *Worcester*, did Marshall recompense for turning his back on the Indians in *Johnson*? Unfortunately, he did not: The principles he established in *Johnson* were invoked and embellished in later decisions that gnawed persistently and jealously at Indian rights in land and self-government.[30] During much of the formative period of American Indian law, political theorists and organized religion contributed, along with the courts, to the demeaning of Native American culture. Religious leaders spoke of the Indians as heathen.[31] Respected writers invoked the doctrine of "waste" to justify the taking of Indian land, the relocation of Indian tribes to desolate areas far from their ancestral homes, and the relentless mining and timbering of the lands to which they were removed.[32]

Could judges and these others have been saved from committing what was beginning to seem like serious moral error in their treatment of the Indians? Indian leaders themselves spoke eloquently of the injustices being perpetrated; they were generally ignored. For example, Mohawk chief Joseph Brant spoke forcefully about Indians' attachment to and love of "those Lands which the great being above has pointed out for our Ancestors & their Descendants, and placed them there from the beginning, and where the Bones of our Forefathers are Laid." He asked "whether the Blood of their grand children is to be mingled with their Bones, thro' the means of our Allies for whom We have often so freely bled?"[33] Shawnee military leader Tecumtha (1768–1813) proclaimed:

> The White people have no right to take the land from the Indians, because they had it first, it is theirs. ... Any sale not made by all, is not valid. ... All Redmen have equal rights to the unoccupied land. ... There cannot be two occupations in the same place. The first excludes all others. It is not so in hunting or traveling, for there the same ground will serve many, as they may follow each other all day, but the camp is stationary, and that is occupancy. It belongs to the first who sits down on his blanket or skins, which he has thrown upon the ground, and till he leaves it, no other has a right.[34]

Narratives such as these, had they been read and heeded, might well have given pause to the religious, judicial, and political figures in the white community who were blithely bent on justifying the taking of Indian land because Indians were unfit, spiritually and morally, to occupy it.

The Chinese Exclusion Case

In the late 1800s, labor unrest and economic dislocation fueled a growing xenophobia, including demands that immigration of nonwhite populations be curtailed. The Chinese Exclusion Case, *Chae Chan Ping v. United States*,[35] was decided in the midst of this nativist resurgence. At issue was whether Chae Chan Ping, who had been granted a federal certificate assuring reentry into the United States following a visit to his native China, could be prevented from returning to this country. During his absence, Congress had rescinded an earlier treaty that would have guaranteed him the right to return to the United States, where he had resided and worked as a laborer for a number of years. In so doing, Congress was taking action in response to popular sentiment that there were too many Chinese flooding the labor market.

Writing for a unanimous Court, Justice Field upheld the government's action in barring Chae Chan Ping's return. Not only did Congress have the power to exclude, Field wrote, but its decision to exercise that power was fully justified:

> [T]he presence of Chinese laborers had a baneful effect upon the material interest of the State, and upon public morals; ... their immigration was in numbers approaching the character of an Oriental invasion, and was a menace to our civilization; ... the discontent from this cause was not confined to any political party ... but was well-nigh universal; ... they retained the habits and customs of their own country, and in fact constituted a Chinese settlement within the State, without any interest in our country or its institutions.[36]

The Chinese Exclusion Case is notorious in the Asian-American community; it typifies the callous, stereotypical treatment our society has afforded Asians at several points in our history.[37] Could Field have avoided contributing this sorry chapter through exposure to a saving narrative? Relatively little Asian-American literature was available in English at the time Field wrote. But newspaper editorials and letters to the editor, many written by U.S. citizens of stature, praised the industriousness of the Chinese and their value to the country.[38] At least one noted clergyman, Otis Gibson, championed their cause. Writing in 1876, he defended the Chinese residing in America from the charge that they presented "evils and dangers ... to these shores."[39] He rejected the charge that the Chinese displaced native labor or caused economic dislocation and defended them against the "absurd" charge of moral inferiority, pointing out that they had developed a superior civilization well before the West.[40] His book, *The Chinese in America*, was available more than thirteen years before Field wrote his opinion in *Chan Ping*. Another book, *When I Was a Boy in China*,[41] was written in 1887 by Yan Phou Lee, who had immigrated to the United States at age twelve. It, too, exploded stereotypes of China as backward and of the Chinese as inhuman, conniving, and inferior.[42]

The Japanese Internment Cases

During World War II the federal government issued a series of executive orders requiring Japanese-Americans living in certain areas to leave their homes and be confined for the duration of the war. The orders had been issued at the request of military officials, who argued that the Japanese posed a threat of sabotage and spying—charges that recent research refutes.[43] Most, perhaps all, of those interned were loyal American citizens who lost houses and businesses as a result of their treatment. In 1943 and 1944 the U.S. Supreme Court decided two cases upholding internment, *Hirabayashi v. United States*[44] and *Korematsu v. United States*.[45] Like the Chinese Exclusion Case, these cases are replete with passages evidencing fear and distrust of outsiders and stereotypes of Asians as untrustworthy.[46] The deference to military judgment was nearly complete; the military's allegations about a risk of sabotage were accepted with little examination.

A dissenting opinion by Justice Murphy calls the "racial and sociological grounds [for these assumptions] questionable," focusing particularly on a portion of the military report that characterized the Japanese as "a large, unassimilated, tightly knit racial group, bound to an enemy nation by strong ties of race, culture, custom and religion ... given to emperor worshipping ceremonies and to 'dual citizenship.'" He dismissed this part of the case against the Japanese as a patchwork of "misinformation, half-truths and insinuations that for years have been directed against Japanese Americans by people with racial and economic prejudices." For Murphy, the Court's approval would "adopt one of the cruelest of the rationales used by our enemies to destroy the dignity of the individual and to encourage and open the door to discriminatory actions against other minority groups in the passions of tomorrow." He argued that hearings could have been used to determine loyalty on a case-by-case basis and described any danger from the Japanese community as minimal or nonexistent.[47]

Murphy's dissent is in itself a powerful counternarrative—not one of those cautious, narrow opinions whose failure to persuade is understandable. It is lengthy, impassioned, and direct. Yet it was not the first statement in support of the Japanese. For example, a widely read novel, Etsu Sugimoto's *A Daughter of the Samurai*,[48] originally published in 1925, was dedicated to Japan and America as her "two mothers, whose lives and environments were far apart, yet whose hearts met in mine."[49] She portrayed Japanese-Americans as loyal to two cultures and sought to dispel stereotypes of Japanese as unrelentingly warlike and forever bound to Japan. Her book found a sympathetic reception; critics praised it for undertaking the difficult task of explaining an unfamiliar culture to the American people. They described the book as not pleading a cause but "tel[ling] a tale with delicacy and taste."[50]

Bradwell v. Illinois

Myra Bradwell, a female resident of Illinois, applied for membership to the bar of that state. Her application met all the requirements for admission, including a certificate of good character and a passing grade on the requisite examination. Illinois denied her application on the ground that she was a woman and hence would be incapable of forming contracts, including those between an attorney and a client. In a brief, dismissive opinion signed by four other Justices, Justice Miller affirmed the state's denial of her application. Admission to the bar, he wrote, is not so basic a right as to be protected as a privilege and immunity guaranteed by the Constitution. A concurring opinion written by Justice Bradley and joined by Justices Swayne and Field went even further. In language dripping with condescension, they wrote:

> [T]he civil law, as well as nature herself, has always recognized a wide difference in the respective spheres and destinies of man and woman. Man is, or should be, woman's protector and defender. The natural and proper timidity and delicacy which belongs to the female sex evidently unfits it for many of the occupations of civil life.[51]

For Bradley, the separation of the sexes was "founded in the divine ordinance, as well as in the nature of things," a separation that rendered the idea of women's practicing a profession other than that of homemaker and nurturer "repugnant." He found support for his notions on women's role in two sources—the law of contract, which in many states prevented women from entering into agreements, and theology. "The paramount destiny and mission of woman are to fulfil the noble and benign offices of wife and mother. This is the law of the Creator. And the rules of civil society must be adapted to the general constitution of things, and cannot be based upon exceptional cases."[52]

Bradley showed few traces of doubt or ambivalence in writing his extraordinary opinion. Yet, at the time he wrote, numerous tracts and books urged women's liberation and condemned the suffocating stereotypes Bradley invoked. The early feminist movement contained powerful voices like Mary Wollstonecraft, Sojourner Truth, and Elizabeth Cady Stanton.[53] These women and others eloquently demanded full recognition of women's possibilities, intellect, and dignity. For example, Margaret Fuller, in a widely disseminated essay—*The Great Lawsuit*, published in 1843—wrote:

> [T]he time has come when a clearer vision and better action are possible—when Man and Woman may regard one another as brother and sister, the pillars of one porch, the priests of one worship. ...

We only ask of men to remove arbitrary barriers. Some would like to do more. But I believe it needs that Woman show herself in her native dignity, to teach them how to aid her; their minds are so encumbered by tradition.[54]

Concerning the roles of wife and mother that Bradley found to exhaust women's possibilities, Fuller wrote:

I have no doubt ... that a large proportion of women would give themselves to [that employment]. ... Nature would take care of that; no need to clip the wings of any bird that wants to soar and sing, or finds in itself the strength of pinion for a migratory flight. ... The difference would be that *all* need not be constrained to employments for which *some* are unfit. ... [55]

We would have every arbitrary barrier thrown down. We would have every path laid open to Woman as freely as to Man.[56]

Buck v. Bell

In 1927, Oliver Wendell Holmes, joined by seven other Justices, upheld a sterilization order issued by a Virginia court in the case of Carrie Buck, an institutionalized person.[57] Ms. Buck had evidently been born to a mentally disabled mother and had herself given birth to a daughter described as mentally disabled. Later commentators have discovered, however, that Ms. Buck's other daughter, who died at the age of eight from a childhood disease, was of normal intelligence.[58]

Holmes found little constitutional difficulty in affirming the Virginia order. His opinion is brief and full of facile analogies.[59] "It is better for all the world," Holmes wrote, "if instead of waiting to execute degenerate offspring for crime, or to let them starve for their imbecility, society can prevent those who are manifestly unfit from continuing their kind. The principle that sustains compulsory vaccination is broad enough to cover cutting the Fallopian tubes."[60]

Holmes's opinion is technically poor—easily his worst. It is nearly devoid of any consideration of Ms. Buck's interests or of less restrictive alternatives. A serious equal protection difficulty, stemming from Virginia's practice of sterilizing only the institutionalized mentally disabled, was summarily dismissed as "the last resort of constitutional arguments."[61] For Holmes, "the law does all that is needed when it does all that it can, indicates a policy, applies it to all within the lines, and seeks to bring within the lines all similarly situated so far and so fast as its means allow."[62] He thus treated Ms. Buck's right to reproduce as an ordinary liberty interest, her equal protection argument like an unreasonable citizen's demand that the state justify its practice of fixing potholes on the west side of town first and those on the east side later.

Could Holmes have saved himself from writing this embarrassing opinion, one that mars the career of an otherwise eminent Justice? Yes, but only by rejecting many of the narratives and accepted wisdoms that constituted his views about the mentally disabled. What would have enabled him to do that? When he wrote *Buck v. Bell*, Holmes was a camp follower of the American eugenics movement, then in its heyday.[63] That movement decried the rapid breeding of the unfit and the purported swamping of America's shores by darker, inferior southern European stock.[64] To Holmes, his depiction of Carrie Buck must have seemed obvious and true. Yet the scientific community, even then, was beginning to turn against the exaggerated claims of the eugenicists. Early editions of the *Encyclopedia Britannica*, for example, refuted such claims and took a more moderate view of the role of heredity in determining mental disorders and illness.[65] At the same time, leading biologists were urging reexamination of many of these issues.[66] Counternarratives were already being found in the public discourse.

Bowers v. Hardwick

When Justice Byron White wrote his 1986 decision upholding Georgia's statute outlawing sodomy, he emphasized the statutory prohibitions still on the books in twenty-four states and the District of Columbia to show that homosexuals have no fundamental right to engage in consensual sodomy in their own homes. He indignantly declared that "to claim that a right to engage in such conduct is 'deeply rooted in this Nation's history and tradition' or 'implicit in the concept of ordered liberty' is, at best, facetious."

For White, the only question before the court was whether homosexuals have a legal right to engage in sodomy. He brushed aside the statute's broad prohibition on all forms of sodomy, including consensual oral sex between married couples in their own homes.[67] He also neglected to consider that even if the right, narrowly stated, is not fundamental, it may nevertheless fall under a broader constitutional principle—for example the emerging right of intimate association.[68] Dismissing the possibility that homosexual behavior may be protected by the Ninth and Fourteenth Amendments, as suggested by such decisions as *Loving v. Virginia*,[69] *Griswold v. Connecticut*,[70] and *Roe v. Wade*,[71] White wrote: "[I]t [is] evident that none of the rights announced in those cases bears any resemblance to the claimed constitutional right. ... No connection between family, marriage, or procreation on one hand and homosexual activity on the other has been demonstrated."[72]

White similarly dismissed on moral grounds the argument that consensual conduct within the home should be free from state interference.[73] White likened consensual sodomy to illegal activities such as possession in the home of drugs, firearms, or stolen goods. His reasoning, of course, begs the question: If these activities were constitutionally protected, we could not make them illegal.

Bowers has already attracted a great deal of criticism[74] and seems destined to join its predecessors, *Plessy*, *Dred Scott*, and *Bradwell*, as flagrantly wrong. Already, retired Supreme Court Justice Lewis Powell has admitted that he regrets signing the opinion and now considers it a mistake.[75] There were ample literary sources to enable the Court to avoid—or at least sense—its error. Walt Whitman, Christopher Isherwood, E. M. Forster, James Baldwin, and W. H. Auden all persuasively describe homosexual relations as potentially loving and constructive.[76] For example, in his novel *Maurice*, E. M. Forster wrote:

> [Clive] flung down all the barriers—not at once, for he did not live in a house that can be destroyed in a day. All that term and through letters afterwards he made the path clear. Once certain that Hall loved him, he unloosed his own love. Hitherto it had been dalliance, a passing pleasure for body and mind. How he despised that now. Love was harmonious, immense. He poured into it the dignity as well as the richness of his being, and indeed in that well-tempered soul the two were one.[77]

In James Baldwin's first novel, *Giovanni's Room*, published in 1956, the narrator describes his thoughts of Giovanni:

> We were both insufferably childish and high-spirited that afternoon and the spectacle we presented, two grown men, jostling each other on the wide sidewalk, and aiming the cherry-pits, as though they were spitballs, into each other's faces, must have been outrageous. And I realized that such ... happiness out of which it sprang yet more so; for that moment I really loved Giovanni, who had never seemed more beautiful than he was that afternoon. And watching his face, I realized that it meant much to me that I could make his face so bright. ... And I felt myself flow toward him, as a river rushes when the ice breaks up.[78]

After reading such passages full of love and excitement over another being, could the authors of *Bowers v. Hardwick* still have written as they did? Unfortunately, we believe the answer is yes, just as the other saving narratives we have identified in this section either did not reach the judges—were not in the canon—or else somehow failed to move them. Let us now examine why this is so.

Law and Literature: The Canon and the Possibility of Counternarratives

Narratives, particularly what we have called "saving," or counternarratives, could conceivably serve as powerful antidotes to serious moral error. As we have seen, most serious judicial mistakes result from the judge's inability to empathize with the litigants or their circumstances. In many cases, a counternarrative was close at hand. The judge might have read the narrative, reflected on it, and written a wiser, or at least more nuanced, opinion. Indeed, this hope constitutes one of the most widely proclaimed advantages of the law and literature movement, whose proponents believe that exposure to great texts can enrich and humanize their readers.

Yet this result has not been realized to any significant extent, even today. This is so for three reasons. As we show later, the canon is always narrow because of limitations inherent in several processes, including anthologizing. Furthermore, a fundamental incommensurability between literature and judging diminishes the liberating effect narratives may have on judges. Finally, we are all situated actors, constituted in large part by the "stories" or narratives by which we understand and impose order on reality. Divergent new narratives, ones that could jar and change us, always spark resistance; we reject precisely those narratives that could save us from history's judgment.

Examining the Current Canon

Saving narratives rarely alter judges' behavior because they are seldom found in the "canon"—the group of texts recognized as valid and legitimate, that is, the "classics"—at any given period in history.[79] If a saving narrative exists at all, it is rarely required reading—rarely found in anthologies, rarely included in the reading lists of busy judges, rarely taught in the best schools.[80] Anthologists, editors, and literature instructors may be somewhat more catholic in their tastes than the average reader, but they are still positioned actors, shaped by the views, preferences, and received wisdoms of their times.[81] Because of a self-selection mechanism (which we discuss more fully later), these guardians at the gates rarely let pass a work or text shocking or divergent enough to challenge the current sensibility. As an example of this effect, we chose a single period, namely the present, and examined one canon—that of the law and literature movement. We recognize that there are many other canons and many other periods that we might have examined. Yet since our findings are so striking, it seems likely that they are generalizable.

To gain a sense of the narratives commonly employed by the current law and literature movement, we reviewed lists of novels, plays, and poems compiled by authorities in that field.[82] We selected these lists because each, prepared in a different era, identifies slightly different benefits to be gained from reading law and literature.

Despite the objective of at least two of the compilers to present aspirational, liberating works and ideas, the range of novels included in the lists is remarkably narrow. Most of the novels were written by white men, who wrote about white men and their experiences. Although some of the works deal with themes of equality and were thought radical at the time of their publication, few can be considered fully emancipatory. For example, we speculated earlier that *Bowers v. Hardwick* may go down in history as one of the moral anomalies of our age—a present-day case embracing serious moral error. Would careful reading of the current canon have saved seven majority Justices from their error? Sadly, the answer is no. Works presenting gay and lesbian relationships in a more loving, sympathetic light do exist and are taught in some universities. But they are not yet part of the legal-scholarly canon. Nor does that canon contain more than token representation of the views of indigenous people, third world nationalists, and radical feminists of color, to name just three groups whose problems are now or may soon be on the law's front burner.

Little can be done to escape this predicament. Because of who we are, we will almost always select texts that supply glosses on or at best provide minor incremental adjustments in our current understanding of social reality. Texts that do more than this strike us as unreal, coercive, "political," and are excluded. Unfortunately, the same forces that lead to serious moral error lead to the formation of a literary canon that is bland, uniform, and unlikely to save us from such errors.

The Appellate Function and Saving Narratives

Recently, a number of writers have begun to question the usefulness of the law and literature movement. Focusing on that enterprise, federal circuit judge Richard Posner has written:

> The functions of legislation and literature are so different, and the objectives of the readers of these two different sorts of mental product so divergent, that the principles and approaches developed for the one have no useful application to the other.[83]

Elsewhere, Posner expands his critique to judging, urging that even great works of literature have little to say to judges, whose objectives are bureaucratic, technical, and narrowly circumscribed and whose work includes a *power* dimension not present in literature.[84]

Although Posner believes that "important opportunities for mutual illumination" between law and literature exist, he finds a danger in exaggerating the commonalities between the two fields.[85] We believe that other reasons counsel skepticism. As we have mentioned, judges, like other persons, are situated actors. Our identities are social constructs; we influence culture and it us. For most persons, perhaps particularly judges, society's dominant narratives will seem unexceptionable and "true," demanding no particular improvement or expansion. Counternarratives will seem foreign or "wrong." The self and culture are reciprocally related; their interaction is powerfully homeostatic. "Power-Knowledge" replicates itself endlessly and ineluctably.[86]

Structural features inherent in the work environment of appellate judges further dampen our faith in the reformative effect of counternarratives. Judges are trained to resolve legal problems on the narrowest possible ground, while literature and narratives point toward expansion. Appellate judges have no juries to serve as reminders that "there may be another story," in addition to the prevailing one, for example, about the police always telling the truth.

Narratives and the Situated Actor

Permeating our reasons for doubt is a sense of our own limitations. Our perception of reality is not a given but rather something we construct. The devices by which we construct and make sense of our social world are largely linguistic, consisting of categories, concepts, and particularly narratives.[87] Exposure to new narratives, texts, and ways of organizing reality may have a very real appeal. Vicarious experience through reading is attractive, can be character-deepening and mind-expanding.[88] Yet the self that meets, selects, as well as deselects and interprets the new narrative also interacts with it and does so in terms of the old narrative. Change is at best slow and incremental. Few of us have been fundamentally changed by reading a single book or even series of them.

Breaking Lockstep:
Two Ways to Avoid Serious Moral Error

We envision two ways to break the lockstep, to avoid the types of mistake we include within the term "serious moral error." The first way is to seek out and disseminate discordant new texts in the hopes that these will enable judges to expand their sympathies and avoid the condemnation of history's judgment. It is unclear, however, how much even conscientious reading of this "outsider literature" will help. Unawareness may be the principal problem; or judges, like most readers, may simply ignore narratives that differ drastically from their own. These differences are perhaps only matters of degree. The same forces that cause an anthologist to exclude a work from the canon cause us as readers to devalue the work even if we happen across it. Placing an arresting, novel piece of outsider literature in the canon is obviously one step in improving the chance of the message's being heard. But because judges wield such significant power, any avenue should be explored. Moreover, judges are interested in transcendence and avoidance of history's condemnation. In a sense, everyone is, but judges perhaps more than most: It is akin to being reversed.

The second is for humanists inside and outside the law to take on the task of critiquing, jarring, displacing, and showing the banal, self-serving nature of many of the current narratives and stories. Creating a genuinely new narrative takes exceptional ability and resources. Further, even if the new narrative is better than the old one, there is no guarantee that it will be perceived as such. Destabilizing and deleting the old edifice of narratives may be easier and is probably a logically prior step toward building a better, fairer world. This task can be carried out in the usual ways, by (1) showing false necessity (the narrative need not have gone that way); (2) showing self-interest behind a story or presupposition; and (3) using irony, humor, and metaphor to destabilize the easy acceptance that surrounds the current tale or understanding.[89]

Could humanists in the law and literature movement take on this role, assuming they desired to do so? Despite their formidable training and skills, might it not turn out that they are just as unable as judges to break free from the constraints of the familiar and move us onto the path of liberation? There are grounds for cautious hope.

First, many of the canonical texts originally had "bite": They were revolutionary and audacious when first written, but have become tame and commonplace through passage of time. The humanists know this better than others; since they know well the setting in which those now-tamed texts were delivered, they know how revolutionary they were for their eras.[90] Further, many of them are experts in textual analysis—they know the multiple meanings and interpretations a passage may be seen to have. Accustomed to discovering hidden riches in familiar material, many of them are more receptive than others to new material, new texts. Moreover, as literature experts they are in a better position than most of us to know developing writers, schools, and ideas. Their training equips them well for the role of critics and appraisers of the extant stock of cultural narratives and stories.

Will they take on this more audacious role? Probably not, unless challenged by outsider writers to do so. Teaching receptive students clever observations on language and text is an easy, enjoyable life. That is, until someone points out to you that *Bowers v. Hardwick* was decided on your watch, that your favorite texts did nothing to stop it, that a highly educated group of judges educated at schools like yours and participating in your culture (the one you helped to create) wrote it, and that no one seems to have found this appalling script lacking. As with judges, there is nothing like the fear of tomorrow's judgment to instill a little needed reexamination into what we do for a living.[91]

3

Why Do We Tell the Same Stories? Law Reform, Critical Librarianship, and the Triple Helix Dilemma

A remarkable sameness afflicts many scholarly articles, books, and doctoral dissertations. Most blame peer review, tenure and promotion requirements, and ivory-tower isolation. In law, additional restraints operate: stare decisis (the insistence that every statement be supported by a previous one), bar requirements, and the tyranny of the casebook.

Although a few legal innovators manage to escape these constraints, an impartial observer casting an eye over the landscape of the law would conclude that most of our stories are notably similar—variations on a theme of incremental reform carried out within the bounds of dominant Western tradition.

We believe that there is an additional and seldom noticed—though much more potent—means by which this sameness is created and maintained: namely, professionally prepared research and classification systems that lawyers employ in researching and understanding the law. We single out three of these in wide use today: the Library of Congress subject heading system, periodical indexes, and the West Digest System. These devices function like DNA—enabling the current system to replicate itself endlessly, easily, and painlessly. Their categories mirror precedent and existing law; they both facilitate traditional thought and constrain novel approaches to the law.

A scholar who works within these systems finds the task of legal research greatly simplified. Beginning with one idea, such systems quickly bring to light closely related ideas, cases, and statutes.[1] They are like a workshop full of well-oiled tools, making work easier. Relying on them exclusively, however, renders innovation more difficult; innovative jurisprudence may require entirely new tools, ones often left undeveloped or unnoticed because our attention is absorbed with manipulating the old versions.[2]

A few legal innovators have risen to this challenge aided, from time to time, by mavericks and reformers in the library science field.[3] On-line word-search strategies promise some hope of breaking the lockstep imposed by older print systems, but even they promise only a partial way out. Nothing approaching a general solution is on the horizon. The categories contained in current indexing systems are like eyeglasses we have worn a long time. They enable us to see better, but lull us into thinking our vision is perfect, that there may not be an even better pair. Even when we obtain that better pair, it, like the old, again eventually sets limits on what we see. This process is inherent in our condition. We move from one set of limitations to another, finding only slightly greater freedom in our new condition. The beginning of wisdom is to understand and, insofar as we may, circumvent our limitations.

Classification Systems in Legal Scholarship

The three principal classification systems in use in the legal world are the Library of Congress subject heading system, which governs library collections; various periodical indexes; and the West Digest System, which classifies legal decisions under various subject headings and "key numbers."

Library of Congress Subject Headings

The *Library of Congress Subject Headings* originated in 1898 when the Library adopted the List of Subject Headings for Use in Dictionary Catalogs as a basis for its own scheme. The first edition was published in parts between 1909 and 1914. Later ones, appearing annually, add new headings, reflect changes in conceptualization, and assure consistency. The current four-volume edition contains 5,091 pages and over 192,000 entries.

The list of headings expands at the rate of approximately 6,000 headings each year. An editorial committee of the Library of Congress Subject Cataloging Division reviews proposals for new headings to determine whether the addition is warranted and congruent with the existing Library of Congress subject headings structure. Although most proposals originate in-house, catalogers at other libraries may also propose changes.[4]

Critics of the Library of Congress complain that its subject heading policy is conservative, excessively cost conscious, and without a coherent philosophy or structure. They also charge that the Library's position of leadership magnifies these weaknesses because other libraries generally follow the Library of Congress's example. Other critics complain that the system of headings replicates majoritarian politics and thought and gives too little attention to new, marginal, or renegade ideas.[5]

Still, many staunchly defend the current system. These defenders point out that the *Library of Congress Subject Headings* was never intended to be an all-inclusive set of categories. When the Library adopted the subject headings, they were adequate for its then small collection. Most libraries, even those with specialized collections, chose to adopt the headings, while the Library of Congress maintained the essentials of the system even as its collection grew. As a result, this system of subject access grew to extend far beyond the task for which it was originally designed. Finally, defenders add that it is reasonable for the Library to take into account the cost of changes (especially when these will be multiplied at other libraries throughout the United States) and that the Library adds new categories when the need for them is shown.[6]

Legal Periodical Indexes

A number of services currently index legal periodicals. We focus on two in wide use: the *Index to Legal Periodicals* and its competitor, *Current Law Index.*

Until 1980 the *Index to Legal Periodicals* was the only comprehensive guide to legal periodicals. When the American Association of Law Libraries published the first volume in 1908, it covered only forty journals. The Association soon broadened its coverage, however, and produced retrospective volumes back to 1898, linking the *Index* with the earlier *Jones-Chipman Index*, which had provided coverage beginning in 1888. H. W. Wilson Co. became the official publisher of the *Index* by 1918 and its owner in 1961. An Index to Legal Periodicals Committee of the American Association of Law Libraries functioned as an advisory body, suggesting new subject headings and consulting with the company on matters of policy. Conflicts over subject headings, breadth of coverage, and other matters caused the Association to dissociate itself from the project in 1978.[7]

The Association's Index Committee then negotiated with Information Access Company to produce *Current Law Index*, which would compete with the *Index to Legal Periodicals*. The new tool first appeared in 1980, indexing 660 periodicals and newspapers—about double the coverage of its competitor.[8] The Information Access Company originally distributed its product in hard copy; it later added a cumulative version on microfilm, laserdisc, and on-line with slightly broadened content. Coverage for *Current Law Index* in any of its forms extends back only to 1980; for articles published before that time the researcher must consult the *Index to Legal Periodicals.*

Both indexing services provide subject access but derive their headings from different but interlinking sources. The *Index to Legal Periodicals* lists *Black's Law Dictionary* (published by West) and West's *Legal Thesaurus/Dictionary* as sources of authority.[9] *Current Law Index* is based on Library of Congress subject headings with modifications.[10] The Library of Congress lists *Black's Law Dictionary* and *Current Law Index* as principal sources used to establish authority.[11] The circle is nearly complete.[12]

The West Digest System

Prior to the development of the West Digest System, there was no comprehensive or uniform indexing of state and federal cases.[13] As a result, late nineteenth- and early twentieth-century lawyers and legal scholars encountered a great deal of difficulty as they struggled with the unwieldy body of American law.[14] As one scholar put it: "In substance our law is excellent, full of justice and good sense, but in form it is chaotic. It has no systematic arrangement which is generally recognized and used, a fact which greatly increases the labors of lawyers and causes unnecessary litigation."[15] Some noted that the inability of lawyers to follow the development of the law threatened stare decisis (the system of precedent) because of the "enormous and unrestrained quantity" of competing reporters, which "discouraged research and inevitably led to a conflict among authorities."[16]

In 1876 the West Company published its first compilations of court reports, *The Syllabi*.[17] By 1879 the company published a permanent edition, the *North Western Reporter*, which included judicial decisions of the Dakota Territory, Iowa, Michigan, Minnesota, Nebraska, and Wisconsin. Facing little competition, West soon blanketed the country with its scheme of regional reporters, which came to be known as the National Reporter System. The system today covers the various federal and state courts, and some sets of statutes.

The West Company built its success on its national coverage, which offered both access to myriad judicial decisions and an efficient means of managing them. To assist lawyers searching for precedent, West provided a uniform plan of headnotes and indexing in all of its reporters. It issued the first *American Digest Annual* in 1887. In its first century, West published about two and one-half million opinions with an average of five headnotes each; it currently publishes about sixty thousand cases a year.[18]

In 1898 the American Bar Association endorsed the *Digest*, reinforcing West's central role in indexing and reporting U.S. case law.[19] Critics have been more guarded. To them, what began as a system abstracted and constructed out of its primary source data—judicial opinions—had transformed itself into a rigid grand scheme into which the law itself had to be fit.[20]

West has weathered this and other criticisms in part by its cautious and somewhat secretive nature. A 1983 article states that eight classification editors assign keynotes to cases; thirty-four general editors who work under them write headnotes and synopses. Change comes slowly: The topic "labor" received a heading only in the 1950s, and until recently West classified "workers' compensation" under "master and servant" law.

West faced a major challenge in 1970 when Mead Data Central introduced LEXIS, the first full-text database containing judicial opinions. The familiar world of print now had to compete with a randomly available on-line universe accessible through any combination of search words the user framed. WESTLAW, West's response to LEXIS, appeared in the mid-1970s and has undergone continual modification and improvement.[21]

Classification Systems and the Replication of Preexisting Thought: The Triple Helix Dilemma

Existing classification systems serve their intended purpose admirably: They enable one to find helpful cases, articles, and books. Their power is instrumental; once lawyers know what they are looking for, the classification systems enable them to find it. Yet, the very search for authority, precedent, and hierarchy in cases and statutes can create the false impression that law is exact and deterministic—a science—with only one correct answer to a legal question.

Moreover, in many instances researchers will not know what they are looking for. The situation may call for innovation. The indexing systems may not have developed a category for the issue being researched, or having done so, may still have failed to enter a key item into the database selected by the researcher, thus rendering the system useless. Indexing systems function rather like molecular biology's double helix: They replicate preexisting ideas, thoughts, and approaches. Within the bounds of the three systems, moderate, incremental reform remains quite possible, but the systems make foundational, transformative innovation difficult. Because the three systems operate in a coordinated network of information retrieval, we call the situation confronting the lawyer or scholar trying to break free from their constraints the triple helix dilemma.

To illustrate this problem, consider the range of related headings found under the general rubric of civil rights. Recently, scholars have begun to question basic premises in this area of law. Some have challenged the utility of majoritarian theory developed in white-dominated academic milieux. Others have called into question key presuppositions of civil rights cases and statutes, observing that present legal remedies generally benefit whites more than blacks and provide relief for the latter only when they do not impose unacceptable costs on elite whites. They also cast doubt on cherished beliefs: for example, that blacks are experiencing steady socio-economic gains, that affirmative action enables many to move ahead in the workplace, and that the foremost challenge facing the civil rights community is attacking individual and institutional racism through education, litigation, and progressive legislation.[22]

These writers have found current legal categorization schemes a hindrance more than a help. A glance at the standard categories shows why: Each system bears a strong imprint of the incremental civil rights approach these writers decry. The *Index to Legal Periodicals* and *Decennial Digest*, for example, lead the reader to works on civil rights, employment discrimination, and school integration or desegregation but contain no entry for hegemony or interest-convergence. The *Index to Legal Periodicals* lacked an entry for critical legal studies until September 1987, nearly a decade after the movement began. The *Decennial Digest* contains few, if any, entries dealing with black urban poverty. To find such cases, one must look in the Descriptive Word Index under "slums," which refers the searcher to "public improvements" under the topic "municipal corporations." Another index contains an entry labeled, simply, "races." As of the time of publication of this book, none of the major indexes contains entries for "essentialism," "legitimation," "false consciousness," "narrative jurisprudence," or many other themes of the "new," or critical race, scholarship. Indeed, researchers who confined themselves to the sources listed under standard civil rights headings would be unlikely to come in contact with these ideas much less invent them on their own.

As an example of the channeling effect of current legal categorization schemes, consider the situation of black women wishing to sue for job discrimination directed against them as black women. Attorneys searching for precedent will find a large body of case and statutory law under the headings "race discrimination" and "sex discrimination." No category combines the two types of discrimination (although computer-assisted research can better approximate a cross-referencing system by combining the two categories in the same search). Attorneys for black women thus have filed suit under one category or the other, or sometimes both. Recently, critics have pointed out that under this approach black women will lose if the employer can show that it has a satisfactory record for hiring and promoting women generally (including white women) and similarly for hiring blacks (including black men). The employer will prevail even if it has been blatantly discriminatory against black women, because the legal classification schemes treat black women like the most advantaged members of each group (white women and black men, respectively) when in fact they are probably the least advantaged.[23]

To correct this problem, legal scholars have recently created the concept of intersectionality and urged that black women's unique situation be recognized, named, and addressed. Of course, more than the absence of an index category created the black women's dilemma. But until the gap was recognized and named, legal classification systems made it difficult to notice or redress. Reform will require disaggregation of the current dichotomous classification scheme, creation of a more complex one, and reorganization of the relevant cases and statutes accordingly.

Word-based computer searches solve only part of the problem. Some key articles and cases dealing with concepts such as civil disobedience and legitimation do not refer to them by name; others that do are not included in standard legal databases.[24] The efficacy of word-based searches depends on the probability that the searcher and the court have used the same word or phrase for the concept in question.[25] Computers may be excellent means of finding cases about cows that wander onto highways. They are less useful in finding cases that illustrate or discuss more complex or abstract concepts. Word-based computer searches provide little assistance to the researcher in coining a concept or word. They are most useful once someone has proposed the concept or word and an editor has entered the text containing it into the database.[26] Finally, computerized research can "freeze" the law by limiting the search to cases containing particular words or expressions. Research is apt to be most creative if it encourages browsing and analogical reasoning. Because it lacks this capacity, computer-assisted research can discourage innovation and law reform.

LEXIS, WESTLAW, and their users are now more sophisticated than in the early days when simple questions stumped the companies' demonstrators, but many of these problems remain. A number of observers suggested adding subject indexing to the LEXIS and WESTLAW systems, thus interposing another human being's subjective judgment between researcher and text—the very element computer-assisted legal research was designed to replace. Natural (that is, non-Boolean) language searching obviates some of this difficulty.

Existing legal research systems thus tug the researcher toward the familiar, the conventional. The researcher quickly discovers preexisting ideas, arguments, and legal strategies and is rewarded for staying on familiar ground. Striking out on one's own is costly and inefficient. Courts, other scholars, and one's adversary will all frame the problem in common terms; the temptation to go along is almost irresistible. Stepping outside the framework is like abandoning a well-known and well-mapped coast for the uncharted sea. We never realize that we cannot embark on certain types of journeys armed only with conventional maps.

Preexisting legal thought replicates itself. The indexes put one set of ideas at the researcher's disposal; it becomes difficult to visualize another or imagine that one could exist. Nevertheless, a few thinkers do manage to escape the trammels we have discussed and propose new ways of thinking about legal reality. The next section explores ways to achieve this innovation, including how to turn the existing classification systems to the advantage of the legal transformer.

How to Break the Circle

We can sometimes break the circle of repetitive thought and scholarship and achieve genuine innovation. Just as in evolution, where organisms regularly appear with traits not present in their ancestors, each generation presents us with a few legal thinkers able to break free from the constraints of preexisting thought and offer striking and effective new approaches.

Often, but not always, these thinkers will be individuals whose life experiences have differed markedly from those of their contemporaries.[27] They may be members of marginal groups or persons who are in other ways separated from the mainstream. In civil rights scholarship, one thinks of Derrick Bell, whose work on interest-convergence, the usefulness of standard remedies, and parables of racial injustice is challenging the civil rights community to reexamine long-held assumptions.[28] We should heed these divergent individuals. Their ideas offer the possibility of legal transformation and growth. Like nature's mutant or hybrid, they offer the infusion of new material needed to retain the vitality of our system of thought.

Can others acquire the skill that some possess at transcending conventional legal categories and modes of thought? In a recent article, one scholar implies that "suspicion" may be an acquired ability, which we can sharpen through experience.[29] We are less sanguine. Creativity is neither widely nor predictably distributed among the human population, nor is it easily acquired. In law and politics innovative potential may be linked with "double consciousness"[30] or life experiences that in some way deviate from the norm. The incentive to innovate may be stronger in persons for whom the current system does not work well. The pressures of a lawyer's life may hinder creativity.[31] Law professors are not free of all those pressures—they have classes to teach, papers to grade, meetings to attend and are distracted by other minutiae of academic life. Perhaps we can only try to look beyond the conventional and applaud those who, often for unknown reasons, actually do so.

Our bondage itself offers a second route to transformation. Categories in the principal legal indexing systems are explicit. They exist externally as well as within our minds. If we examine them, we will see an outline of the structure of traditional legal thought.[32] That structure will reveal what previous courts and writers have recognized and indexers faithfully recorded. By inspecting this record, we may gain a glimpse of the very conceptual framework we have been wielding in scrutinizing and interpreting our social order. We may then inquire whether that framework is the only, or the best, means of doing so. We may turn that system on its side and ask what is missing, or how that which is there is organized. (See, for example, the telltale patterns of symposium publishing detailed in Chapter 5.)

Our review of the way civil rights categories limit thought and innovation showed that open-minded inquiry is not easy. Yet, a skeptical examination of what exists may sometimes prompt a researcher to ask why something else does *not* exist. For example, a feminist study group recently explored a legal issue affecting women. Although the members knew of several cases that dealt with the problem, West indexers had created no category for it. Thus, the only way to find the cases was to know about one and search for others that followed it or perform a computer search employing as many descriptive terms and synonyms as possible. The feminists, sophisticated in the workings of patriarchy and mindset, concluded from their experience that the oversight was not merely inadvertent, but was rooted in the structure of male-dominated law. Less sophisticated users might have blamed themselves for their inability to find the right section of the Digest or concluded that the absence of a category was an isolated oversight attributable, perhaps, to bibliographic lag that would be cleared up in the next edition.[33]

Going beyond standard legal categories and conventional wisdom is difficult even when we are only looking for moderate, incremental reform that does little to tax one's imagination or the traditional legal system. There are a few means by which we can sometimes escape the constraints of current legal categories to examine the framework that underlies legal reality. These strategies enable us to discover the intricacies and limitations inherent in our framework, make allowances for them, and so view reality in a truer, fairer light. Yet, an expanded framework will in time become a further shackle, requiring yet another struggle to break free.[34] We can only hope to progress from one degree of nonfreedom to another, slightly less confining, one. Vigilance and effort are required to achieve even these modest gains.

PART TWO

On the Difficulty of Hearing
What Our Prophets Are Saying

Sometimes a failure of imagination lies at the heart of resistance to reform. If we surmount that obstacle a different one often appears—namely, a failure of perception—just as a reform movement crystallizes and gathers force. The reformers' message disconcerts: If true, our world would need to change. There would be confusion; power would shift. Accordingly, we ignore or trivialize what they say or translate their concerns into more familiar, less challenging terms. Chapter 4 deals with ways in which mainstream (even liberal) legal scholars marginalize outsider writing. Chapter 5 discusses a second mechanism—gathering with the like-minded—by which we cope with fragmentation and trouble. Chapter 6 addresses translation and failure-to-see as responses to radical new claims. This chapter examines the reactions of a number of writers and social scientists to the suggestion that hard-core pornography needs to be regulated because it injures women.

4

The Imperial Scholar:
How to Marginalize Outsider Writing

Ten years ago one of us wrote a law review article, "The Imperial Scholar: Reflections on a Review of Civil Rights Literature,"[1] that became one of the more controversial pieces of its era. It has been cited innumerable times, as often without approval as with. Even as sympathetic a coreligionist as Derrick Bell describes it as "an intellectual hand grenade, tossed over the wall of the establishment as a form of academic protest."[2]

The article showed that an inner circle of twenty-six scholars, all male and white, occupied the central arenas of civil rights scholarship to the exclusion of minority scholars. When a member of this inner circle wrote about civil rights issues he cited almost exclusively other members of the circle for support. This exclusion of minority scholars' writings about key issues of race law caused the literature dealing with race, racism, and American law to be blunted, skewed, and riddled with omissions. Among the reasons for the curious citation practices were (1) the mistaken belief that minority authors who wrote about racial issues were not objective; (2) the mainstream writers' need to remain in control, thus ensuring that legal change does not occur too quickly; and (3) the sense of personal satisfaction this group derived from being at the forefront of a powerful social movement.[3]

The essay concluded by urging minority students and teachers to question insistently the unsatisfactory scholarship produced by the inner circle and encouraged white liberal authors to redirect their energies toward other areas. Although provoking a storm when they appeared, many of the article's premises and assertions seem commonplace today.[4]

This chapter, a sequel to "The Imperial Scholar," addresses the "second generation" question: What happens when a group of insurgent scholars gains admission to the inner circle and earns the credibility and credentials that warrant consideration by mainstream scholars? Are these new scholars promptly granted equal standing, integrated fully into the conversations, colloquies, footnotes, and exchanges that constitute legal-academic discourse on issues of race and equality? Or are they still marginalized, muffled, and kept in limbo—to be seen, perhaps, but not heard?

This inquiry focuses on two groups of insurgent scholars—critical race theorists and radical feminists—who were barely beginning to make themselves heard at the time "The Imperial Scholar" was written. Ten years later, members of these groups teach at the top law schools, publish in the best law reviews. Their work is subject to commentary by distinguished colleagues and critics,[5] their controversies covered by the *New York Times* and *The Nation*.[6] Even if not in the living room, they are plainly somewhere "inside the door." What reception are they receiving?

We examine the treatment of these new writers at the hands of two groups. First, we analyze their treatment by the original twenty-six "imperial scholars." Have this latter group's practices changed for the better, perhaps as a result of exposure to works such as "The Imperial Scholar"? Second, we examine how the two oppositional groups are cited by mainstream scholars generally. Our conclusion is that writers in the scholarly mainstream, ones who control the terms of discourse, marginalize outsider writing as long as possible. In what follows we do not attempt to "prove" this conclusion in any scientific sense. Our intent is not to bring the guilty parties to justice; some may yet change their ways. Rather, our hope is that mainstream writers who recognize themselves in these pages will reevaluate their scholarly practices with respect to insurgent scholars. At the same time, we hope that what we say will assist outsider scholars in articulating their criticisms of attempts to keep them on the margin.

The continuing marginalization of outsider scholars, although perhaps distressing for the cause of social reform, should not come as a surprise. It is what studies of narrative theory and paradigm shifting would predict. Reform tends to be slow and incremental; new knowledge strikes us as extreme, coercive, "political," or strange. Yet even if natural, this resistance is unfortunate and self-defeating, depriving us of points of view that we need for a more comprehensive view of the world. Sometimes, though, we suspect that resistance is based upon inertia, entrenchment, or sheer hostility to that which is new. Whatever its cause, the phenomenon is widespread enough to suggest that without real effort resistance to reform may become a standard feature of our intellectual landscape.

What the Outsiders Are Saying:
A Brief Analytical Summary

Outsider jurisprudence takes three principal forms: critical legal studies (CLS),[7] feminism,[8] and the "new" or critical race theory (CRT).[9] Critical thought, in general, traces its origins to European writers such as Marx,

Martin Heidegger, Antonio Gramsci, and Michel Foucault, as well as to the work of the Frankfurt school that flourished during the 1920s. Critical thought first gained a foothold in philosophy, literature, sociology, and anthropology, where criticalists challenged received ideas such as universality, objectivity, neutrality, and the notion that every text had a single or determinate meaning.

Law lagged behind other text-based disciplines in incorporating these new approaches. For example, hermeneutics, the science of textual interpretation, had entered the study of scriptural texts through the nineteeth-century writings of Friedrich Schleiermacher; in the 1970s, structuralism and deconstruction added a new dimension to the interpretation of literary texts.[10] Not until the 1980s, however, did critical legal scholars introduce deconstruction into law.

They also borrowed the idea of indeterminacy and applied it to law, urging that legal reasoning rarely, if ever, has just "one right answer."[11] Instead, there will be multiple interpretations of the available precedent from which judges may choose in resolving the case before them. Other criticalists look behind legal reasoning to the panoply of presuppositions, agendas, and hidden assumptions that make up legal culture—the baseline from which legal argument proceeds. Duncan Kennedy, for example, analyzed *Blackstone's Commentaries* and showed how its underlying structure reflected and advanced the values of Western liberal-capitalist thought.[12] Other scholars have applied deconstructionist techniques to specific areas of law such as contracts, property, and civil rights.

Critical legal studies influenced two additional movements—feminist legal thought and CRT. Feminist legal scholars write about the ubiquitous patriarchy of the law and other social institutions.[13] Scholars such as Catharine MacKinnon and Robin West have focused on pornography,[14] divorce laws,[15] and sexual harassment[16] in the workplace. Other writers have decried law's embrace of universality, urging instead an emphasis on context, particularity, and "voice."[17] Feminist legal scholars also have examined legal education, addressing such issues as bias in the curriculum, silencing in the classroom, and lack of opportunities for women following graduation.[18] They have challenged male bias in law school appointments, promotion, and tenure standards.[19] Some have written critiques of standard casebooks that exclude women or their point of view.[20] Others have written women's legal history and biography.

Criticism is not aimed exclusively at mainstream legal thought, however. Within feminism itself, two debates currently are being waged. In one, feminist scholars debate the extent to which feminism can be incorporated within traditional jurisprudence or whether, by contrast, it has a unique methodology.[21] A related issue is the necessity or advisability of defining a unitary ("essential") position for the movement.[22] Feminists of color, for example, have been urging that the privileging of white women's perspectives leads to marginalization of their own experience and inattention to their unique needs.[23] The differences in perspective and agenda that feminists find between themselves and the dominant male framework must be carried further to include differences within the female community itself.[24] Writers such as Kimberlè Crenshaw, Mari Matsuda, and Leslie Espinoza have been raising such issues in connection with race-remedies law, hate-speech, employment discrimination, and other areas.[25]

Critical race theory took root in the late 1970s when Derrick Bell first questioned the adequacy of conventional race-remedies law to achieve its self-professed aims. Minority scholars in this movement expressed dismay that the gains of the civil rights era were unstable and indeed were being rolled back in the late 1970s and 1980s. New approaches were needed to take account of the complex interaction among race, racism, and American law.[26] A central theme of much of this scholarship is interest-convergence—an idea developed by Derrick Bell—which holds that the majority group advances the cause of racial justice only when it suits its interest to do so.[27] Some even argue that civil rights law furthers and deepens the dilemma of persons of color. Some explain that race-remedies law serves a homeostatic function, assuring that racial progress occurs at just the right slow pace. Too-rapid change would be terrifying for the white majority; too-slow change could prove destabilizing.[28] Other writers use critical tools to address classic civil rights issues, such as federal Indian law,[29] reparations for blacks and Asians,[30] remedies for racist speech and hate crimes,[31] immigration policy and bilingual education,[32] sentencing and capital punishment,[33] and the elimination of bias in civil litigation and alternative dispute resolution.[34]

Many of these writers employ innovative forms of writing, such as parables, narratives, poems, and chronicles, to address racial injustice in ways not possible in conventional legal style.[35] After many years of effort, nonmainstream scholars seem to have gained some level of acceptance. The Association of American Law Schools chose as its theme for its 1990 annual meeting in San Francisco, California, "A Time for Sharing: Speaking Difference, Sharing Strength." Plenary speakers and workshop panelists of color addressed such critical issues as narrative theory and race, the current retrenchment of American race-remedies law, and majority mindset in legal institutions.[36]

Will this recognition continue and grow? For this to happen, critical scholarship must reach a wide audience, must begin to be absorbed by the intellectual mainstream. This chapter and the following one examine whether this is likely to happen.

Reception by the Elders

Ten years ago, "The Imperial Scholar" showed that when insurgent scholars begin knocking at the door, they are ignored as long as possible. Once they gain admission,[37] the situation becomes more complex. Some inner-circle writers abandon the field. Others remain but retain the habit of ignoring scholarship they wish not to recognize. Still others use a series of mechanisms to muffle and tame the new, divergent scholarship. Finally, some members of the inner circle have begun to integrate the outsiders' scholarship into their own writing and thought.

Abandonment of the Field

Most civil rights writing (by which we mean to include writing about women's rights) published in current top legal journals is written by women and minorities. As new writers have entered the field, established ones have either reduced their production or left the field entirely. What a famous federal judge called the "minstrel show"[38]—black rights being enforced and interpreted by white men—is finally coming to an end. Part of the abandonment is simply due to increasing age: Some of the great names of ten years ago have died or retired. Others are moving into the golden part of their careers, during which heavily documented and supported scholarship can give way to "reflections," opinion pieces, and musings that rely not on the careful analysis and painstaking research of traditional articles but on the strength of a reputation built by such analysis and research. The aging of the inner circle alone, however, does not account for the entire shift in the demographics of authorship on race or gender and the law.

Instead, many inner-circle writers have moved on to other fields. Perhaps they do not see race and women's issues as the urgent topics they were in the 1960s and 1970s. Many are now writing about jurisprudence, federal courts, constitutional interpretation, and strict construction—issues our more conservative times have placed on the front burner. In the case of some, it could be argued that they moved on to bigger and better things.

It may be, as well, that as recognition of female and minority voices progresses some members of the inner circle find their efforts neither as necessary nor as productive as they once were. When a middle-class, white male scholar sees articles written by outsider scholars published in the top law reviews, he may well ask himself why he should continue writing about those same issues (with which he has a much more tenuous connection). Perhaps he wrote, in part, out of generosity or a sense of social obligation. Now that others have taken up the torch, his efforts may seem less necessary.

Antidiscrimination law has not been given over entirely to minority and feminist scholars, however. Nor should it be. For one thing, white males are affected to some degree by issues of racial justice. Moreover, we certainly do not need ghettoization; the cross-fertilization resulting from integrated scholarship can be as beneficial as recognition of long-neglected voices. The inner-circle writers who continue to write about civil rights are examined next.

Those Who Stayed

The original inner-circle scholars who continue to write about civil rights can be divided into three groups. Some have proceeded as they always did, virtually oblivious to the voices of those who are in many ways the subjects of the imperialists' writing. These scholars we call the Unconverted. A second, more interesting group has acknowledged the new scholarship but developed an arsenal of mechanisms for taming and restructuring it. These are the Latter-Day Imperialists. A third group recognizes the outsider scholars, agreeing and disagreeing with them as they do with their inner-circle colleagues. This is the Road to Damascus group, for they have seen the light.

The Unconverted

A few from the original group continue to ignore the new voices of color and the feminists. This practice leads to many of the scholarly deficiencies noted in "The Imperial Scholar," deficiencies extending far beyond failure to give recognition when it is due. The author of a recent article on the right to an abortion, for example, slights feminist analysis and describes the woman's interest as lacking any constitutional or moral foundation. He frames the issue as the right to destroy third-party life, cites mainly male authorities, and gives short shrift to feminist commentators, mentioning but three in passing footnotes.[39]

Others do cite the new literature but opt for the most familiar, safest versions. For example, when Harvard professor Laurence Tribe writes of the critique of constitutional determinacy, he often refers to writers such as Mark Tushnet, ignoring the even sharper criticisms by feminists such as Catharine MacKinnon and critical race theorists such as Derrick Bell.[40] This results in a softened and incomplete picture of the debate about liberalism's defects.[41] It produces works like a recently updated textbook on civil rights legislation that cites nearly every inner-circle author but gives only one grudging "see generally" cite to a famous feminist and another to an emerging young female scholar of the fem-crit school.[42] The impression one could receive from reading these otherwise impressive works is that the liberal system of law and politics that has reigned since 1930 is largely intact and that the challengers are doing little more than raising variations on a familiar theme.

The Latter-Day Imperialists

There comes a time when most scholars can no longer ignore the work being done by previously excluded writers. At this point, two responses are possible. One is thoughtful inclusion of outsider work. The other is limited, grudging, or calculated acceptance, coupled with resort to a panoply of devices to reduce its impact. The old-line, inner-circle scholars have employed three types of mechanism to lessen the threat of outsider scholarship; newcomers to the field have developed even more.[43]

Mechanism One: Oh yes, before I forget—The afterthought. One way to acknowledge outsider scholarship without fully assimilating it is to cite it at the end of a long footnote. In the main text the author can continue to rely on the familiar list of friends and acquaintances.[44] This approach allows the author to show that he is familiar with the new work, while avoiding fully accounting for it in his analysis. The approach also conveys the message that minority or feminist writing is deservedly obscure and worthy only of passing mention.

Mechanism Two: The stereotypical dismissal. An established author can dismiss a troublesome radical by caricaturing her or appealing to the reader's preexisting assumptions about her writings without treating those writings seriously.[45] Alternatively, the author can call the new voices utopian, daring, "interesting," or not really doing law.[46] These approaches enable the writer to avoid confronting what the criticalist is saying. The teeth of the criticism are thus drawn, and it emerges in more innocuous form than if it had remained unmentioned.

Mechanism Three: I'm so hip. The Establishment writer cites to his familiar inner circle for 95 percent of his article. Then, for a proposition that cries out for citation to a critical race theorist or feminist, the author will cite to one: "Aren't I hip!" The author appears to be recognizing and assimilating outsider scholarship while actually doing little to integrate it into his own.[47] For example, a scholar writing or teaching about developments in evidence law considers feminist thought only in connection with his treatment of rape. He then writes the rest of his article or teaches the rest of his course as he has always done—linearly, hierarchically, and with little thought to its impact on women or the poor.[48]

Those on the Road to Damascus

A few original inner-circle authors have understood and incorporated the writings of the critical race theorists and feminists. Instead of dismissing their writings or ignoring them outright, the mainstream author engages their propositions or ideas in a forthright manner.[49] When an author raises an issue from outsider scholarship and takes the time to discuss his agreement or disagreement with it, he recognizes its validity and relevance; it is not simply brushed aside or ignored.[50]

This thoughtful treatment of outsider scholarship encourages expansion of the civil rights canon. It constitutes an awareness on the part of members of the inner circle that civil rights writing has not really been composed of two different strains but instead of parallel traditions that must inevitably lose their Euclidean separateness and become one integrated tradition. There is nothing magical about this merging. It is a matter of scholarship as usual. Relevant, important work exists; it is read, criticized, and cited. The only thing remarkable about this scholarship as usual is that, in law, in a few places, it is finally happening.

Reception by the New Generation

"The Imperial Scholar" showed that the bulk of writing in the areas of equality and civil rights was done by a small circle of approximately two dozen white male scholars publishing in the top reviews and teaching at the top law schools.

Since then, however, newcomers have arrived on the scene. Many of them are white; most are male; some have brought reputations achieved in other areas of the law. As with the old-line group, we find that a few of the new scholars are relatively egalitarian in their scholarship, citing critical race theorists and radical feminists about as frequently as one might fairly expect. Some new scholars, however, steadfastly rely on the familiar stalwarts. A third group, the "neo-imperialist" scholars, for our purposes the most fascinating, has deployed an almost baroque variety of ways to minimize, marginalize, co-opt, soften, miss the point of, selectively ignore, or generally devalue the new insurgent writers.

Mechanisms Four and Five: The hero, the zero. As with the original inner-circle scholars, the new majority-race writers include both heroes and zeroes. Duncan Kennedy, Alan Freeman, Alex Aleinikoff, and Gary Peller cite the new voices, sometimes agreeing and sometimes taking issue with them.[51] Other new entrants, however, either ignore the oppositional scholars or treat their work diffidently. One dynamic young majority-race writer, for example, in an otherwise helpful article refers to dozens of white male writers but collects works by women and minority authors in a single footnote, doing little to distinguish, quote, or refer to particular passages from them.[52] Another author offers two "special interest" references, one for feminists and one for critical race theorists.[53] In an article on slavery and slave law, a third only once cites to Bell's *Race, Racism and American Law,* a standard work[54]—she cites several well-known white scholars more often—and at no time mentions Leon Higginbotham's well-regarded history, *In the Matter of Color.*[55] A fourth wrote a stinging footnote chastising a number of the new-voice authors for dangerous reliance on notions of class-based harm and redress.[56] Unlike some, this author at least cited oppositional scholars for a proposition, if only to attack it.

Mechanism Six: "Yeah, yeah"—No need to tell me more. Many of the new writers in the field of civil rights cite work by women and minorities as perfunctorily as the old-timers do, but with a difference. That difference consists of citing an early page of an article or book—for example, page 3, not page 403. When an author does this regularly, it raises the suspicion that he has not bothered to read the entire article or book but has merely leafed through the article's preface or introduction in search of a general proposition he can cite with a minimum of effort. The author discharges his obligation to refer to the new voices but avoids the hard work of reading and dealing seriously with the entire piece. The number of references to the middle or latter pages of Catharine MacKinnon's writing on pornography is much smaller than those to its opening pages, a treatment some other radical feminists receive as well.[57] Women will recognize this treatment as a conversational gambit many men use—interruption. The male listens to a woman's opening words, then bursts in to finish her sentence, saying "Yeah, yeah. I get it; no need to go on ... now, what do you think about *my* idea?"[58] Derrick Bell also garners references of this sort.

Mechanism Seven: "I know"—The facile (and safe) translation. This mechanism translates a novel, hard-edged, and discomfiting thesis by an outside writer so that it becomes familiar, safe, and tame. Often the translation forces the thesis into liberal-legalist terms that the original author did not intend. For example, some scholars translate MacKinnon's work on pornography into an "intriguing First Amendment hypothesis." MacKinnon, of course, does not consider pornography a First Amendment question but a near-crime, a civil rights offense against women. Once translated into a First Amendment framework her proposal loses much of its urgency and original character.[59]

Mechanism Eight: "I loved Dan's idea." A number of the new writers show familiarity with ideas feminists and critical race theory scholars have been proposing but either forget where they heard them[60] or cite a derivative source—a critic or a majority-race commentator—to summarize the outsider view in question. For example, some scholars rely on Randall Kennedy, a critic of critical race theory, for a summary of that theory; others cite men such as Cass Sunstein for radical feminist views developed by Catharine MacKinnon and others. One writer cited Deborah

Rhode for "reasoning from the bottom,"[61] a view associated at least as much with critical race scholar Mari Matsuda.

This approach corresponds to another experience familiar to most women—co-optation. A woman proposes an idea; no one in the group reacts. Twenty minutes later, a male restates and puts forward the same suggestion, which immediately wins widespread praise and thereafter becomes "Dan's idea."

Mechanism Nine: "I know just how you must have felt"—Co-optation of others' experience. Some of the new writers, and a few of the original ones, make an effort to identify with the stories and accounts the outsider narrativists are offering but in a way that co-opts or minimizes these stories.[62] The majority-race author draws a parallel between something in the experience of the outsider author and something that happened to him. There is nothing wrong with using analogies and metaphors to deal with the experience of others; that is how we expand our sympathies. If, however, we analogize to refocus a conversation or an article toward ourselves exclusively, something is wrong, especially if the experience to which we liken another's is manifestly less serious. For example, the author of one article on campus racial harassment observes that everyone experiences "insulting" or "upsetting" speech at one time or another. What is so special, she asks, about the racist version?[63]

Mechanism Ten: "Pure poetry"—How poignant, touching, etc.—Placing outsider writing on a pedestal. Some writers of majority race praise the new writing for its passionate or emotional quality. The writing is so personal, so colorful, so poetic—so "moving."[64] This approach marginalizes outsider writing by placing it in a category of its own. Women and minority writers feel more deeply than we; they have "soul."[65] The writing is evaluated as a journal of the author's individual thoughts and feelings, not as delivering uncomfortable truths about society and injustice.

Mechanism Eleven: Assimilation/co-optation—"We have been saying this all along." This mechanism dismisses the feminists and critical race theorists as saying little that is new; we have been making the same points about brotherhood, equality, and civility for hundreds, if not thousands, of years. Plato, Aquinas, John Austin, Roberto Unger, and any favorite male author urged that society be arranged justly, that all members should be treated with respect.[66] Of course, on some level, every truth is foreshadowed by or included in every other. Yet one might argue that earlier authorities wrote inadequately, spoke poorly to our condition, because that condition persists today. If outsider voices are addressing new or old grievances in new ways, one ought not dismiss what they are saying merely because someone else previously said something remotely similar.[67]

Mechanism Twelve: "She wrote just one" (And I'll cite it, too). Some of the mainstream authors treat the new voices as though each of them had written exactly one article or book.[68] Susan Estrich is cited for her book on rape, Mari Matsuda for "Looking to the Bottom," Derrick Bell for *And We Are Not Saved,* and Richard Delgado for "Words that Wound." Each of these writers has written many works, arguably of comparable merit to the one cited. Routinized, stereotypical citation gives the impression the author wrote only the one. It also conveys the message that insurgent writers can only write one work, probably an anomaly, the result of a gigantic effort or internal convulsion that they are capable of producing only once in a lifetime.[69]

Mechanism Thirteen: The all-purpose citation. The author has a flash of insight, for example, into the way constitutional equality works. Midway through the article it dawns on him that he had better cite a minority. What better place to do so than for the propositions that (1) racism is terrible, (2) discrimination still exists, and (3) we all must work really hard at dealing with it? Most authors of color surely say these things somewhere, so the author chooses one. How about Crenshaw?[70]

"At the Margin": Why We Always Fail to Recognize New Stories

Even though the new voices are finding their way into the pages of the top reviews and journals, as we have seen they are not being quickly and easily integrated into the conversations and dialogues of traditional legal scholarship. Some of the resistance may be intentional and mean-spirited—why should I cite that outsider after the things she said about me or my friends?[71] Resistance may also be the product of inflexibility and an unwillingness to entertain new positions—I'm forty-five years old; why do I have to read all these new authors anyway?

But most mainstream legal writers are neither mean-spirited nor lazy; the most likely explanations for the mechanisms detailed lie elsewhere. Current legal scholarship is radically transforming itself. Formalism, case-crunching notes, and articles running a hundred pages or more, littered with hundreds of footnotes, are passing into history. Even legal process and interdisciplinary "law and" scholarship have lost much of their momentum. In their places a subtler yet more audacious form of legal writing has appeared, with roots in postmodernism, critical thought, and narrative theory. The authors, format, and authorities cited are radically different from those that came before. If this is not a full-fledged paradigm shift, then something like one seems to be happening. As sociologists of knowledge have pointed out, such shifts are at first resisted by those steeped in the old regime; the paradigm changes only when the costs of resisting it become unacceptable compared to the gains of adopting the new one. Resistance to new voices, then, may be as natural as that which the Langdellians and "mechanical jurisprudes" mounted to legal realism early in this century. All change is costly. What more natural reaction than postponing dealing with it as long as possible?

A second, related explanation applies insights from narrative theory. As many have pointed out, reality comes to us not as a given but in terms of narratives, mindsets, or stories—interpretive structures by which we construct and come to terms with the world around us. We are all the products of a large number of such understandings by which we reduce the diversity of daily life to manageable proportions. In a sense, we are our stock of stories and they us.[72]

When a feminist or critical race theorist offers a radically new account, we evaluate it in terms of the one we currently hold. If it seems too different, we are apt to reject it as extreme, coercive, political, harsh, or untrue. Imagine, for example, the reaction of most liberal law students on hearing Derrick Bell's interest-convergence hypothesis for the first time.[73] The first response is often reinterpretation—softening or qualifying it on the ground that Bell could not have intended to interpret the search for racial justice in such pessimistic fashion. Yet for many radical race reformers, the hypothesis seems commonplace and true.

Both mechanisms lead to a melancholy truth: We postpone confronting novelty and change until they acquire enough momentum that we are swept forward. We take seriously new social thought only after hearing it so often that its tenets and themes begin to seem familiar, inevitable, and true. We then adopt the new paradigm, and the process repeats itself. We reject new thought until, eventually, its hard edges soften, its suggestions seem tame and manageable, its proponents elder statespersons to be feared no longer. By then, of course, the new thought has lost its radically transformative character. We reject the medicine that could save us until, essentially, it is too late.

Nearly ten years ago "The Imperial Scholar" identified an inner circle of white male scholars who systematically excluded minority voices from the central arenas of civil rights scholarship. Almost a decade later many of the actors have changed, but the situation is not greatly different. With a few notable exceptions both the original group and the newcomers rely on a panoply of devices—ranging from the dismissive Afterthought to the wishful Translation—to muffle and tame the new voices.

Thus, although critical, feminist, and minority writers are increasingly appearing in the pages of our top journals, they are still not being integrated fully or easily into the colloquies, exchanges, and dialogues of legal scholarship. Some of the resistance may be intentional, but we believe most of it results from quite ordinary forces: preference for the familiar, discomfort with impending change, and a near-universal disdain for an account or "story" that deviates too much from one upon which we have been relying to construct and order our social world.

Cultural momentum tends to be preserved. All discourse marginalizes. We resist transformative thought until it has lost the power to transform us. If we are right, imperial scholarship will be with us a long time.

5

Gathering with the Like-Minded: Symposium Battles

Outsider scholarship with a reformist agenda has been developing rapidly in many fields. In law, radical feminists are challenging law's ingrained maleness and patriarchial assumptions. Critical race theorists and others are raising doubts about many doctrines and legal theories by which we have been ordering our social world.

How are the new views being received? As the previous chapter showed, mainstream figures ignore the new ideas as long as possible. And when the new voices become impossible to ignore, they push them to the periphery, tame and marginalize them, to avoid having to deal with what the newcomers are saying. This chapter describes another mechanism that comes into play during times of paradigm shift and change: Grouping together with others like us. The new voices strike us as strange and disconcerting. What more natural response than to form a think tank, convoke a symposium of the like-minded? This way, we regain the solidarity that seems to be slipping away.

This effect is most vivid within the setting of the law review symposium. Most such symposium issues are designed to bring together a group of scholars with common interests and ideas. This chapter describes how the symposium has developed and what its current status is. We believe symposium publishing, like other expressions of beleaguered collectivity, can serve both exclusionary and inclusionary purposes. We describe these contradictory purposes and show how they play themselves out on the pages of our most influential legal journals, both braking and propelling change at the same time.

The Symposium

Since publication of the earliest known law review symposium in 1889,[1] tens of thousands of symposia, colloquies, and special issues have been published. During the period 1980 to 1990 alone, almost 14,000 symposium articles were listed in commonly used legal databases. Few issues of the weekly *Current Index to Legal Periodicals* do not contain a listing for at least one symposium. Indeed, the number of symposium-type issues has nearly doubled in the last decade alone.

What accounts for this increase? We believe that law review symposia have become a form of search for meaning. Human beings demand meaning, coherence, and order. During times of social crisis and fragmentation, this search becomes particularly urgent. Moreover, toward the end of any era, society usually demands even more certainty than usual because of a felt need for closure.[2] In this last decade of the twentieth century we live in crisis and also approach the end of a millennium.

Law does not escape these social forces. The recent literature is replete with articles by scholars attempting to discover, impose, clarify, and defend meaning in the law. Indeed, a recent scholarly movement holds that "interpretive communities" or "communities of meaning" are, if not the most important factor in legal judgment and interpretation, at least a key element.

Yet, contrasting notions about the relevant meanings, and how to determine them, abound. Does legal meaning lie in the current context or original intent? Does principled adjudication consist in following precedent, or has deconstruction irretrievably destroyed that notion? Is social life about community, freedom, order, equality, or something else? Several respected legal commentators have observed that legal scholarship is undergoing the type of ferment associated with a paradigm shift. Following the lead of social philosophers and literary critics, they bring to legal thought postmodern insights in understanding our condition in order to cope with that change. Others are convinced that we need less scholarship of this type, not more.[3] They hold that much recent legal writing strays too far from the canon—that is, it is not grounded in tightly adduced reasoning from the body of legal thought that preceded it. These arguments are played out in the pages of the law reviews.

In a typical symposium, a group of four to fifteen writers sharing a common interest explore, develop, destroy, or build meaning around that subject. For example, consider a symposium focusing on feminist jurisprudence or critical legal studies. The authors will undoubtedly share the conviction that those two movements have something to offer—if only that they are significantly wrong. The authors will discuss first principles, methodology, the relationship between their movement and mainstream liberal thought, the movement's basic themes and agenda, its history and future, and so on.

Every symposium, then, has a theme or core subject that the contributors explore. Within this thematic framework, symposia appear to break down into three broad time orientations: future, past, and present. Future-oriented symposia bring together writers who wish to establish new meanings or challenge old ones. Past-oriented symposia (anniversary issues, for example) celebrate or examine a past event. Contributors share a conviction that this event contains meanings we should preserve because of their continuing value. Present-oriented symposiasts present "developments in" or "current aspects of" the law. For these writers, the relevant search for meaning is pragmatic, concerned with the daily problems of practitioners and clients.

History and Development

The symposium takes its name from the title of one of Plato's dialogues[4] in which the poet Agathon gives a banquet to celebrate his victory in a drama contest. Symposium literally means "a drinking party; a convivial meeting for drinking, conversation, and intellectual entertainment."[5] In Plato's *Symposium*, Pausanias suggests to the other guests, among them Aristophanes, Phaedrus, and Socrates, that they avoid heavy drinking and they agree. Eryximachus proposes that each guest make a speech in honor of love—a subject they all consider praiseworthy. Each guest, in turn, declares, argues or distinguishes the different ways love can be valued and understood. Alcibiades arrives drunk and has his say. A band of revelers enters, confusion reigns, and the symposium comes to an end. But the speakers succeeded in creating, if only for a brief time, a community of meaning.

The earliest known American law review symposium issue appeared in 1889. Published by the *American Law Review*, it included responses to a query regarding the future of legal scholarship in the twentieth century. The role of the editors seems to have been limited to selecting the topic, extending invitations to several law publishers, and a spare editing of the manuscripts. Thereafter, symposia—though not always labeled as such—appeared intermittently. For example, in its first issue the *Yale Law Journal* published a set of four articles solicited from legal educators at Yale, Columbia, New York University, and Harvard on legal pedagogy.[6] In 1893, the *Harvard Law Review* published articles in four consecutive months[7] about the Torrens system of land transfer. Each of the writers referred to the others, elaborating on or taking issue with their views. Although the articles appear without any editorial statement, it is likely that the grouping was not accidental.

By 1933, the symposium issue was well established. That year, the Duke University Law School faculty started the journal *Law and Contemporary Problems* for the sole purpose of publishing such issues. The stated intent of the faculty editor and advisory board was to broaden perspectives on the law, include nonlegal specialists on law-related subjects, and present "contrasts and conflicts as well as ... reconciliations."[8] Recent issues have focused on attorney fee shifting, children with special needs, vice, and the economics of contract law.

After World War II large numbers of students sought admission to the law schools. In response, many schools that did not have a law review established one; others started a second one. Specialty law reviews began to flourish. The number of journals indexed in *Index to Legal Periodicals* grew from 188 to more than 300 during the period 1946 to 1961. The number of pages to be filled increased; concomitantly, more symposium issues were published. Our survey focused only on the years 1980 to 1990.

Competition over Meaning: Past, Present, Future

How shall we understand the steady growth of the symposium idea? After reviewing thousands of symposium entries, our overall impression is that symposium issues can be seen as competing struggles over what law, the legal profession, and justice are to mean. Leaving aside whether meaning is embedded in text or context, or whether it is supplied by writer or reader, we can safely say that the more closely two or more persons assent to common norms and values, the more likely they are to interpret text or events similarly. Some symposium issues present articles on various aspects of their subject with little conflict or disharmony among the authors. Other symposia offer conflicting interpretations of what their subject is about. Yet, at some basic level symposium issues are efforts to establish, reestablish, or otherwise emphasize similar ways of understanding the enduring issues with which law is concerned. All such meanings are, to a large extent, communal. They require that others be persuaded to think, see, and speak as we do. One cannot easily establish a new meaning or value by oneself. The creation of meaning is, virtually by definition, communal.

What constitutes a community or a community of meaning? Robert Post defines a community as "a social formation that inculcates norms into the very identities of its members," an inculcation that is always partial, "a matter of degree ..."; "some persons can share some norms but not others ... the meaning and application of [those] shared norms can give rise to debate and disagreement."[9] Symposium issues illustrate Post's observations.

Sometimes the search-for-meaning idea is only implied in the timing and structure of a symposium. Other times, the editors lay bare the authors' collective effort to establish, or debate, norms and meanings. This is particularly so in connection with future-oriented symposia. A random survey of introductions and forewords to symposium issues revealed the following typical examples: The *Texas Law Review* symposium on law and literature "brought renewed debate over the underpinnings of the legal system."[10] The *Stanford Law Review* symposium on critical legal studies "offer[ed] a set of viewpoints, descriptions, and prescriptions that vary substantially from those embraced by the mainstream legal culture."[11] The *Southern California Law Review* symposium on interpretation declared it was "valuable to try to identify whatever common elements can be found, to see how far they may extend across the entire universe of interpretative contexts."[12]

Past-oriented symposia likewise undertake a collective search for meaning but with roots in the past: The *Western Legal History* special issue on the Bill of Rights in the American West stated, "The articles in this issue reflect a common theme that runs throughout the history of the Bill of Rights. ... They serve to remind us that a true commitment to the Bill of Rights requires eternal vigilance—here and now, each day—lest we are doomed to repeat the violations of the past."[13] The *Rutgers Law Journal* symposium on the twenty-fifth anniversary of the Model Penal Code explained, "The Code has given criminal lawyers everywhere in the country a common language, a common understanding."[14]

The largest number of symposia are oriented in the present; we find the usual search for meaning in this category as well. Symposia in this group explain, interpret, and analyze a current legal problem or trend. They are often intended for practitioners or legislators and their aim is often utilitarian: To clarify a body of law considered important for a region or group of lawyers. A *Rutgers Law Review* symposium on current issues in mental disability law noted, "As recently as twenty years ago there was no systematic body of law that could be labeled mental disability law. ... Highlighting some of the most significant current issues in mental disability law, the Symposium demonstrates how much this field has grown in a relatively brief period."[15] A *Law and Contemporary Problems* gun control symposium explained, "[T]his symposium tends merely to help bring the discourse closer in balance. ... The time has come to begin the process of learning more about the issues raised in this symposium, so that future arguments may rely on far more thorough and reliable data."[16] A *Kentucky Law Journal* equine law symposium stated, "From the days when horse races on Main Street entertained crowds and disrupted life in Lexington and other communities ... Kentuckians have demonstrated an uncommon devotion to the horse. ... Given what this industry means to the people of the Commonwealth, it is my hope that this issue of the *Kentucky Law Journal* will advance the understanding of legal questions surrounding various aspects of the industry. ..."[17] An *Idaho Law Review* symposium on managing the Pacific Northwest salmon and steelhead industry explained, "Just as the rivers tie together a geographically diverse region, refusing to recognize ecological or political boundaries, the fish provide a common element. But fish, like rivers, divide as well as unify. ... New legal structures for managing the fishery have been created within the last decade. Appraising where we are requires some understanding of where we have been."[18]

In short, law—like other areas of human endeavor—is a shifting, jostling mass of competing understandings and accounts, some challenging, some blending, others overlapping. Symposium issues illustrate this aspect of law and legal scholarship even more clearly than other forms of faculty scholarship such as publication of casebooks or nonsymposium articles. The quest for order, for agreement—for communities of meaning— is the single most dominant impression that emerged from our examination of thousands of symposia items.

Particular Findings

If we are right that symposium issues do represent an effort to establish communities of meaning, there still remain a set of secondary questions: Is the search for community successful? Are symposium issues worth the trouble? How many symposium issues are there and what are they about? Is the number increasing, and if so what accounts for the increase? Is the market becoming saturated?

Quantitative Issues: What Subjects Are Presented, Who Writes, Who Sponsors, and to What Effect?

The subject matter distribution of 1,807 symposium issues in the eleven-year period is fascinating: In some respects it mirrors the social and legal issues that occupied our national consciousness in the 1980s. Reaganism and Republican leadership focused considerable attention on federalism, federal courts, and state-law alternatives. These subjects generated at least 58 symposia. Related perhaps to the new federalism, 25 symposia focused on judges and judicial efficiency.

Rising public concern with the quality of life brought heavy coverage of issues of environmental law. Acid rain, air pollution, energy, land use, toxic torts, waste management, and water quality accounted for 103 entries. Business, governmental, judicial, and legal ethics, as well as white-collar crime, received attention in 47 symposia. Health care, AIDS, bioethics, and elder law accounted for 84 symposia. Reflecting the increased focus on world economics, international law, transnational law, and law of the sea received over 86 entries.

Traditional bread-and-butter legal issues, administrative regulation (10), tax (11), torts (14), legal education (8), corporations (14), employment discrimination (4), and labor law (28) received less coverage than one might perhaps expect. At the same time "crisis type" issues such as terrorism (8), poverty (3), homelessness (3), and public-interest law (1) received some but not heavy treatment, while crime (7), drugs (11), criminal law (15), and the criminal justice system (36) received more extensive coverage.

Increased concern with the breakdown of the family and the by-products of divorce (15) also brought eighteen symposia on the status of children and their rights, while issues dear to the hearts of radicals and reformers—prison law reform, critical movements of all types, and freedom of speech—received somewhat lighter coverage.

The decade's listing included certain unusual topics or ones of regional concern: one each on whales, lying, excuses, ski law, error, soap operas, tobacco, salmon-and-steelhead law; and three on equine law.

Each of the time focuses was amply represented. Almost all substantive issues were dealt with in a "current issues" or "developments in the law" format. These present-oriented symposia were the most numerous; retrospective and "future of" somewhat less. Many of the substantive symposia contained a mixture of articles, some looking to the future, some to current law.

Why These Subjects—and Are They Skewed? Who chose these subjects, and are they representative—that is, do they differ from the distribution to be found in ordinary, "mixed" issues of law reviews? Occasionally the symposium introduction or foreword will explain how the topic was chosen.[19] The available evidence suggests that symposium topics come from a variety of sources. A local faculty member or law review sponsor may persuade the law review to publish a symposium on his or her favorite topic. Individual law review editors or outside scholars may propose one as well.

Our overall impression, after reviewing hundreds of symposium issues, is that themes lean slightly more toward the concrete, at least in the middle-ranked law reviews, than do topics presented in nonsymposium issues. In the relatively few top-tier reviews, the opposite is true—symposium issues tend toward future-oriented or jurisprudential topics, while nonsymposium issues reflect a mix of practical and theoretical writing.

Who Writes? Who writes for symposium issues? Reviewing all 13,000-plus entries for 1980 to 1990, one is struck by a number of patterns. A typical symposium contains between 4 and 9 writers—one contained 2,[20] another 84.[21] As might be expected, a large majority are middle-aged, male, white, and law professors. Some symposia include more practitioners, political figures, or social scientists than others. Interdisciplinary symposia contain more coauthored articles than others. In general, hard-core legal areas such as securities law or intellectual property have a high proportion of male authors; areas such as family and juvenile law, feminist legal theory, and pornography have larger numbers of women.

To focus more narrowly on the composition of symposium issues, as well as on a number of other aspects discussed later, we chose a single year—1988—because it contained a large number of entries, as well as a broad cross-section of subject matter and approaches.

Although the year contained a slightly larger proportion of articles written by women and minorities than had earlier years, nevertheless, male authors dominated the tables of contents of symposium issues—1,412 men to 244 women. Women contributed about one-seventh of all symposium articles published that year—a significant underrepresentation given that in 1988 women constituted 23 percent of the law professorate[22] and tended to be younger—and hence probably more active writers—than men in general. As was generally true in all years, women authors were invited to write in areas of law concerned with caregiving, family and juvenile law, health care, and aging.[23] The number of authors of color was even smaller—fewer than thirty known minorities in over 1,600 entries. The most male-dominated symposia were in areas such as jurisprudence, constitutional law, and antitrust law. Even when the subject was an aspect of "left," or radical, law, women and minorities were poorly represented.

The patterns we found in 1988 seemed to hold true generally. The 1985 *Southern California Law Review* interpretation symposium,[24] for example, featured 26 white male authors. Of five symposia on critical legal studies,[25] only two included a woman author, and those included only one each. Constitutional, particularly bicentennial, symposia of the kind that began to appear around 1986 were equally unisex; few included women—one included a minority, Vine DeLoria, Jr., a Native American scholar.[26] In two symposia on law and community, where one might expect to find more women writers, the author mix reflects the six-to-one male-female ratio found in symposia subjects generally.

Who Publishes? In general, the top-tier law reviews published fewer symposia than those outside this group. During the eleven-year period the top twenty law reviews[27] published 116 symposia, whereas a comparison group produced 172.

The time orientation varied considerably between the two groups. Law reviews outside the top tier published more symposia, with more pragmatic focus, than did those in that tier. One can only speculate why this is so. It may be that law reviews outside the top group reflect the greater practice-orientations of their schools. It may also be that faculty and law review advisers encourage them in that direction. Also, many middle-tier law reviews have a traditional annual symposium, sometimes in a specific area of law.

What explains the larger numbers? Less prestigious law reviews may use the symposium to increase the quantity and quality of articles they publish. Every year Harvard and Yale receive thousands of submissions while other journals receive barely enough to fill their pages. Targeting particular authors, especially ones that have some connection to their schools or the subject of their symposia, greatly increases the editors' chances of receiving a manuscript of publishable quality.

With bar journals and faculty-edited or special-interest law reviews, the reason for symposium treatment is clearer. Particular substantive areas are apt to undergo sudden change in response to new legislation or case law. Frequently, law reviews of these types cover the changes for the benefit of their readers, mostly practicing attorneys.

Growth in Number. As we mentioned earlier, the number of symposium issues is rising rapidly. In reviewing symposia published during the eleven-year period, we noticed two remarkable trends. Between 1980 and 1990 all symposia in general moved away from a present to a future orientation. Indeed, in almost every year the percentage of future-oriented symposia increased. Why this increase? The current fragmentation in legal scholarship may have caused an intensified need for coherence, for redefining communities of meaning, and for a return to solidarity. It seems likely as well that the coming end of the century, heralded by the approach and passing of 1984, has brought with it a need for closure.[28] One exception stands out: The percentage of past-oriented symposia increased markedly in 1987, reflecting a nationwide focus on national origins and the foundations of our political system.

Qualitative Issues: Publish and Flourish?

Some of the questions one might ask about the symposium vehicle are less subject to quantitative determination.

Stronger Cast of Authors? Can apt selection of a symposium topic (one that catches a cresting wave of legal writing) coupled with diligent solicitation of authors enable a middle-ranked law review—one outside the top twenty—to attract more renowned writers than would ordinarily be the case? Measuring the prestige of writers is difficult and subjective. We chose two simple, readily determined measures—the rank of an author's institution, and his or her general reputation in the community of legal writers.

Examination of the year 1988 disclosed that a number of highly visible and accomplished scholars were indeed publishing in law review symposia sponsored by law reviews outside the top ten. For example, a symposium on reason, passion, and "The Progress of the Law" sponsored by *Cardozo Law Review*[29] contained over a dozen legal writers of the first rank.

A symposium sponsored by *Mercer Law Review* on law and literature[30] featured several well-known figures. A third, sponsored by *Northwestern Law Review,* on law and social theory,[31] contained another remarkable cast. Finally, *Notre Dame Law Review* sponsored a retrospective on the fiftieth anniversary of the Federal Rules of Civil Procedure;[32] many of its well-known authors ordinarily publish in law reviews of the very top tier.

It appears, then, that a law review may indeed attract a stronger group of authors for a symposium issue than nonsymposium issues. This is especially so just outside the ten or twenty most prestigious reviews. In these "strong second-tier" reviews, intelligent selection of an appealing topic will, sometimes at least, enable the journal to attract leading authors. It may be that, for these reviews, the work entailed in thinking of the symposium topic pays off by getting the attention of the established writer and persuading him or her that the review's editors are discerning and serious. It may be also that authors merely like to be asked.

It may also be, simply, the pull of community. The life of a writer even at the top level is apt to be a lonely one. The lure of participating with others, even at distant institutions, in forging a new approach to a social or scholarly issue may be powerful. This presumably is particularly so if, as sometimes is the case, the law review or law school hosts an on-site conference of authors who then have the opportunity to meet one another, the editors, and the discussants and to present their topics in a collegial atmosphere.[33]

Are the Articles Better? A related question is whether symposium articles, in general, have a broader impact than nonsymposium pieces. One easily ascertained measure of an article's impact is the number of references by other writers or judges that it garners in a designated period.[34] To carry out this comparison, we selected 1984 because it is far enough in the past so that patterns of citation would be evident. Within that year we chose a sample, by employing a table of random numbers, of thirty symposium issues. We compared both types of articles—symposium and nonsymposium—appearing in the volume year for each of the thirty reviews. We calculated the rate of citation per page for each type of article.

The results are striking. Symposium issues attracted a larger number of citations, but only in the top or high middle-tier reviews. For reviews outside this group, the reverse effect appeared—*nonsymposium* articles in these reviews were cited more frequently than symposium articles. Symposium publication, even with the added pull of community, thus is no guarantee of success for a middle-tier law review—at least as measured by citation impact. Far from having a "catch-up" effect to raise a law review's visibility, symposium publication may only result in the rich getting richer while middle-tier reviews remain at the same level.

We can only speculate why this might be so. It may be that the middle-ranked reviews lack access to the networks that would enable them to target the right topics or writers. It may be that the market is saturated, so that prestigious authors receive more symposium solicitations than they can accept and turn down offers from all but top or strong second-tier reviews. Finally, it may be that an invitation to become a part of a community whose members one has never heard of is less attractive than one to join with persons one knows, if only by reputation.

Intellectual Incest? Insider Groups and the Danger of Group-Think. Community may be ennobling, even necessary, but it may also pose the risk of conformity and group-think. Thus, a question one may have about symposium publishing is whether the same authors predominate, resulting in insider networks and exclusion of new fresh voices.

We did find some evidence that this is happening. Of the more than 13,000 symposium articles published during 1980 to 1990, a high percentage of authors appeared only once or twice, but a small number appeared several times. Equally interesting is that certain authors tended to appear together often. Is there an "imperial communitarian" phenomenon in which like-minded communitarians nominate each other, making it difficult for an outsider to break in?[35] Symposium editors do seem to take pains to solicit divergent views—the landmark *Stanford Law Review* symposium on critical legal studies (CLS), for example, contained several articles that criticized that movement. Yet most of them were written by "insiders"—well-known mainstream scholars whose reactions to CLS were fairly predictable. Few mavericks or new writers were included.

The "Sociogram"

Groupings of symposium authors yielded a sharp, well-defined pattern of who publishes with whom—perhaps one of the most striking results of our entire survey of law review symposium publishing. The twenty most frequent writers and the number of symposia in the top twenty law reviews in which they appeared between 1980 and 1990 were Mark Tushnet (13), Richard Epstein (12), Michael Perry (11), Cass Sunstein (11), Richard Posner (10), Sanford Levinson (9), Jonathan Macey (9), Frank Michelman (9), David A. J. Richards (9), Frederick Schauer (8), Lea Brilmayer (8), Paul Brest (7), Frank Easterbrook (7), Judith Resnik (7), Milner Ball (6), Stephen Carter (6), Daniel Farber (6), Daniel Fischel (6), Duncan Kennedy (6), and Martin Shapiro (6).[36]

Moreover, certain authors frequently appeared together. For example, Tushnet appeared with Brest and Richards three times each, with Perry and Schauer four times each. Perry and Richards appeared together three times. Carter, Epstein, Kennedy, Levinson, Michelman, Posner, Shapiro, and Sunstein each appeared with another twice. Brilmayer and Resnik, high-publishing women, were nearly isolated—none of the top male symposiasts appeared with either of them more than once. Among minorities, only Carter appeared in as many as six symposia, and the number of times his work appeared linked with others of the top group was small: twice with Shapiro, once with one of seven others.

Given that there are over 6,000 law professors, many of whom could be considered highly distinguished, we found these data surprising. Each of the frequent contributors is, of course, eminent—but so are many others, including women and minorities. Expertise alone also seems unable to account for such patterns; many of the authors who achieved renown in an area such as constitutional law were solicited to write for symposia in other, not closely related, areas such as legal history or interpretation.

Two possibilities occur to us. The top authors may nominate each other, neglecting to call attention to promising newcomers, women, and minorities. Or more innocently, it may simply be a product of name recognition. When one's name begins to appear frequently on the "symposium circuit," editors and faculty advisors think of one as a possible contributor for their own symposium. It may also be a product of the insecurity or "herd mentality" of student editors.

Whatever the explanation, the clubby quality of the law review symposium is troubling. If symposium publishing is a means of stating, declaring, and defining community, the contours of that community have some striking exclusionary overtones.

Is a Writer's Symposium Work as Valuable as His or Her Other Work? Are symposium articles by a given author as valuable, as carefully crafted, as his or her nonsymposium work? In other words, if a law review does manage to attract a noted writer to contribute to its symposium, is the resulting article likely to prove as thorough and well reasoned as that author's previous work—the work that brought his or her name to the review's attention? Is there, as a colleague puts it, a "schlock effect" in which noted authors dispatch hastily drafted, less intensively researched work for the symposium issue? This supposition gains plausibility, for once an author agrees to write for a symposium, most reviews will feel obligated to publish whatever he or she sends. The editors realize the other symposium authors may have agreed to write in reliance upon the noted author's inclusion; rejecting his or her article may cause disappointment or a sense of betrayal on the part of these other writers.

To address this possibility, we selected ten authors whose work appeared frequently in symposium issues between 1980 and 1990. As might be expected, each of these authors also published widely in a nonsymposium format. We then examined and compared their articles appearing in (1) middle-tier symposium issues and (2) nonsymposium issues of top reviews. Employing this admittedly small sample, we did find some of the symposium contributions were briefer and more impression-istic than the author's usual (nonsymposium) pieces and garnered fewer citations. To be sure, other symposium articles by those authors were as lengthy and cited as frequently as their nonsymposium work—in a few cases even more so.

This effect diminished but did not disappear when we compared (3) symposium issue articles from top reviews and (4) nonsymposium issue articles in top reviews—both written by the same author. Although many of the authors' symposium articles received roughly the same number of citations as their nonsymposium work, slightly over 60 percent received fewer.

Do Symposia Create Communities of Meaning, and How Can Law Reviews Achieve That Effect? Most symposia clearly create "communities of mean-ing" for the participants at some level because (1) they give presenters and commentors opportunities to interact; (2) they validate the expertise of the authors; and (3) they legitimize a subject area in which a handful of com-mitted people might be working.

Perhaps the classic symposium, however, is one that focuses on a new way of ordering reality (CLS),[37] delineates new perspectives on the law (Excluded Voices),[38] or maps out a paradigm shift (Normativity).[39] Often, in such cases, a cluster of writers previously working in relative isolation become identified with, or identify themselves as, a new movement. They become part of a community; they create, intentionally or de facto, a com-munity of meaning.

The significance of a symposium is sometimes not seen until long after its publication. A future-oriented symposium, years later, is often seen as a benchmark or signpost—"we have come this far,"[40] "we are going this way."[41] With a few inspired exceptions, the top-tier law reviews seem more able than others to pinpoint cutting-edge subjects for their sympo-sia, and given their resources, will likely continue to do so.

As we have seen, symposium publishing has both practical and theo-retical aspects. The practical aspects include who publishes in symposium issues, on what subjects, with what effect, and whether or not there exists an "in-group" network that dominates the pages of the most prestigious symposia.

The theoretical insight, which grew in certainty as our work pro-gressed, is that these issues are in a highly significant sense searches for communities of meaning. Authors who share a common concern or per-spective bring their work together to analyze, clarify, or advance that way of seeing law. Past-oriented symposiasts find meaning and solidarity aris-ing out of some past event or individual. Present-oriented writers discuss a problem or issue of immediate current concern, frequently of a practical nature. Future-oriented symposium contributors are concerned with change, with introducing or defending new meanings, and with new values in law and legal scholarship.

Regardless of the type of symposium, however, we detected a troublesome tendency on the part of editors and authors to state the same themes and invite the same participants. Perhaps community and exclusion are inextricable—unless strenuous and intentional efforts are made to reduce the latter. As our culture continues to fragment and social change increases in pace, the need for commonality and for dialogue will only heighten. So long as symposium issues are seen to answer this need and give shape to the communitarian impulse, they are likely to remain a significant feature of the scholarly landscape. But their exclusionary tendency will require attention, or symposium publishing will inhibit innovation and variety of thought.

6

Pornography and Harm to Women: "No Empirical Evidence"?

In this book, we have been addressing a number of forces that render transformative legal thought so halting and slow. Chapter 1 examined the history of popular depiction of four ethnic groups of color, showing that racism is so deeply embedded in our culture that it is for all practical purposes invisible. Chapter 2 examined limitations on the judicial imagination. Inscribed in the master narrative, racial stereotypes function as organizing principles by which we understand and construct the social world. As such, they are highly resistant to reform, even at the hands of highly competent and ostensibly fair-minded judges.

This chapter employs a different example, pornography, which many people believe is connected to another social ill, female subjugation. Even more than media racism, pornography has begun to be named and attacked by a number of vocal reformers, including many feminists. The attack on pornography thus brings into play late-stage dynamics; exploring it reveals mechanisms the general culture deploys to slow the advance of a reform movement that is well under way.

We begin by giving a brief history of media depiction of women, including pornography. As we shall show, popular depiction of women takes on different forms at different periods. But running through the various images is a constant thread: *functionality*. The pictures we coin and circulate adjust women and their images to serve the needs of groups with the power to insist on that adjustment. This process is true of pornography as well. Most members of society's elite groups today profess to find pornography distasteful; they only disagree on whether it should be regulated. One of our findings, however, is that pornography is a tacitly recognized *good* that the dominant group depends on to achieve certain ends and is naturally reluctant to relinquish.

But we cannot allow ourselves to see this. Accordingly, we deploy various strategies, including refusal to see pornography as a serious harm. Some opponents translate feminists' claims into versions unlikely to succeed. Further, they ignore evidence that might argue for reform because the very images of women that society circulates disable persons in the culture from seeing the injuries associated with these images. Drawing on cognitive psychology and narrative theory, we show how these mechanisms work. We conclude with a few suggestions on how to minimize their soul-deadening sway.

A Brief Functional History
of Pornography and Female Depiction

There is no necessity to the notions that women are more passive than men, more domestic, less venturesome, or that they should have primary responsibility for the care and nurture of children. Our ideas about women and women's roles are constructed, contingent rather than necessary, their maintenance a product of reinforcement and conditioning.[1] The tools of this construction are both verbal and visual—words, images, pictures, and stories. For the sake of brevity, we denote this collection of representations "narratives."

History of Female Depiction in General

In the early years of this nation, women were needed for domestic and farm labor on the frontier and newly developed areas of the West and prairie regions.[2] Accordingly, images of women in the narratives of the day depicted them as pious, God-fearing, resourceful, able to make fires, mend clothing, fend off Indian raiders, raise children and help their husbands in the fields from morning to night. Not particularly sexual (at least in the image), the woman of this era derived her main satisfaction from work, raising children, and standing by her man.[3] Dime novels of the period depicted frontier heroines such as Hurricane Nell, Bess the Trapper, and Mountain Kate—rugged women who rode, roped, toted guns, and confronted grizzlies while constantly maintaining a proper feminine demeanor. Their ultimate reward was that supposedly sought by all members of their sex: an idyllic and fruitful marriage.[4]

Later, the nation's attention shifted from survival to consolidation and economic development. The independent, resourceful image of westward expansion receded, replaced by a much more confined, "ladylike" one.[5] Women's magazines of the period advised their readers to use caution in exercising because their frail constitutions could bear only moderate exercise; women's "fibres are thin and weak," they explained, and "[t]heir feeble arms cannot support severe and long-continued labor."[6] Even women writers of this time had to conform to popular taste; they wrote novels and stories upholding virginity, thrift, and similar virtues.[7] During this period, male industrialists and developers were firmly in charge. Independent, venturesome women would have been threatening; large numbers of women workers were not yet needed in the workplace.[8] Women's images reflected these needs and conditions.

The late nineteenth century saw the first waves of feminism. Women's suffrage leaders and novelists such as Kate Chopin urged that women could be independent, had intellects, needs, and a sensuous nature of their own. Most readers were taken aback. Chopin was seen as a radical; the early suffragists were derided and ignored.[9] For example, the 1848 Seneca Falls Convention Declaration was belittled in newspaper articles as "a most interesting document" because of its "amusing" assertion of women's "equality."[10] The public preferred women dreamy, frail, innocent, and romantic, a preference that played itself out both in literature and the scripts of the early film period. D. W. Griffith, for example, in *Birth of a Nation, Intolerance,* and other films showed Lillian Gish playing the role of the innocent and virginal child-woman who relies on men for protection.[11]

With the outbreak of World War II, a contrasting image reminiscent of the depictions in the early westward expansion period surfaced—the strong, independent woman. These characterizations tend to appear during times of stress when the nation faces an impersonal challenge, such as war or depression, that requires women's active engagement. Wartime propaganda featured workers such as Rosie the Riveter, who labored in the factory while her husband or male friend fought overseas.[12] Those women who did not work in the factories were portrayed as cheerfully shouldering additional household responsibilities while waiting faithfully for the man's return.[13]

Immediately following World War II, women's image changed again. Women returned from the workplace, providing the "baby boom" that stabilized the nation's numbers and compensated for the low birth rate during the war. Accordingly, films, magazine advertisements, television programs, and stories of this period depicted women happily engaged in domestic tasks and roles.[14]

With the return of feminism in the late 1960s and early 1970s, images modestly broadened to incorporate the new vistas the civil rights movement had opened for women and minorities. But even then, publications promoted submissive roles for women. For example, confession magazines often presented accounts of rapes or rape-fantasies in which the victim precipitated the event and in which "the rape functioned as a positive catalyst for the heroine in her never-ending quest for a new boyfriend or an improved relationship with a husband."[15] Even well-known women authors followed well-trod tracks. Lois Gold's *Such Good Friends* and Erica Jong's *Fear of Flying* were permutations of old narratives: The woman strays, explores adventure and sex, then returns to husband or old lover at the end.[16]

As we found with ethnic minorities of color, the dominant stereotypes of women in any era are thus either limiting or demeaning, yet rarely perceived as such at the time. Rather, they are seen as natural, inevitable, "the way things are." Moreover, the images change to accommodate society's need for labor, sex, reproduction, independence, or its opposite. The nation needs workers, Indian fighters, breeders, or temptresses, and the creative community obligingly responds. All this takes place largely at an unconscious level; rarely, if ever, does there seem to be anything like a conscious conspiracy.

A Brief History of Pornography and the Debate over Regulation

Pornography, a particular form of female depiction, responds to many of the same forces that shape female depiction generally, but often with a reverse twist. For example, during westward expansion the dominant image of women was relatively traditional—defender of home and hearth. Yet, because there were not enough women to go around, vaudeville, music and burlesque halls flourished. "Bawdy women" spoke and sang of sexual themes, engaged in low humor, and made rude observations on forbidden subjects. They took the preexisting image of Eve, the sexual woman, and portrayed it as socially forceful, lusty, natural. They depicted women courting men, enjoying conquests, and making fun of it all. Antiprudes and naughty, they mocked society's reigning view of women as demure and submissive.[17]

Early pornography and erotica were largely the province of wealthy gentlemen. By today's standards it was relatively tame and refined; those who collected it often pretended it was something else and described their interest in it in scientific, delicate, or euphemistic terms. Some described their interest as "hygienic"—as controlling, studying, or understanding prostitution and other forms of social "vice."[18]

By 1800, the industrial revolution was well underway, however, and with it middle-class ideas and conventions gained ascendancy. Sexual morality, at the public level at any rate, became more limiting as religious fervor coupled with economic pressure to force women back into subordinate positions. The pornography of this time lacked the subtlety, finesse, or literary merit of earlier periods. A dominant theme became the factory girl who left home, succumbed to the wiles and temptations of her new environment, but sadder and wiser lived to tell all. There were also risque novels with male Civil War heroes being seduced by amorous ladies.[19]

By the end of the nineteenth century, early feminists and social reformers were inveighing against prostitution, pornography, and the demon rum. These "social purists" believed that enabling women to take their places along with men in the workplace and government would bring about a more virtuous, temperate society.[20] Soon, however, Freud, Richard von Krafft-Ebing, and Havelock Ellis would begin writing about the naturalness of sex and the eroticization of much of life. And although the movement assisted in efforts at self-determination for women and the repeal of repressive or paternalistic legislation, including the Contagious Disease Act, its antipornography strain soon lost momentum.[21]

By the time of the feminist revival, pornography in the United States was well established. Even by 1902, privately screened films with graphic scenes of adult sexuality were available. Running between ten and twelve minutes without sound or color, these "stag" films generally avoided dealing with female sexual pleasure.[22] The encounter was impersonal; the woman almost did not exist.

With the advent of the women's movement of the 1960s and 1970s, however, pornography took on a sharper edge. Photographs and films became more explicit, and a substantial portion—as high as one-third—came to include force by the male against the female. By the 1980s, pornography had become a large business with distributors, 165,000 full- or part-time workers, theater chains, and technological advances such as home videos, subscription television, dial-a-porn, and computer sex subscription services widely available. The industry today accounts for 10 to 15 percent of the videocassette market; for 5 million adult magazines and 2 million X-rated movie tickets purchased weekly.[23]

As we have seen, pornography, like female depiction generally, responds to forces emanating from the broader society. Pornographers create and respond to a market that in turn wants women passive, active, or abused and repressed. Always at the extreme end of a continuum of female depiction, pornography marks transitions from one understanding of woman to the next. During times of change it teaches women what may be done to them, shows men what they may do, and adds new content to the social construct of women.

The Controversy over Pornography's Regulation

Proposals to ban pornography can be traced to the early temperance movement, when reformers inveighed against its evils along with those of prostitution, venereal disease, and alcohol. Beginning in the late 1960s, the American feminist movement gave the campaign against pornography a secular, feminist cast. Instead of portraying pornography as harmful principally to men (the usual consumers) or to society at large (for example, through its impact on public morality), the new critics charged that pornography harms women.

Antipornography feminism and fundamentalist religion have sometimes found themselves on the same side of the controversy, an alignment that civil libertarians and some feminists deplore, asserting that conservative churches are antiwoman and that making common cause with them is dangerous and unwise. For their part, religious conservatives base their objection to pornography on the belief that sex outside marriage is a sin and that pornography increases disrespect toward conjugal love.[24]

In 1983, many of these issues came to a head when Catharine MacKinnon and Andrea Dworkin helped introduce the nation's first antipornography civil rights ordinance in Minneapolis. The ordinance, which was enacted by the city council but vetoed by the mayor, would have made trafficking in, and coercing persons into, pornography civil harms.[25]

Women who opposed the ordinance formed the Feminist Anti-Censorship Taskforce (FACT),[26] an organization that successfully opposed a similar ordinance that the city of Indianapolis enacted a few years later.[27] Just as antipornography activists were criticized for aligning themselves with the religious right, MacKinnon and others charged that their liberal sisters in FACT were in league with right-wing libertarians and the pornography industry and were collaborating with male power.[28] Members of FACT responded that MacKinnon's ordinance violated freedom of choice, reinforced the double standard, and rested on a dubious causal link. Others argue that pornography legislation relieves rapists and perpetrators of other sexual violence of responsibility because they can argue that "porn made me do it."[29] MacKinnon replied that pornography objectifies women, expropriates their sexuality for men's use, and teaches sex roles in which women are subordinate, degraded, or subject to physical abuse.[30]

A number of American cities and the U.S. Congress have enacted or are considering enacting antipornography regulations, some along the lines proposed by MacKinnon and Dworkin. Recently, the Supreme Court of Canada upheld a Canadian antipornography statute, a decision widely viewed as a vindication of MacKinnon's position.[31]

"No Empirical Evidence": Why We Fail to Find Anything Seriously Wrong with Pornography

As we have shown, the dominant depictions of women in any era are not seen as particularly injurious at the time. These images teach those in the culture the role of women and how they may act toward them. They enable us, in short, to construct the idea of woman, one that serves varying purposes at different times. Once the images are in place, they guide what we see.

Pornography, a particular type of negative depiction, flourishes when the needs and expectations of the dominant group with respect to women are not being met in some respect. When, as now, we are in such a period, a predictable sequence occurs: (1) women protest the images; (2) researchers profess to search for evidence of its harmful nature; and (3) researchers find no such empirical evidence. These events occur, we believe, because the broad system of female depiction renders most of the harms ordinary and normal, part of "the way things are." Society reserves the terms "shocking," "brutal," and "misogynist" for treatment that deviates from the norm—that falls outside the range the narratives mark out. Thus, a male researcher may genuinely and sincerely look for violence following the showing of an antiwoman movie or television program and find none, neglecting to notice the joke, putdown, comment, leer, pointed offer of a drink, and pressured sex that go on daily.

Narrative theorists and outsider scholars have been writing of the way context and experience shape perception. An example of this mechanism occurred at the sentencing of Mike Tyson. In his statement before the court, Mike Tyson exclaimed, "I didn't hurt nobody. Nobody has a black eye or broken ribs."[32] His statement reveals a common misperception: An act constitutes rape only if the victim suffers injuries as a result. Mike Tyson and those who share his point of view are unable to understand the victim's viewpoint, namely, that sex without consent is inherently forceful and therefore constitutes rape. Frequently, the man may envision a seduction in which he is being commanding, she coy. However, a woman may experience the same encounter as a degrading violation of her will.[33] In similar fashion, our engrained ideas of womanhood and male-female relations determine what will strike us as abnormal as well as what we might count as evidence against pornography. The very images under study become internalized; we then use them to judge their own real-world efficacy. In what follows, we show a number of ways in which this occurs.

Translation: How to Avoid Hearing What the Feminists Are Saying

One mechanism by which opponents of pornography's regulation have been able to avoid the feminists' attack is *translation*. MacKinnon and others maintain that most forms of pornography degrade and injure women and ought to be controlled. Many opponents of this position say they are unable to verify that claim. For example, one well-regarded constitutional scholar rejected the MacKinnon-Dworkin proposal because the scientific case for a link between exposure to pornography and commission of later antisocial acts is not established.[34] The studies relied on by a recent Attorney General's Commission on Pornography, for example, show only correlation, not causation. The few controlled experiments that do seem to indicate such a connection can be explained by observer effects or the artificiality of the laboratory setting.[35]

The scholar, like many in the antiregulation camp, fails to recognize that for many feminists pornography is a *per se* harm, namely, that of being derogatorily constructed as passive, hypersexual, masochistic, a sexual plaything, and so on.[36] This harm occurs irrespective of what happens later; there is no need to show copycat offenses the next day. But this injury becomes invisible if one translates the feminists' claim into a causal one to be investigated in the usual way—by conducting interviews, looking at crime statistics, exposing laboratory subjects to particular stimuli. The error consists in treating a novel claim, with roots in postmodernism and the social construction of reality, as an ordinary empirical one.[37]

"No Empirical Evidence": How Not to Find Documentation by Looking for the Wrong Thing

The case against other forms of pornography, however, *is* based on its tendency to encourage antiwoman acts. For example, many feminists believe that glorified depiction of sexual violence teaches men that this behavior is acceptable—the victims actually enjoy it.[38] Yet many researchers (and others) fail to find the connection that feminists believe must be there. We believe this failure occurs for two reasons: (1) researchers fail to take account of certain types of evidence that if counted would tend to corroborate the feminist claim; and (2) when many observers do find instances of crime incontrovertibly linked to pornography, they deem them abnormal, bizarre, and idiosyncratic.

Looking for the Wrong Thing. One reason why some fail to find later-committed acts associated with pornography is that many such acts strike the observer as ordinary and unremarkable.[39] How many of us would find the following events significant enough to record on a clipboard as evidence of sexual oppression: aggressive flirting, conspicuous leering, remarks on a woman's appearance, unwanted requests for a date? Incidents such as these may well be highly correlated with pornographic consumption, yet our system of female depiction renders them ordinary and invisible, blinding us to the large amount of daily "low-grade" hassling that goes on. For example, when Stroh's beer ads were criticized, the company saw no link between bikini ads and sexual harassment in its workplace, even though women complained of constant leering, touching, and sexual approaches.[40] The images define what is normal and ordinary; what is ordinary cannot be a harm; therefore, pornography, if it only results in *this*, cannot harm women. Pornography functions like a thermostat, setting our threshold at a high level. Once it is set, we fail to notice or consider important much that goes on around us.

Denial and Dismissal: What Happens When We See Evidence We Cannot Ignore. Sometimes, however, pornography is followed by an event, for example a "copycat rape,"[41] that appears incontestably linked to it. But because we are not accustomed to thinking that images have causal efficacy, we often respond by deeming the perpetrator deranged. Mere imagery should not have that effect, we say to ourselves. So by a sort of backward reasoning, we dismiss events that might substantiate pornography's efficacy as idiosyncratic and the product of individual pathology[42] despite evidence to the contrary.[43]

A Third Method: Deprecation

Some segments of society employ a third approach to minimize the case against pornography: deprecation. If one begins with the premise that pornography is a relatively harmless form of expression, individuals arguing against it must be intolerant and puritanical, bent on depriving men of innocent pleasure, women of free expression of their sexuality.[44] This criticism gains superficial plausibility because some feminists do in fact preach against the evils of patriarchy, do speak unkindly of some men's sexual intentions.[45]

But is opposition to pornography necessarily intolerant and puritanical? Maybe, but only if one assumes that all sex is voluntarily entered into and is a manifestation of freely expressed love and eroticism carried out by two partners of similar standing and ability to choose. Some feminists question those assumptions. For them, male-female relations are carried out against a background of radical inequality. What many men consider innocent courtship often looks dangerously like coercion, dangerously like rape. The first camp seems antimale, antisex, and puritanical to the second; to the first camp, the second seems only interested in maintaining current power relations.

Why Legal Reform Is So Difficult:
A Few Suggestions

Resistance to regulation of pornography illustrates a stage or moment in a more general pattern of reaction to transformative thought. These patterns of resistance take certain recurring forms almost irrespective of the cause championed. They reappear because resistance stems not so much from the nature of the reform movement as from that of the actors called on to position themselves with respect to it.

Earlier chapters have described particular mechanisms of resistance. The very tools of thought our lawyers use channel them into safe, familiar directions, making legal reform difficult even to imagine. If one somehow surmounts that problem, aided perhaps by an inspired and determined client, there is no guarantee that the judge before whom one argues the case will be able to. Conservatives or moderates, deploying antiessentialist arguments, will rise up to challenge one's standing. Or, as the next chapter shows, a conservative savior may enter the arena just in time to siphon off the reformist impulse into safe, moderate directions.

Finally, as with pornography, members of the empowered group may simply announce to the disaffected that they do not see their problem, that they have looked for evidence of harm but cannot find it. Later generations may well marvel, "How could they have been so blind?" But paradigms change slowly. In the meantime, one may describe oneself as a cautious and principled social scientist interested only in the truth. And one's opponent, by a neat reversal, becomes an intolerant zealot willing to trample on the liberties of others without good cause. The mechanisms we have identified are deeply inscribed; every reform movement evokes them. But perhaps most insidious is the one described in this chapter, for once one declares invisible the problem the reformers agitate about, any need to deal with it dissolves.

Can anything be done? First, we may act decisively in the cases of social evil we do see, treating them in effect as proxies for those that we do not. With pornography, for example, we might enact laws prohibiting the worst forms of violent imagery (for example, "snuff" films), saving treatment of the more general problem for another time. Second, we should be alert to the way current practice may appear different in history's light. For example, we now see many earlier stereotypes of women and minorities as demeaning. Yet, at the time, artists and consumers did not see them that way. (See, for example, Chapter 1.) We should bear in mind that our current treatment of female imagery may in time come to seem similarly inexcusable.

To avoid ensnarement by the mechanisms we have discussed, we should empower outsider speakers, including radical feminists, and listen closely to their message. Their reality, although surely not the only one, may well prove to be the one that a later era adopts. We should pay attention even to the most alienated, seemingly extreme elements of a movement. The message of more moderate factions may well appear to us more reasonable, sensible, and true. Yet what we know about narrative theory puts us on notice: During times of change and paradigm shift, it is precisely the familiar that holds the greatest danger.

Understanding how the dialectic of resistance and reform works can enable us, perhaps, to avoid the worst forms of narrow-mindedness, the most devastating of history's judgments. A modest hope, certainly. But if we are right, it may be all our predicament as situated actors, limited by our own range of experience and empathy, admits.

PART THREE

Why We Always Embrace Moderate Solutions (or Saviors)

At some point, society decides that reform is in order. A problem like date rape or environmental deterioration becomes so serious that everyone realizes something must be done. But how far should we go? The answer frequently is as little as possible. Chapter 7 examines the role and reception of moderate reformers, who often appear on the scene at exactly the right moment with a compromise solution the majority will accept but that leaves the original agitators dissatisfied and much of the problem unaddressed. Chapter 8 explores the way "objective" legal rules and formulas cause reformers' demands to appear intemperate, "subjective," and unfair. We tend to resist transformation and new thought until they have lost their urgency and novelty—or until conditions worsen, at which point the proposals then strike us as moderate and necessary responses to a serious crisis.

7

"Our Better Natures": A Revisionist View of the Public Trust Doctrine in Environmental Theory

In 1970, law professor Joseph Sax proposed a strikingly simple, intuitively appealing approach to environmental protection, namely, that natural resources ought to be regarded as held in common. Because these goods are to be enjoyed by all, the government must assume a trust-like duty not to waste or expend them for the benefit of just a few. Further, the state must take into account future users—later generations who will be harmed if society depletes or damages the environment in irreversible ways.[1]

At the time Sax wrote, the environmental movement was in a state of agitation and flux. Commentators were writing about plastic trees and whether we should bestow legal rights on natural objects. The Green Movement was beginning to take hold in Europe, and in the United States scholars, activists, and ordinary citizens were calling for greater attention to decreasing quality of life, increasing pollution, and overdevelopment of the nation's farmlands and wilderness.[2]

The time was exactly right for Sax's article. The public was becoming concerned that the nation's natural resources and parklands were limited commodities that, if too rapidly consumed, would not be available to us and later generations.[3] Sax argued that we should address these concerns by regarding ourselves as trustees who hold these precious goods for the benefit of all. The nation's rivers, beaches, and other natural resources are not ours alone to spend; we must deplete them judiciously, setting aside as much as prudence dictates for our own use and for that of future generations. To enforce this idea, courts should consider that the government holds parklands and other natural resources in a trust-like fashion.

Sax's proposal caught on quickly, influencing legislation and national policy.[4] His article is discussed in virtually every environmental law casebook; courts have cited it heavily.[5]

We believe Sax's public trust doctrine is a wrong, or, at least, a seriously flawed, solution to our environmental crisis. Its oversimplified answer— to regard the nation's environmental resources as goods held in trust— forestalled more searching reconsideration of our environmental predicament and postponed, perhaps indefinitely, the moment when society would come to terms with environmental problems in a serious and far-reaching way.

Sax's trust approach illustrates a general problem for social reformers. Most serious movements fail because society prefers incremental rather than wide-ranging change. In a version of the maxim that "bad money drives out good," we are almost invariably drawn to doomed, moderate approaches like Sax's when society needs more sweeping, ambitious ones. We resist precisely the medicine that could save us. We turn to strong solutions only when it is either too late or when our thinking has advanced so far that the solutions seem commonplace and tame.

Sax's Public Trust Approach to Environmental Law

Sax derives his doctrine from Roman law and traces it to early U.S. Supreme Court decisions in which the Court used trust language to protect shores, rivers, and other water-related resources.[6] Although Sax initially applied the trust doctrine to water conservation, later commentators have urged the doctrine's extension to protect dry beaches, wildlife, parks, and the scientific study of all of these,[7] a suggestion that some states have adopted.[8] The status of the theory today seems secure; it has been incorporated into legislation, case law, and, indeed, our basic thinking about the environment. The National Environmental Policy Act (NEPA) reflects trust notions,[9] as do the federal Clean Water Act,[10] Endangered Species Act,[11] and environmental statutes in many states.[12] The public trust theory has been criticized by a few conservative scholars as an impediment to economic development[13] and by a few on the environmental fringe as unduly homocentric.[14] Yet it seems to have withstood all such criticism. Even in areas where direct influence is difficult to trace, the doctrine marked out a realm of the "ideal," a kind of background against which policymakers operated.

Defects of the Trust System of Environmental Protection

Despite its widespread approval and influence, Sax's theory inhibited the development of other approaches that would have enabled us—and might still—to cope better with our environmental problems. Before turning to these other approaches, however, we shall briefly explain our reservations concerning the public trust doctrine as a means of environmental protection.

First, the model is inherently antagonistic to the promotion of innovative environmental thought. A trust, by its nature, is conservative; its purpose is to protect a thing or good and put it to some use. The idea is to protect what one has, to reduce the risk of improvidence or improper expenditure. Trusts are established to serve an already defined purpose, not to prompt consideration of what that purpose should be. One establishes a trust for a child's college education, for example, once one has decided the child should attend college, not to prompt the child to reflect about his or her future or about whether he or she should attend college (much less about whether college education, as currently constituted, is good or ideal).[15]

In this view, the trust theory arrived on the scene too early in our debate about the environment. It was adopted before we had explored adequately humanity's relationship with the environment. The fit between it and the stage of social dialogue at which it appeared was poor. Yet something about it attracted and made us seize on it before we knew precisely what we were protecting and why. The trust theory froze thinking on our relationship to nature into the form in which it was articulated in the early 1970s. Serious reflection on environmental questions continued, of course,[16] but it was marginalized, confined to the pages of fringe journals and books of the radical environmental movement. It was no longer center stage as it was during the period before Sax's theory appeared on the scene.

Second, the public trust theory is poorly suited to advance natural values. The approach places protection of the environment in the hands of a trustee, generally some agent of the sovereign, who is issued a set of instructions and told to protect the environment accordingly. Unfortunately, the trustee in whose hands the environment is placed is not in the classical position of trustee who has the expertise and concern necessary to promote the trust's purpose. With environmental protection a government agency will often be in no better position to understand how the environment is to be protected than ordinary citizens are.

Frequently, the impulse for setting up a trust is lack of confidence; we fear that we may act irresponsibly with respect to the valued good (say, a sum of money), so we place it in the hands of another whom we instruct to act in accord with our better natures—in the way we would act if we were trustworthy. Consider educational trusts, for example. In our society, men often are conditioned to measure their success by material gains while women are conditioned to value responsibility to others, particularly their children. Men often set up trusts for their children's college education because they fear that otherwise they might spend the money on a sports car or European vacation. Women—and men who have developed a more immediate connection with their children—are less likely to resort to a trust; spending the children's college money on a consumer item simply is not a serious temptation. To the extent that these generalizations remain true, one might say that Sax's reliance on a trust model is a particularly male approach to guarding against overconsumption of limited resources.[17]

One of the reasons why we establish trusts, then, is that we sense in ourselves a dark impulse to act in ways that go against our better natures. This is particularly true with respect to environmental values. All of us, especially men, know that we have impulses to hunt, mine, dam, or cut things down—to treat nature, in short, in ways that contravene our stated collective ideals. Both men and women, in addition, often desire an easier, more resource- and energy-intensive life. Sax and other serious environmentalists know this: If we are left to balance environmental values against short-term pleasure or economic gain, we are likely to favor the latter. But this goes against our ideal natures, hence we relinquish control over the valued object, like Odysseus who lashed himself to the mast to avoid succumbing to the sirens' song.[18]

There is nothing inherently wrong with the trust model. It can be a useful device in many situations. But in wilderness preservation, the trust approach is unlikely to succeed because the trustee will share the same values we hold and have the same weaknesses and propensities.[19] He or she will construe our trust instructions against a background of the very cultural assumptions and meanings that render us poor defenders of the thing in question.[20]

This is much more troublesome in connection with the environment than with areas where bright-line treatment is possible ("Issue Junior four hundred dollars a month as long as he remains a full-time student with a GPA above 2.5"). Environmental protection entails trade-offs and judgment calls, embracing such issues as clear versus selective timbering, grazing on public lands, and building roads and parking lots in national parks. If the trustees are prone to make the same mistakes we would, there is likely to be little gain from transferring defense of the environment to them.[21]

This is, of course, what has happened. Government trustees at both the federal and state level have done little to stop deterioration of air and water quality, to protect endangered environments from the growing problem of toxic wastes, and to protect endangered species.[22] Although there have been some recorded successes, federal and state bureaucrats have generated little in the way of creative, wide-ranging thought about environmental questions; their role has been routinized, administrative, and contained. Yet the public and scholarly community have reacted as though environmental issues are solved or at least in capable hands. Self-scrutiny virtually has ceased, with the result that several promising approaches to humanity's relationship with the natural world have not been developed.

What Sax's Theory Displaced—
Three Approaches to Environmentalism
That Were Not Seriously Explored

The adoption of Sax's approach into statutory law effectively pushed aside other promising approaches to environmental policy and protection. Three such theories were: (1) Aldo Leopold's system of earth-centered ethics; (2) Native American thought; and (3) ecofeminism.

Aldo Leopold's Sand County Almanac—
Earth-Centered Environmental Ethics

In 1949 Aldo Leopold wrote a short book, *A Sand County Almanac*. Its core message is contained in one passage: "A thing is right when it tends to preserve the integrity, stability, and beauty of the biotic community. It is wrong when it tends otherwise."[23] For Leopold, the traditional approach to environmental ethics was wrong. It placed man at the center and asked what use we might properly make of nature. Instead, Leopold urged, we are just one of many members of the land community. Earth does not exist for our use; we have no special, privileged status. Our interests, desires, and wishes should count for no more than those of other creatures; our stability and comfort no more than those of a rock, bird, or mountain valley.[24] Leopold's book quickly became an underground classic. Then, in the late 1960s and early 1970s, it began to receive serious attention.

Kenneth Boulding, in his essay *Economics of the Coming Spaceship Earth*,[25] echoed many of Leopold's ideas when he wrote that we must soon abandon a "cowboy" mentality and economy, based on ceaseless development, and move toward a concept of "spaceship earth," according to which we should be self-sustaining and conscious of our own limits. Although Leopold's and Boulding's ideas remain popular among hard-core environmentalists, they no longer command the attention they once did. Their disappearance coincided with, and is almost certainly one of the effects of, the ascendancy of Sax's trust approach. The broader perspectives afforded by these other approaches could have led to better solutions to some of the environmental problems we are facing today. Discussion of them faded, however, with the adoption of Sax's scheme.

Native American Thought

The late 1960s and early 1970s saw a general revival of interest in Native American thought, particularly that aspect concerning our relationship to land.[26] Early in our history, Native American spokespersons decried the white man's seizure and use of their lands. For example, Chief Seathe (Seattle), when signing the treaty of Port Elliot, is said to have proclaimed:

> Every part of this country is sacred to my people. Every hillside, every valley, every plain and grove has been hallowed by some fond memory or some sad experience of my tribe. Even the rocks which seem to lie dumb as they swelter in the sun ... thrill with memories of past events connected with the fate of my people. ...
> The braves, fond mothers, glad-hearted maidens, and even little children, who lived here ... still love these solitudes. Their deep fastnesses at eventide grow shadowy with the presence of dusty spirits. When the last red man shall have perished from the earth and his memory among the white men shall have become a myth, these shores shall swarm with the invisible dead of my tribe.[27]

In other passages, tribal leaders and wise men spoke of the Native Americans' reverence for the land, animals, forests, and nature. Anthropologists, environmentalists, and anthologists were beginning to collect these and other passages into a coherent, spiritually based view of the environment.[28] But this general approach, too, was largely stilled by Sax's theory.

Ecofeminism

A third movement, in its infancy during the period when Sax was writing on the public trust theory, is ecofeminism. Unlike the other two approaches, ecofeminism remains relatively vital today.[29] Yet it may well have commanded even more serious attention had not the public trust doctrine sprung up when it did.

Ecofeminism, as its name implies, is an effort to link feminism, the study of women and women's values, to exploration of environmental issues. Ecofeminists believe that patriarchy—men's mistreatment and subordination of women—and environmental despoliation are linked. Both stem from a view of the world that countenances harsh, unloving treatment of defenseless things and persons. For many ecofeminists a developer's cutting down a forest in order to build a shopping center is akin to spousal battery and other abuses men inflict on women. They urge that women's values and priorities should infuse and shape environmental thinking. Only when our current approach is supplanted by a more loving, feminist one will we be able to enjoy and protect nature fully.[30]

Each of these approaches to environmental protection was put on the back burner when Sax's public trust theory was adopted. In the meantime, our environmental problems have worsened. Halfway measures have been ineffectual, and within the near future we surely again will have to reconsider our relationship to the natural world. We missed an opportunity in the 1970s, a loss we have only recently begun to appreciate. Was this inevitable? And what does this missed opportunity mean for our prospects for achieving social and legal reform in general?

The Career of Sax's Public Trust Theory: What It Portends for Reform

We believe it is possible to distill from society's experience with Sax's public trust theory of environmental protection a basic truth about legal reform. One way to view the debate over environmental values is through the role of normativity.[31] It is almost a commonplace that normative thought (such as religion) usually increases during times of social unrest. The scholarly analog is that academic writing increases in normativity just before and during times of paradigm change. Just before such a shift, defenders of the old regime marshal normative arguments to defend the old and condemn the new as dangerous, extreme, and immoral. As Thomas Kuhn and others have pointed out, this has been true of virtually every scientific advance.[32] It is true in law and in the social sciences as well. Mainstream scholars resisted critical race studies, males resisted feminism, law deans invited members of critical legal studies to leave the academy, and so on.

If the new paradigm nevertheless catches hold, normative analysis plays a second, more subtle, role. Everyone now rejects the old paradigm (slavery, quantum physics, legal formalism) as antiquated. We rejoice in our modernism and liberality. Yet this rejoicing enables us to avoid even more far-reaching changes and to confine reform to comfortable dimensions. Normative analysis, then, serves as a kind of social homeostat, ensuring that change occurs at just the right pace—not too early, not too fast, and not too far. Like other homeostats, prescriptive thinking prevents us from slipping back to the now-condemned position or paradigm. It thus has both a forward- and a backward-looking thrust; it is conservative and progressive at the same time. It is at this second stage—the stage of consolidating gains—that Sax's article played an important role in our history, one with lessons for every other legal reform movement, such as feminism, critical legal studies, legal realism, law and economics, and postmodernism—all of which evoke the same response at key times.

To explain our thesis more fully, it is essential to recapitulate briefly the recent history of environmental activism. During the middle years of the century, American society began to realize that unlimited exploitation of our natural resources could not continue much longer. We began to doubt the old ethic that prevailed during our period of rapid expansion—permitting practically any form of development or use of public lands that did not positively injure another person and that a majority of the citizenry would tolerate. After several decades of increasing ferment (which included a proliferation of creative essays and books addressing such basic environmental questions as: Why protect the natural environment? What status shall we afford natural objects and our wilderness heritage?), matters were ripe for a revolution in consciousness. Americans reached a collective decision that something had to be done. Business and other interests resisted change; members of "deep ecology," admirers of Aldo Leopold, and ecofeminists advocated far-reaching ones.

Hoping to capitalize on the manifest failures of the old mine-it, dam-it, cut-it-down approach, members of the latter groups wrote books, spoke at rallies, and organized political campaigns around issues of environmental protection. Their programs were not particularly normative; they did not need to be. Instead, they rested on shrewd observation and imaginative (and for some, unflattering) reconceptions of how our relationship to nature could be.

Normativity was turned against them, however. As is generally the case when a paradigm change is in the wind, society deployed normative analysis to (1) praise and embrace the just-begun reforms; and (2) condemn the more ambitious reform programs as extreme and dangerous. There almost always arises, at exactly this point in history, a savior—an individual who captures the legitimate need for reform as well as society's need to assure that matters do not change too far or too fast; an individual who sincerely condemns the old order, thereby assuring that the revolution has a ratchet effect—won't slip back—yet offers the assurance that the new paradigm is not too different from the old.[33] We condemn and abandon the old order only when we are certain that the new one is not more discomfiting than necessary.

In the environmental revolution, that savior was Joseph Sax, whose trust theory, *Mountains Without Handrails,* and other landmark works rightfully established his credentials as a serious reformer and condemner of the old order. At the same time, his public trust article dealt the coup de grâce to legal scholars and environmentalists who were pushing for a radical transformation in consciousness. His theory, then, was in some ways forward-looking, an imaginative, pragmatic, even gallant, effort to save the environment from further deterioration.[34] Yet the theory won wide support largely because it did not promise far-reaching environmental protection. It offered exactly what society needs during the middle and late stages of a revolution—a way of confining change to a manageable level.

Sax's public trust doctrine was attractive because it offered protection from our base instincts.[35] It enabled us to tell ourselves that we no longer needed to worry about the dark sides of our natures, enabled us to tell ourselves and each other that we had finally done something about the environmental problem. Yet by placing control over natural resources and wilderness areas in government agencies run by people like us, we could feel confident that familiar, comfortable values would shape and restrain environmental decisionmaking. The ecofeminists and others advocating sweeping change were shut out. The problem was taken care of in a way that would not change anything too fundamentally—which was all to the good.

The public trust theory, although deeply compromised, solidified a partial revolution in social thought on the issue of environmental protection. It prevented that thinking from slipping back and, thus, provided some protection against retrenchment during the Reagan years. Yet it also delayed more serious consideration of humanity's relationship with the natural world. Three approaches to natural resources and wilderness preservation law would have gone further than Sax's theory, but his theory forestalled their serious consideration. This experience mirrors a general pattern in all law reform movements. At certain points in a paradigm shift a savior, like Sax, always arises offering an approach that enables us to condemn the old order and solidify gains so that we are in no danger of slipping back. Yet the new approach also causes the public to lose interest in more far-reaching strategies that would push our thinking too far forward and threaten stability. We turn to strong solutions only when they no longer seem, or are, strong. Meanwhile, the problems that called forth the new thinking proceed largely unabated, until they again become so serious that we once more engage in introspection and examination. Yet another savior arises, and the process continues in an unending cycle with few heroes, few villains—and little basic change—until, fundamentally, it is too late.

8

Shadowboxing: An Essay on Power

It is important to know when we are being gulled, manipulated, and duped.[1] It is even more important to know when we are unwittingly doing this to ourselves—when we are using shopworn legal scripts and counterscripts, going around endlessly in circles, getting nowhere.[2] Understanding how we use predictable arguments to rebut other predictable arguments in a predictable sequence—"The plaintiff should have the freedom to do X," "No, the defendant should have the security not to have X done to her"; "The law should be flexible, permitting us to do justice in particular cases," "No, the law must be determinate; only bright-line rules are administrable and safe"[3]—frees us to focus on real-world questions that do matter. We can begin to see how what we do as citizens, lawyers, and legal scholars advances or retards causes we hold dear. We can see where the scripts come from and, perhaps, how to write new and better ones.

An Example: "Subjective" Versus "Objective" Standards

In many areas the law prefers "objective" over "subjective" standards for judging conduct. Tort law uses the reasonable person doctrine, contract law applies objective rules to determine when a contract has been formed and what its terms mean, and so forth. An objective standard focuses on the average, reasonable person—what would such a person have meant, thought, understood, or done—whereas a subjective standard focuses on what a particular individual meant, thought, or did.[4] Where does this preference come from, and what does it say about ourselves and our legal culture? Does the objective-subjective distinction hold up under analysis? When we rehearse the familiar arguments in favor of one approach or the other, what are we doing, and what is at stake?

We approach these questions by means of three examples: cigarette warnings, informed consent to medical treatment, and date rape. Tobacco companies defend their marketing of a product known to cause cancer, heart disease, and a host of other illnesses by invoking the narratives of *freedom* and *consent*. The warnings they place on cigarette packages are visible and easy to read. Purchasers who smoke despite these warnings must be deemed to consent to the risks of that activity; any more effective measure would unacceptably impair freedom of action. To the objection that some consumers are addicted, will ignore the warnings, or will bow to social pressure, the manufacturers reply that the warnings are what an ordinary consumer living in our society would expect when purchasing a somewhat hazardous product and that no further effort on their part is necessary. The objective warning on the package is a clincher.

One aspect of the cigarette warning debate was recently before the U.S. Supreme Court. In *Cipollone v. Liggett Group, Inc.*, a widow whose husband died of smoking-induced lung disease sued a large cigarette manufacturer for damages.[5] The issue on appeal was whether federal law, which requires only the current labeling, supersedes state tort law, under which a stricter standard of liability might be applied to cases like the Cipollones'. Not surprisingly, Liggett advocated application of the more objective, and more easily satisfied, federal standard; plaintiffs like the Cipollones, the more flexible state-law tort approach. The Supreme Court predictably held that state law failure-to-warn claims were, indeed, preempted by federal law.

The law of informed consent to medical treatment[6] operates in similar fashion. Before performing medical operations or other invasive procedures, doctors must tell the patient what a reasonable person would want to know about the material risks and benefits of the procedure and obtain the patient's consent. It is irrelevant that the patient may have an undisclosed or highly personalized fear or preference that, if known, would have called for further information or a different course of action. The law requires only the doctor's initial disclosure of "objective" information.

Some physicians, to be sure, may go further, asking, "Is there anything else you are concerned about?" But the law does not require this, and it is the rare doctor who asks the patient about her specific feelings and attitudes toward pain, incapacity, dependency, death, risk aversiveness, reproductive faculties, and religion—a few of the matters that could bear significantly on a medical decision. Answers to these questions might suggest to the doctor the necessity of further discussions with the patient, further disclosures, and a different course of treatment.

The case law of informed consent makes clear, however, that the physician's duty to disclose is simpler and more easily satisfied. The leading case in this area, *Cobbs v. Grant*,[7] requires that the doctor disclose to the patient the reasonable risks and complications of the contemplated procedure and, beyond this, what a competent member of the medical community would disclose. More exacting standards requiring physicians to probe into the patient's need for information have been proposed[8] but are not yet the law.[9]

The debate on date rape is similarly structured: Men generally prefer an objective standard, women a more broad-based, subjective one.[10] If a man can truthfully report that a woman accompanied him without protest, did not resist his advances, and began disrobing when he did, the man wants those actions to be deemed consent. For many date-rape activists, however, that is only the beginning of the story. Under a subjective standard, other factors would be relevant to the issue of consent. We would need to know whether the woman felt coerced or intimidated. Perhaps they were at a party where they drank too much liquor. Perhaps the woman felt social pressure to pair off. Perhaps she was afraid to say no, afraid of ostracism, or of having to go home alone in the dark if the man grew disgusted and left. Perhaps the atmosphere was such that a woman could not easily say no.

Men generally find this type of response infuriating: In their view, women just want to be able to change their minds depending on what happens later—how he behaves (Did he send flowers?), how she felt in the morning, whether or not she became pregnant.[11] Men want the woman's outward behavior at the time to be conclusive: If a reasonable observer would interpret her actions to signal willingness to have sex, that should end the inquiry. A more individualized approach would chill legitimate courtship behavior, encourage bogus claims, and be impossible to adjudicate.[12] It might also patronize, encouraging women to see themselves as weak, easily led, and in need of protection.

What the Subjective-Objective
Debate Shows—and Conceals

Underlying these stylized debates about subjective versus objective standards is a well-hidden issue of cultural *power*, one neatly concealed by elaborate arguments that predictably invoke predictable "principle."[13] These arguments invite us to take sides for or against abstract values that lie on either side of a well-worn analytical divide having remarkably little to do with what is at stake. The arguments mystify and sidetrack, rendering us helpless in the face of powerful repeat players like corporations, human experimenters, action-loving surgeons, sexually aggressive men.

How does this happen? Notice that in many cases it is the stronger party—the tobacco company, surgeon, or male date—who wants to apply an objective standard to a key event.[14] The tobacco company wants the warning on the package to be a stopper. The doctor wants the law to require disclosure only of the risks and benefits the average patient would find material. The male partygoer wants the law to ignore the woman's subjective thoughts in favor of her outward behavior. Generally, that's the way it is—the law complies.

What explains the stronger party's preference for an objective approach and the other's demand for a more personalized one? It is not that one approach is more principled, more just, or even more likely to produce a particular result than the other. Instead, we think the answer lies in issues of power and culture. It is now almost a commonplace that we construct the social world.[15] We do this through stories, narratives, myths, and symbols—by using tools that create images, categories, and pictures. Over time, through repetition, the dominant stories come to seem true and natural, "the way things are." Recently, outsider jurisprudence[16] by persons of color, women, gays, and lesbians has been developing means, principally "counterstorytelling," to displace or overturn these comfortable majoritarian myths and narratives.[17]

The debate on objective and subjective standards touches on issues of world-making and the social construction of reality. Powerful agents, such as tobacco companies and male dates, want objective standards applied to them simply because these standards always, and already, reflect them and their culture. These actors have been in power; their subjectivity long ago was deemed "objective" and imposed on the world. Now their ideas about meaning, action, and fairness are built into our culture, into our view of male-female, doctor-patient, and manufacturer-consumer relations.[18]

It is no surprise, then, that judgment under an "objective" or reasonable person standard generally will favor the stronger party. But not always: Rules that too reliably favored the strong would be declared unprincipled.[19] The stronger actor must be able to see his favorite principles as fair and just—ones that a reasonable society would use in contested situations. He must be able to depict the current standards as integral to justice, freedom, fairness, and administrability—to everything short of the American way itself. Notice that when a subjective test would strengthen the hand of a powerful agent or institution, the law will often oblige—as is illustrated by the "intent" tests used in antidiscrimination law.

How Objectivity Does Its Work

We have thus cleverly built power's view of the appropriate standard of conduct into the very term *fair*. The stronger party is able to have his way and see himself as principled at the same time.

Imagine, for example, a man's likely reaction to the suggestion that subjective considerations—a woman's mood, her sense of pressure or intimidation, how she felt about the man, her unexpressed fear of reprisals if she did not go ahead—ought to figure into determining whether the man is guilty of rape. As we mentioned, many men find this approach offensive; it requires them to do something they are not accustomed to doing. "Why," they say, "I'd have to be a mind reader before I could have sex with anybody!"[20] "Who knows, anyway, what internal inhibitions the woman might have been harboring?" "What if the woman simply changed her mind later and charged me with rape?" (A variation of the age-old objection that rape is a charge easily made but hard to defend against.)

What we never notice is that women can "read" men's minds perfectly well. The male perspective is right out there in the world, plain as day, inscribed in culture, song, and myth—in all the prevailing narratives. These narratives tell us that men want and are entitled to sex, that it is a prime function of women to give it to them (after a suitable period of courtship, of course), and that unless something unusual happens, the act of sex is ordinary and blameless.[21] We believe these things because that is the way we have constructed women, men, and "normal" sexual intercourse.[22]

Notice what the objective standard renders irrelevant: a downcast look (which the man interprets as modesty or delicate anticipation); ambivalence; the question, "Do you really think we should?"; slowness in following the man's lead; a reputation for sexual selectivity; virginity; youth; and innocence (the greatest prize of all!). Indeed, only a loud, firm "No!" counts, and probably only if it is repeated several times, overheard by others, and accompanied by forceful body language such as pushing the man and walking away briskly.

Yet society and law accept only this latter message (or something like it) and not the former, more nuanced ones, to mean refusal. Why? The "objective" approach is not inherently better or more fair. Rather, it is accepted because it embodies the sense of the stronger party, who centuries ago found himself in a position to dictate what permission meant. Allowing ourselves to be drawn into reflexive, predictable arguments about administrability, fairness, stability, and ease of determination points us away from what really counts: The way in which stronger parties have managed to inscribe their views and interests into external culture, so that we are now enamored with that way of judging action. First, we read our values and preferences into the culture; then we pretend to consult that culture meekly and humbly in order to judge our own acts. A nice trick if you can get away with it.

Why Not a Subjective Standard?
On Being Unprincipled on Principle

"But it wouldn't be *fair* to require more. A man would virtually have to carry out a half-hour cross-examination before going to bed with a woman." (Men, of course, have no difficulty quizzing women—or each other, for that matter—at length when deciding whether to enter into a business partnership or deal, by looking for ambivalence, doubt, or strength of motivation.) "A cigarette manufacturer would have to place a blinking neon sign on every pack of cigarettes." (Fine—cigarette manufacturers do just that when they install billboards aimed at creating demand and convincing new consumers that placing a burning carcinogenic object in their mouths is desirable and a path to social acceptance.) To get their message *into* your minds, stronger parties are perfectly willing to go to great effort and expense. But to find out whether you are *willing* to do what they want, we must rely on simple, easily ascertained "objective" factors.

The subordinate party, naturally, prefers the subjective standard. No matter how limited one's resources or range of options, no matter how unequal one's bargaining position, at least one's thoughts are free. Small wonder that the recent legal-storytelling movement has had such appeal to people of color, women, gays, and lesbians.[23] Stories inject a new narrative into our society. They demand attention; if aptly told, they win acceptance or, at a minimum, respect. This is why women demand to tell their account of forced sex,[24] why cancer victims insist that their smoking was a redressable harm despite the tobacco companies' pathetic warning, why patient advocates demand a fundamental restructuring of the doctor-patient relationship.

A Final Example and Conclusion

We began by observing that law-talk can lull and gull us, tricking us into thinking that categories like objective and subjective, and the stylized debates that swirl about them, really count—when in fact they either collapse or appear trivial when viewed from the perspective of cultural power. If we allow ourselves to believe that these categories do matter, we can easily expend energy replicating predictable, scripted arguments. In this way, the law turns once-progressive people into harmless technocrats.

But this happens in a second way as well, when we borrow *their* tools for *our* projects without sensing the danger in that use. For example, a recent article by a critical race scholar proposes a novel approach to the impact-intent dichotomy in antidiscrimination law.[25] The author observes, quite correctly, that most persons of majority race, including judges, are not prepared to see subtle forms of "institutional" or "latter-day" racism. Impact alone is not enough—a vicious intent must be shown. To bridge the gap between unintentional discrimination and the redressable, intentional kind, Charles Lawrence proposes that the law recognize a third, *unconscious* form of redressable discrimination. So far, so good—a fine insight. But his article goes on to propose a "cultural test" for this sort of unconscious racism.[26] Under it, unconscious racism would be redressable if, in light of prevailing cultural meanings and understandings, the action is racist. It would be no defense that the actor did not *intend* racial harm; if persons in the culture would reasonably interpret his act as racially offensive, the court will as well.

Although the proposal has won an enthusiastic reception from mainstream writers, the cultural-meaning test deprives it of any real force. Majority society has *defined* racial reality in such a way that relatively few acts are seen as carrying a racist meaning.[27] Racism is limited to those rare individual (not institutional) acts of a vicious, indefensible, shocking sort. It tends to be associated with persons of another class, who have little political influence and lack the ability to structure society in such a way that our forms of racism—yours and mine—are condemned. Lawrence would have done better to couple his suggestion with proposals to *change* the legal culture, as the storytelling movement sets out to do. Instead, he proposes a relatively small doctrinal adjustment within that culture that will prove ineffective because it neglects the system of power and knowledge within which all interpretive acts take place.

* * *

Sometimes a gestalt switch is necessary.[28] As in a drawing by M. C. Escher, a figure will stand out only if we focus on the background and ignore the foreground at which we have been staring. If we constantly skirmish with the legal foreground when it is the background that has causal efficacy, we are unlikely to get anywhere. We propose that in many cases it will behoove us to examine the legal background—the bundle of assumptions, baselines, presuppositions, and received wisdoms—against which the familiar interpretive work of courts and legislatures takes place. Sometimes, all the rest is shadowboxing.

PART FOUR

Supreme Court (and Other) Rhetoric: How the Way Powerful Institutions Talk Can Devalue and Marginalize Outsider Groups

This final part considers what happens when reformers persist despite the many obstacles of imagination and reception they face. Their movements gain force. Prisoners clamor for reform in their conditions of confinement. Consumers demand protection from unsafe products. Women insist on access to professions that formerly excluded them. At this stage, many judges and other authoritative speakers depict the reformers in unflattering terms. They are seen as shrill, unreasonable, and extreme, asking for things that they do not deserve. Not only are we entitled to resist such unreasonable demands, we have a duty to do so. The first part of Chapter 9 discusses language of scorn and ridicule in Supreme Court opinions and in popular discourse. The final part of the chapter examines a devastating trope our society deploys against reformers whose movement has gained ground: the figure of *imposition*.

9

Scorn and Imposition—How We Use Language, Consciously or Unconsciously, to Derail Reform

The language we use in thinking and talking about something often has real-world consequences. It marshals opinion, constructs images, contributes to a culture in which certain ideas and persons have high prestige and validity and others have less. The terms and images we use also reflect our attitudes and sense of things—they provide a mirror into our collective consciousness.

This final chapter analyzes the rhetoric courts and other opinionmakers deploy with respect to reform movements. We focus on two devices that we deploy in connection with movements that do not meet our approval for some reason. We employ the first, *scorn*, in connection with movements that are in their middle stages—that are beginning to gather force. Later, when the movements become genuinely threatening, we deploy the second, *imposition*.

Scorn

Every year, the Supreme Court issues between one and two hundred written opinions. The more than five hundred volumes of Supreme Court Reports occupy over one hundred feet of shelf space in a library. This body of work can be regarded as a corpus, analyzed for style, argument, use of rhetorical strategies. Such an analysis may reward us with insights into the way the Court sees itself as an institution, into the way it thinks of itself and of law.

It is said that if you want to know what a person is like, all you need to know is whom he adores, admires, and tries to emulate. We believe that the opposite is also true—that to understand how a person's mind works, it is helpful to know whom he scorns, laughs at, regards as low and outside his circle of concern. First, we describe various types of scathing speech, including satire, parody, mockery, irony, and sarcasm. Next, we explain the ways the Justices deploy these types of humor—against litigants, against lawyers who come before them, against legal ideas, and against each other, giving examples from Supreme Court opinions. After that, we propose when it is legitimate for a powerful institution, like the Court, to engage in scornful discourse, and when it is not. We argue that the most caustic types of humor are permissible only when deployed against the high and the mighty, when used to call attention to the foibles, weaknesses, pomposities, and abuses of those more powerful than oneself. A root meaning of "humor" is humus, bringing low, down to earth.[1] On this theory, it is never justifiable to use destructive humor at the expense of someone weaker, of a lower station than oneself.

This distinction also corresponds to a key function the Supreme Court is supposed to serve, namely, its countermajoritarian role. In a standard theory of judicial review, the highest court is charged with policing excesses of powerful actors, like the military and other branches of government. To these, the Supreme Court owes a duty of *suspicion*. To the poor, the outcast, and "discrete and insular minorities" unable to fend for themselves in the democratic process, the Supreme Court owes respect and solicitude. The Court is their defender, the only arm of government capable of redressing injustices they suffer at the hands of the majority.[2]

Our concern is that the Supreme Court has quietly brought about a stunning reversal. It is applying suspicion—cool, sometimes disrespectful treatment—to blacks, welfare recipients, prisoners, gays, and other disempowered litigants. And it is treating with exaggerated respect the military, large corporations, arms of government, and other empowered actors. The study of scornful discourse brings this reversal into sharp relief. If we are right, the Court today is verging close to becoming an illegitimate institution.

Scornful Discourse

One can distinguish scathing words according to their audience, their target, and their intent and effect, as well as their character or genre.

A scornful or satiric speaker can have high or low prestige. When he wrote his famous satires of French society, Voltaire was a respected writer whose prestige and power were only somewhat lower than those of the wealthy whose vices he mocked.[3] A columnist writing today about the excesses of government spending is an example of a writer of moderate social power writing about an institution of even greater power. When Jonathan Swift wrote his satire of humanity's foibles, *Gulliver's Travels*, his target was powerful in the aggregate but weak individually.[4] Marie Antoinette's notorious remark about the poor illustrates a powerful individual speaking cavalierly about those of much lower station.[5] As we shall see, Supreme Court opinions sometimes employ humor in each of these ways.

Humorous discourse also can be distinguished in terms of its intention or effect. Some of the classic exponents of satire used wit with what they considered an educative purpose, to improve or edify. For example, Alexander Pope wrote about what he saw as the frailties and vanities of women. His purpose seems not to have been intentionally unkind, however, but rather to amuse and entertain while gently poking fun.[6] Others, however, made fun at the expense of women or weak social groups, such as dunces, bumpkins, and rustics. On the whole, however, most of the classic writers reserved their arrows for society's favored few.

Finally, scornful discourse can be aimed directly at the target group, someone else, or both together. If aimed at the target group, the impact is apt to be more immediate; therefore the satirist often moderates his or her remarks accordingly, writing with a little more restraint or delicacy than usual. But if the target is a large group or humanity in general, feelings are less exposed and the writing is apt to have a more no-holds-barred quality.

According to most theorists, humor always has a social dimension wherein a speaker and an audience tacitly acknowledge certain beliefs or norms of behavior. Much of it is also aggressive, using words to rearrange the distance between speaker and target, reiterating or calling into question the social hierarchy.[7] This feature is prominently in evidence in satire.

Satire has a long history. Many early cultures used satiric utterances to drive away evil spirits. The Greeks had no word for the genre, but Aristophanes's comedies ridiculed the Athenian elite mercilessly and are today considered early exemplars of satire. Juvenal, the most famous Roman satirist, also aimed his quill at the upper class. According to one classicist, "the 'smart set' of Domitian's Rome was sufficiently corrupt to furnish innumerable targets for his barbed shafts."[8] Though some medieval bawdy plays made fun of both kings and clergy, satiric discourse did not flourish in the Middle Ages. But by the seventeenth century, French society was so rife with religious and social hypocrisy that Molière was able to mock those who piously feigned humility while privately scheming for worldly wealth and position.[9] Satire reached its apogee in eighteenth century England when Jonathan Swift composed his diatribes exposing the venality of the British ruling class. The tradition was later carried on by Mark Twain, who wrote about the foibles of America's upper class, and in the twentieth century by such writers and commentators as H. L. Mencken, Sinclair Lewis, and Russell Baker.[10]

"Satire" derives from the Latin *satura*—a poetic medley characterized by a mocking spirit or tone. Satire is a deliberately distorted image of a person, institution, or society written to entertain. It can take the form of beast fables, imaginary voyages, character sketches, anecdotes, proverbs, and homilies. The writer marshals social themes and narratives to expose the incongruity between what is said and what is done. As will be seen, courts employ satire in a remarkable variety of these senses.

Closely related to satire are parody and caricature. In parody, the writer imitates a person or work in an exaggerated way so as to make him or it appear ridiculous. An early classical Greek poet used parody to mock and mimic Homeric epics by describing a battle between frogs and mice in grandiose language. In recent times, Victor Borge imitates Liberace, Jay Leno and Dana Carvey parody a U.S. president, and a battery commercial mimics other products. Caricature likewise relies on exaggeration, taking a single trait of a person or thing and focusing on that feature alone, distorting through oversimplification to produce a desired effect. Dickens's character Pecksniff and William Hogarth's drawings are classic examples.[11]

Ridicule raises laughter against a person or thing by making him or it the object of jest or sport. Sarcasm intensifies the tone of ridicule, making the gibe or taunt more biting. Mockery jeers and scoffs. It makes a counterfeit representation of something, mimicking and distorting with ridicule, derision, and belittlement.[12] Irony is a figure of speech in which the intended meaning is other than that which is expressed. It can take the form of mock seriousness, insincere praise, or showering attention on minutiae while ignoring what is important.[13]

Scornful Discourse in the Supreme Court

Courts use humor and satire, often quite legitimately. Humor can brighten an otherwise dry and technical opinion, relieving a discussion that without it would be dull and lifeless. It can also have an educative function. As we have seen, many of the world's great writers employed wit and satire to change the behavior of their readers. The Supreme Court also has a supervisory and educative function. When it deploys humor to admonish an overstepping governmental figure, unresponsive bureaucrat, or tedious, long-winded attorney, no one could object. But at other times, the Court's use of wit goes beyond these uses.

When the Target Has High Social Standing

The Supreme Court directs humor or sarcasm at institutions or persons of high prestige less often than at ones of lower prestige, and when it does its language is apt to be relatively restrained: It uses a scalpel, not a sledge hammer. For example, the Supreme Court recently upheld a challenge to the F.B.I.'s policy of exempting disclosure of its records compiled in the course of a criminal investigation. The Bureau had insisted that virtually all documents it obtained in the course of a criminal investigation were confidential, despite a federal statute that required them to establish that each requested document could be expected to disclose the identity of, or information from, a confidential source. Despite the agency's clear violation, the Court's language was relatively mild. It only noted that it held as it did in order to remain consistent with its obligation to construe the Act's exemptions as narrowly as Congress intended.[14]

Sixteen years earlier, the Court considered a challenge to federal action under the Endangered Species Act of 1973. It determined that the government had continued to spend public funds for a certain project, even after congressional committees were made aware of the impact upon the survival of the snail darter, in violation of a law that required federal departments to cooperate with the Secretary of the Interior in protecting wildlife. It found the breach flagrant enough to warrant comment but only noted that the plain language of the Act and its legislative history showed that the balance between economic development and conservation had been struck in favor of the latter.[15]

The degree of restraint employed reminds one of that found in the more famous case of *Brown v. Board of Education*. In 1954, the Supreme Court finally declared that separate but equal schools violated the Equal Protection Clause of the U.S. Constitution. The case was of historical importance. The Court might conceivably have taken the occasion to chastise the many school boards across the nation that had been operating segregated schools, yet it did not do so. It described Topeka's action as generating a feeling of inferiority and its policy of segregation as at most inherently unequal. Instead of demanding immediate desegregation, it permitted local authorities to proceed to dismantle separate systems with "all deliberate speed" and enjoined them to "make a prompt and reasonable start towards full compliance."[16]

These examples are only suggestive, and it is possible to find opinions in which the Court rebukes a governmental figure somewhat more harshly.[17] On the whole, however, the Court keeps its sharpest weapons sheathed when dealing with figures of high prestige, even when it clearly finds they have transgressed.

When the Target Has Relatively Low Status

As we mentioned earlier, the Supreme Court has deployed humor and satire more frequently in connection with disempowered litigants. When it does so its language is apt to have a sharper, more acerbic quality than when it directs its wit upward. Curiously, the Court seems to take little note of early cases in which its own caustic language became notorious.

Two of those cases are *Buck v. Bell* and *Plessy v. Ferguson*. As the reader may recall, in *Buck v. Bell* Justice Holmes upheld an order providing for the sterilization of a young, sexually active woman asserted to have been mentally retarded and herself the mother of a child also said to be retarded. With little consideration of the mother's interest or of less restrictive alternatives, Holmes upheld the order. The opinion is curt and full of facile analogies. Holmes rejects a plausible equal protection argument as one of last resort and concludes with the dismissive pronouncement, "Three generations of imbeciles are enough."[18] A few decades earlier, Justice Brown, in *Plessy v. Ferguson*, upheld a state provision requiring blacks to ride only in railroad passenger cars for blacks. Brown found that the rule did not violate the requirement of constitutional equality because the blacks' car was equal to that of whites. The plaintiffs maintained that the very separation of passengers by race degraded them, violating the Fourteenth Amendment. Brown dismissed this argument, holding that the law could and should not attempt to redress social inequality. Moreover, if the blacks found the railroad's separate treatment offensive it was "only because of the construction they put upon it."[19]

These lines are, of course, now notorious. Yet that notoriety has stopped neither today's Court nor individual Justices from issuing opinions as sarcastic and high-handed as the early ones. For example, in *United States v. Sioux Nation of Indians* the tribe sued the government for the value of lands in the Black Hills region of South Dakota promised them in the Fort Laramie Treaty of 1868 but later taken by the United States. The majority opinion presented a detailed history of the issue on the way to holding that the Sioux were indeed entitled to compensation. Justice Rehnquist offered his own historical presentation, drawn, he maintained, from historians "not writing for the purpose of having their conclusions or observations inserted in the reports of congressional committees."[20]

This jab at the other members of the Court and the historians upon whom they relied did not content Rehnquist. He went on to quote from Samuel Eliot Morison's description of the Sioux, in order to describe the plaintiffs as barbaric:

> The plains Indians seldom practiced agriculture or other primitive arts, but they were fine physical specimens; and in warfare, once they had learned the use of the rifle, [were] much more formidable than the Eastern tribes who had slowly yielded to the white man. Tribe warred with tribe. ... They lived only for the day, recognized no rights of property, robbed or killed anyone if they thought they could get away with it, inflicted cruelty without a qualm, and endured torture without flinching.[21]

Even if true, the historic description Rehnquist read into the record has little to do with the claim the Sioux nation was maintaining against the government. It can only serve as backdrop for his claim that "the Indians did not lack their share of villainy either,"[22] one that at best only tangentially advanced resolution of the issue before the Court. Justice Rehnquist scorned the Indians, pure and simple, thinking his readers would do so as well—just as Holmes thought in *Buck v. Bell*. He misjudged his audience. He failed to persuade a majority of his fellow Justices. And among Indians and Indian lawyers at least, his opinion acquired an instant notoriety.

In the short time he has been on the bench, Justice Antonin Scalia has distinguished himself for his quick tongue and acerbic wit. In two cases having to do with environmental standing (that is, who is entitled to sue in environmental cases), he may have crossed the line between lively language and impermissibly caustic speech. Until recently, the Court had recognized a fairly generous basis for standing in such cases—environmental harm. But in *Lujan v. National Wildlife Federation* the Court severely restricted the previously liberal "personal stake" requirements of individuals seeking environmental standing. There Scalia held that "[this requirement] is assuredly not satisfied by averments which state only that one of respondent's members uses unspecified portions of an immense tract of territory. ... It will not do to 'presume' the missing facts because without them the affidavits would not establish the injury that they generally allege. That converts the operation of [the rule] to a circular promenade."[23] His "circular promenade" comment might strike many readers as gratuitous, but it is positively restrained in comparison to his approach in *Lujan v. Defenders of Wildlife*.

Defenders centered around the standing of an environmental group to bring suit under federal regulations governing the application of the Endangered Species Act. Members of an environmental organization had submitted affidavits stating that they had used the precise lands in question, but Justice Scalia, writing for the Court, held that "the affiants' profession of an 'inten[t]' to return ... is simply not enough." He ridiculed even the terms in which the plaintiffs framed their suit, including an "inelegantly styled 'ecosystem nexus' ... 'animal nexus' ... and 'vocational nexus' approach."[24] A dissent by Justice Blackmun turned the ridicule on Scalia, pointing out that "a Federal Torts Claims Act plaintiff alleging loss of consortium should make sure to furnish this Court with a 'description of concrete plans' for her nightly schedule of attempted activities."[25]

When the Target Is an Idea or Legal Argument the Judge Thinks Ridiculous

Justice Scalia's derision in *Defenders of Wildlife* extends beyond the plaintiff personally, illustrating a third category of cases in which the Court deploys humor against an entire legal idea or argument. In *Defenders*, Scalia made plain that he thought the idea of expansive standing in environmental litigation bordered on the ridiculous. Prison and law-reform cases often provoke the same reaction. For several centuries, prisoners have employed the historic writ of habeas corpus to challenge the conditions under which they were confined and confinement itself. Recently, conservative judges have begun cutting back on the writ's scope by imposing hurdles in the path of prisoners attempting to employ it. Judge Richard Posner, for example, has complained that prison writ-writers file so many requests because they have too much free time on their hands; they would be better off rehabilitating themselves and thinking about their sins.[26] Recently, the Supreme Court echoed this view. In *Gomez v. United States District Court*, a prisoner on death row filed a writ challenging California's use of lethal gas in executions. A per curiam opinion dismissed, explaining that "Equity must take into consideration the State's strong interest in proceeding with its judgment and [the prisoner's] obvious attempt at manipulation. ... This claim could have been brought more than a decade ago. There is no good reason for this abusive delay, which has been compounded by last-minute attempts to manipulate the judicial process."[27] In dissent, Justices Stevens and Blackmun described in length the horrors of death by cyanide gas. They also made the obvious point that if execution by gas is unconstitutional, delay in bringing the claim can hardly endow the state with authority to continue the practice.[28]

When the Target Is an Attorney, or an Attorney in Addition to a Client or an Idea

Rule 11 of the Federal Rules of Civil Procedure has provided an outlet for yet a fourth type of judicial derision, namely directed against the attorney who was foolish enough to bring a groundless case. The rule allows a court to impose "sanctions" against lawyer and party when it finds that a motion, document, request, or the entire lawsuit was unfounded and frivolous. As many feared, it seems to be used disproportionately to punish attorneys and clients who bring civil rights or other suits seeking to vindicate unpopular or new interests.

Because of the rule's relatively brief history, most of the case law is found at the district or circuit court level. For example, in *Szabo Food Services, Inc. v. Canteen Corp.*, a minority firm sued over Cook County's failure to comply with its own minority set-aside program. The district court found that Rule 11 sanctions were inappropriate and the defendant appealed. Circuit Judge Easterbrook, in remanding the case to the lower court to fix the amount of the sanctions, stated that "an absurd complaint does not even invoke federal question jurisdiction." Moreover, he reasoned, "If the complaint is indeed too silly to create subject matter jurisdiction, attorney's fees should be an ordinary incident of the award of costs."[29]

The plaintiff had to endure more than being labeled silly, absurd, and the drafter of a specious complaint, however. Easterbrook went on to ridicule one of his arguments as follows:

> You can only get so far with the comparison to a suit never filed. ... Suppose the plaintiff files a suit, seeks a TRO, in the midst of the hearing asks to approach the bench, emits a Bronx cheer, punches the judge in the nose, and as the judge reaches for a handkerchief to staunch the bleeding tenders a dismissal under Rule 41(a)(1)(i). In reply to the inevitable citation for contempt of court, the plaintiff could not say, "I wasn't there in the eye (nose?) of the law; nothing happened for which I am responsible; for 'it is as if the suit had never been brought.'"[30]

After a few more pages detailing plaintiff's derelictions, the opinion concludes with: "Szabo-Digby's theory of due process is wacky, sanctionably so."[31]

Other judges have imposed penalties on plaintiffs who lost civil or prisoners-rights cases, using such terms as "fantasies," "shocking," "absurd," "unsubstantiated," "self-serving," "contradictory," and "inconsistent" to explain their decision.[32] The Fifth Circuit described one such suit as "patently meritless," "frivolous," and calculated to "try even the most patient members of this court." It said it "[would] not dignify by discussion the merits of the case," directed that the plaintiff "file no further action in any court in this circuit until the sanction levied by the district court is satisfied," and warned "that such continued abusive conduct will trigger increasingly severe sanctions, including the ultimate denial of access to the judicial system absent specific prior court approval."[33]

Recently proposed amendments to Rule 11 may reduce the amount of litigation brought under the rule by providing that offending parties compensate the court, not their adversary, and by making sanctions discretionary rather than mandatory. But while the rule has been in effect it has provided a revealing mirror into the way judges think about racial discrimination, prisoner, civil rights, and similar suits.

When the Target Is Another Court, Another Justice, or the Supreme Court of Another Era

Justices of the Supreme Court sometimes vent their spleen at lower courts, each other, or a predecessor version of the Court itself. Three civil rights decisions from the modern era illustrate scorn and sarcasm directed by one member or wing of the Court at another. In two the Court found for a minority plaintiff, while conservative justices in dissent blasted their more liberal colleagues. In a third, in which the Court chose not to play its countermajoritarian role, liberal justices in dissent excoriated the majority.

In *Metro Broadcasting, Inc. v. F.C.C.*, the Court held that the F.C.C. could employ racial preferences in granting licenses in order to redress long-standing imbalances in the radio broadcast industry.[34] In dissent, Justice O'Connor derided the F.C.C. as a know-it-all agency, stating "[t]he FCC has concluded that the American broadcasting public receives the incorrect mix of ideas."[35] Of course, the F.C.C. was not maintaining that it knew *what* ideas the public should receive but rather that minority broadcasters (and their ideas) were being excluded, a much different proposition. Justice Kennedy went even further, accusing the liberal majority of reinstating a regime of race consciousness, thereby recreating the error of *Plessy v. Ferguson*. He evoked the horrors of that era by quoting passages from a South African publication about apartheid.[36] The liberals, of course, merely opted for a rule that *increased* the number of minority-owned stations.

Justice Rehnquist provides a second example, not only of scorn and derision but of a remarkably patronizing tone. In *F.C.C. v. League of Women Voters* the Court struck down an F.C.C. regulation that prohibited government-funded public broadcasting stations from editorializing. This made Rehnquist unhappy; his "Little Red Riding Hood" response is as follows:

> All but three paragraphs of the Court's lengthy opinion in this case are devoted to the development of a scenario in which the Government appears as the "Big Bad Wolf," and appellee Pacifica [corespondent with the League of Women Voters] as "Little Red Riding Hood." In the Court's scenario the Big Bad Wolf cruelly forbids Little Red Riding Hood to take her grandmother some of the food that she is carrying in her basket. Only three paragraphs are used to delineate a truer picture of the litigants, wherein it appears that some of the food in the basket was given to Little Red Riding Hood by the Big Bad Wolf himself, and the Big Bad Wolf had told Little Red Riding Hood in advance that if she accepted his food she would have to abide by his conditions.[37]

In *Richmond v. J.A. Croson Co.* the Court abandoned its countermajoritarian role. This gave liberal justices in dissent an opportunity to exercise *their* skill at scorn and derision. Because it is directed upward at a Court upholding the power of the majority, this could be said to constitute a rare example of "benign" scorn. In *Croson*, the Court considered a minority business enterprise quota adopted by the city of Richmond. The plan required construction contractors dealing with the city to employ, if possible, 30 percent minority-owned subcontractors, a percentage the City Council considered reasonable in a city roughly 50 percent black. The majority disagreed, holding that the 30 percent quota rested "upon the 'completely unrealistic' assumption that minorities will choose a particular trade in lockstep proportion to their representation in the local population."[38] This is a mischaracterization: Lockstep proportion would be 50 percent; moreover, if one wanted to quarrel over numbers, the starting point would need to be the actual minority representation among recipients of prime construction contracts in Richmond of 0.67 percent.

The factual distortions and second-guessing of the decisions of the Richmond City Council, which was five-ninths black, were based on the majority's view that the city council action was "simple racial politics." The dissent disagreed. Given Richmond's history, "to suggest that the facts on which Richmond has relied do not provide a sound basis for its finding of past racial discrimination simply blinks credibility." Moreover, Justice Marshall wrote: "[T]he ... view that remedial measures undertaken by municipalities with black leadership must face a stiffer test of Equal Protection Clause scrutiny ... implies a lack of political maturity on the part of this Nation's elected minority officials that is totally unwarranted. Such insulting judgments have no place in constitutional jurisprudence."[39]

As we have seen, members of the Court can use blunt language with each other and even harsher language with attorneys and parties appearing before them. Occasionally the Court has an opportunity to employ similar words when discussing its own previous actions or those of a lower court. In *Minnick v. Mississippi*, the Court chided the state court for failure to uphold the rule that an interrogation must cease upon the accused's request for counsel. Mississippi's mistake could not be allowed to stand because of the clear and unequivocal guidelines stated in earlier decisions. The Supreme Court admonished the state court to protect the rights of the criminally accused more zealously and in the future to avoid extracting admissions of guilt contaminated by the coercive pressures of custody.[40] The language is relatively temperate and restrained.

In summary, the Supreme Court reserves its sharpest language for civil plaintiffs, particularly ones for whom the Court feels little empathy, and criminal defendants. With the latter two groups, the sarcasm is apt to be heavy and blunt, falling into the categories of ridicule or derision as we have defined them. When the target is broader or more abstract, such as an entire legal theory or group of plaintiffs, the language is apt to be more refined, if no less scathing. Perhaps because judges respect legal reasoning, the adversary is treated to greater attention and deference. We have fewer "Little Red Riding Hood" tales but more deftness, detail, and wit. The level of writing at times approaches that of true satire, with metaphors marshaled, comparisons made, literary allusions deployed. When the target is another court, the level of asperity is apt to fall somewhere in between—more gentle and solicitous than that aimed at a seriously offending attorney but not so mild as that directed against its own ruling or precedent. The degree of sharpness ranges between what we have described as caricature and irony. We found no case of the Supreme Court, in recent history at least, treating in any seriously satirical way the action of a federal agency, the military, an upper-level law enforcement figure, or a large, multinational corporation. The Court reserves its most withering language for law reform cases or ones brought on behalf of groups like prisoners, gays, environmentalists, and blacks, groups it sees as falling outside its circle of concern.

The Judicial Function: A Theory of the Appropriate Role of Satire and Humor

As we mentioned earlier, our theory of humor and satire is relatively straightforward: Satire should be reserved for targets of higher status and power than the speaker, never lower. We now explain and defend our thesis in greater detail.

A root meaning of "humor" is *humus*, bringing low, down to earth. Although humor and ridicule can of course be directed at the lowly and the weak, it appears that a principal function in all ages has been that of calling to account the high and the mighty. Early Greek playwrights and satirists made fun of the foibles and vices of the gods, the ruling class, and sometimes mankind in general. Early Roman emperors used a slave to march or stand with them during victory parades and other state occasions and whisper periodically, "Thou art but a man."[41] Early European royalty employed court jesters to mock and make light of their own mannerisms and excesses.[42] Although the early meaning of humor, of course, is not decisive, it nevertheless gives some indication of what humor's central function might be today.

Past practice also argues for our general thesis. Throughout history, the best humorists and satirists have aimed their arrows either at the ruling class or at some group that in the aggregate could be described as empowered.[43] Thus, Molière mocked the vanities and absurdities of his nation's aristocracy or of the nouveaux riches. Voltaire reserved his best barbs for social climbers. Jonathan Swift wrote his sliest, most savage denunciations of heartless bureaucrats and rulers. Today's newspaper satirists concern themselves with abuses of power, and so on.

It is possible to find exceptions, to be sure: A famous author tells a dunce tale at the expense of an industrial worker who loses a finger by accident, is recompensed, and decides to lose another;[44] women were a common object of humor in the Classical period;[45] snobs of all ages would sometimes enjoy a laugh at the expense of the naive or unsophisticated.[46]

Sinclair Lewis, H. L. Mencken, and Aldous Huxley made fun of the middle class; Orwell of the "proletarians."[47] And in our time, one sees an upsurge of misguided humor aimed at women, minorities, and immigrants. Yet, "it is no longer considered proper to laugh at the crippled and the insane, as it was in Shakespeare's day."[48] We tend to find such humor mean-spirited, "mere invective." It lacks the detachment, indirection, subtlety, or social reformist quality of the better forms of parody, irony, and satire. When satirists tirelessly "attack individuals in public life and in institutions ... [the] awe of greatness vanished. ... And whereas there had once been discussions of the divine rights of kings, these were succeeded by candid admissions that monarchs were as susceptible to error as any of their subjects."[49] In our time, Jay Leno, host of NBC's *Tonight Show*, explained that he favors "topical humor, hammering political figures," rather than "four-letter words ... and testosterone-laced ranting against women, gays and various ethnic groups." He joins such comics as Will Rogers, Bob Hope, Garry Trudeau, and Johnny Carson in carefully aiming humor upward, dissecting the habits, pointing out the foibles, and puncturing the pomposities of society's elites.

Both the etymology of the terms and the practice of their best exponents thus argue that humor and satire should never be aimed at the lowly. This is in accord with intuition as well. In a dozen areas of life, ranging from playground protocol to international politics, we believe that it is wrong to bully a weaker adversary, that one should always "pick on someone your own size." The Bible, for example, admonishes that we should look after the poor, the lame, and our weaker brothers. The Declaration of Independence justifies the colonies' break with England, in part, on a series of abuses and tyrannies the older country perpetrated on its fledgling outpost. A hundred myths, novels, sagas, and songs celebrate defenders who champion the causes of weaker persons or groups.

Humor is a powerful social tool. In humor one laughs, bares one's teeth, looks at and invites others to laugh with one, often at the expense of another. It can as easily lend itself to bullying as to the redress of injuries. In our view, only the latter use is the appropriate one. Consideration of the judiciary's function argues that this is even more true when humor is deployed by courts. A leading theory of judicial review holds that courts, particularly the Supreme Court, are charged with exercising a countermajoritarian function. The judiciary is the only branch of government capable of intervening to protect a "weak and insular minority" from discrimination at the hands of the majority.[50] At the same time, the Supreme Court may often prove the only institution capable of redressing excesses and abuses by other branches of government, the military-industrial complex, multinational corporations, and other powerful entities. This is why judges have lifetime tenure, are not easily removed from office, and are kept distant from the pressures of political life.[51] Courts owe a duty of *suspicion* toward the mighty, just as they owe a duty of solicitude to the weak; with them, the rude remark, brusque dismissal, and sarcastic or mocking treatment will rarely be in order. Both the theory of humor and that of the judicial function thus coincide: Sarcasm and invective should be reserved for the high and powerful, never the lowly.

Humor distances. It emphasizes the separation between the one who employs it and the one who is its butt. It invites the reader or listener to join in laughter at the folly or plight of another. Indeed, theorists believe that this distancing is one of humor's constitutive features. Yet this quality renders humor and satire troublesome when deployed by a court, especially against the lowly: Racial minorities, mental patients, the poor, prisoners, and others are already lowly. They come before the Court in hopes of improving their situation, of correcting some injustice they have suffered. Humor threatens to lower them even further, place them even further outside our concern. It tends to weaken empathy, already in short supply.

The opposite genre, *tragedy,* will often prove a more fitting model for courts considering what language to apply in such cases. Tragedy emphasizes the commonalities in human experience, humanizes by reminding us of our common fate. Courts cannot, of course, compose a work of great tragic literature every time they write an opinion rationalizing their treatment of a young death-row prisoner or welfare recipient. But they can restrain their instinct to laugh, to make fun at the expense of those less fortunate than they. They can aim for a tone that is sober and respectful, reserving their barbs, their wit, their flourishes for more worthy targets— for empowered actors who have distanced themselves from the rest of us, who have violated the public trust and deserve to be brought low. They can deploy humor, tragedy, respect, and iconoclasm appropriately, selecting their tone and language with a view to the features of the situation facing them. They can keep their countermajoritarian role constantly in their consciousness, reminding themselves, if necessary, of the way history has treated their most serious lapses.

*   *   *

It is not easy to control what will strike us as ridiculous and unworthy of belief. We all have an internal canon—a group of ingrained ideas that seem to us self-evidently true, sensible, and just—indeed, that we use in evaluating new ideas to see whether they are true, sensible, and just. Ones that deviate too drastically from those we believe are apt to appear wrong and extreme. But merely because we have a tendency to scoff at that which is new or different, it does not follow that we should. If our research teaches anything, it is that consciousness changes, so that the day's commonplace—separate railroad cars for blacks and whites; three generations of "imbeciles" and no more—in time may look quite different.

How can judges and others protect themselves against history's judgment? We have proposed a simple, easily recalled rule: Satire, sarcasm, scorn, and similar tools should only be deployed upward, at actors and institutions more empowered than oneself. The Supreme Court today has been breaching this rule with increased frequency, treating powerful litigants with exaggerated respect and deference and affording curt, sometimes scornful treatment to society's outgroups. This trend is troublesome on a number of levels. It can mar the reputations of otherwise eminent justices long after they leave the bench. It can do damage to particular litigants, demoralizing them and causing them to lose faith in the judicial system. And, if continued, it portends serious damage to the legitimacy of the Court as an institution.

Imposition

In one of the prison-rights cases mentioned earlier, the Seventh Circuit rejected a plea brought by an inmate who had already filed a number of others. Describing him and other prison writ-writers as petty and litigious, the court went on to declare their constant hounding of the authorities and refusal to come to terms with their own guilt further proof of their unregenerate condition.[52]

Courts, including the Supreme Court, have been employing more and more such expressions of exasperation lately in cases brought by prisoners, minorities, and other outsider groups. As with terms of scorn, we find this trend intriguing. An examination of such cases has shown that the court system, like society generally, deploys terms of *imposition* at key moments in the history of a reform effort. Before that point, society tolerates or even supports the new movement. We march, link arms, and sing with the newcomers, identifying with their struggle.

At some point, however, reaction sets in. We decide the group has gone far enough. At first, justice seemed to be on their side. But now we see them as imposing, on the offensive, asking for concessions they do not deserve. Now they are the aggressors, we the victims. At precisely this point in a reform's history, we begin to deploy what we call imposition language, language of encroachment. We decide the group is asking for "special" status. We find their demands excessive, tiresome, or frightening. The imposition narrative delegitimizes the reform movement, portraying it as unprincipled. But by a neat switch, it also enables us to feel comfortable about withdrawing our support, paints us as morally entitled to oppose the movement and bring it to a halt.

First we consider words that focus on the reformer personally or on some trait or quality that renders him unreasonable, a nuisance. We next focus on words that impugn the outsider's motives and then ones that focus on his or her external actions. A fourth category focuses on the implications or effects of reformist behavior. In general, society attaches the imposition label only to individuals or groups whom we already see as bearers of a stigma. We rarely hold our friends guilty of imposition; it is only outsiders, persons whom we have already rendered "other," whose behavior we can deem imposition. *Satirical* language can be soft or mild—or hard-edged and dismissive. *Imposition* language almost always falls on the latter end of the continuum.

Words That Impugn the Outsider Personally

Supreme Court Opinions. Four cases dealing with racial minorities or women illustrate what we call the imposition *per se* approach. In *Dred Scott v. Sandford*, the U.S. Supreme Court considered for the first time a direct challenge to the institution of slavery. Writing for the majority, Justice Taney reviewed the history of Negro slavery beginning with early colonial times, concluding that blacks had always been regarded as property. The early colonial leaders and framers were "great men," who regarded the institution of private property, including the ownership of slaves, as the basis of civilized government. Consequently, Taney found it "impossible to believe that these rights and privileges [of citizenship]" extended to slaves. His opinion showed little contrition, sorrow, or inner tension, in effect chastising the petitioner for having asked the Court to do something absurd on the face of it, given his status as a Negro.[53]

In *Bradwell v. Illinois*, the Supreme Court held that a woman's desire to practice law did not constitute a "privilege of citizenship" protected by the Constitution. If permitted to practice law, women might want to "engage in any or every profession, occupation, or employment"—something the Court obviously considered outlandish. The Court used words of imposition to show how unreasonable Myra Bradwell was in making her request: "In the nature of things it is not every citizen ... that is qualified for every calling and position." The Court found Ms. Bradwell, who had already performed an apprenticeship and passed a written examination, unqualified by virtue of her womanhood, and peculiar for wishing to follow a course more characteristic of "the sterner sex."[54]

In *Chae Chan Ping v. United States*, the Supreme Court upheld the Chinese Exclusion Act limiting immigration from that country. Justice Field pointed out that Chinese immigration had increased rapidly because of the Gold Rush in the middle of the century. Many of the Chinese settlers were hardworking and frugal, which led to friction between them and their white neighbors. By holding to their own customs, language, and norms in a new land they struck others as clannish and aloof. A convention to consider the problem found that the Chinese were a "menace to our civilization" and had a baneful effect on national life. Writing for the majority, Justice Field emphasized that control over immigration is necessary for "security against foreign aggression and encroachment" and from "vast hordes of ... people crowding in on us." These dangers are especially acute when the foreigners are of a "different race" unlikely to "assimilate with our people."[55] The imposition language could not be plainer. The characterization of Chinese as undesirables who do not deserve to be here could not be more manifest.

More recently, in *Maher v. Roe,*[56] the Supreme Court considered a challenge to a Connecticut funding program that paid fully for the cost of an indigent woman's childbirth but did not fund abortions that were not medically necessary. The Court held that Connecticut's program did not violate the Equal Protection Clause, even though an earlier decision, *Roe v. Wade,*[57] had found abortion to be a fundamental right. Because Connecticut did not create the petitioner's indigence, it had no obligation to make her abortion free or affordable. Her poverty, in other words, gave her no special standing. The Court saw no difference between what Ms. Roe was demanding and a hundred other possible claims an indigent woman might make for welfare support. It stopped just short of telling her she did not understand her role as a poor woman—namely, to be as quiet, prudent, and nondemanding as possible. Although not as blatant a case of exclusion as the previous three, *Maher's* effect is just as serious: Women who cannot afford abortions will not be able to obtain them. The opinion's indignation over the woman's effrontery is practically as plain as that of the nineteenth-century cases.

General Popular Discourse. Although the Supreme Court today uses imposition *per se* language somewhat less frequently than before, certain social commentators have no such inhibition. For example, Mickey Kaus, in a recent issue of *The New Republic,* published a scathing review entitled "The Godmothers: What's Wrong With Marian Wright Edelman." For Kaus, Ms. Edelman's book on the plight of poor children avoids the root cause of their troubles, namely, their parents' dependency and unwillingness to work. Her interpretation thus constitutes for him a kind of double hubris. Her clients overstepped in the first place by being poor and making us feel guilty. And she overstepped as author by blaming society for neglecting its schools and children. Kaus charged Edelman with opportunism, implying that she wrote as she did in order to increase funding for her organization.[58]

Linda Chavez, writing in the same magazine, ridiculed in the title of her essay Hispanic groups who insist on calling themselves "Latino."

How tiresome—yet another new name, yet another imposition on our good natures! Her article also described Latino demands as amounting to quotas and the group's troubles as its own fault for refusing to legalize and assimilate into the culture as earlier immigrants have done. There is little to indicate that Chavez wrote as she did to exhort her countrymen to do better. She described their traits in fatalistic terms, as though they are inborn and unlikely to change.[59]

The English-only movement supplies further examples of inherent imposition. Supporters speak of immigrants who wish to maintain their culture with an irritation that sometimes verges on revulsion. They are unpatriotic and unfit to reside here, their presence (in their unreformed foreign-language speaking condition) calculated only to precipitate white flight. Certain Latino and Asian groups' insistence on speaking their own language with each other merits special scorn.[60]

In an ironic twist, Asians who succeed can also draw unfavorable attention. Recently, U.S. Representative Roscoe G. Bartlett (R.–Md.) noted that of recently awarded scholarly prizes, "half went to those with Oriental names, a sixth ... to Indian names, and the rest to what we consider normal Americans." Bartlett later explained that he meant "normal" only in the sense of average and admitted that he had used "poorly chosen words." He maintained that he did not mean to offend anyone and that the news media had distorted his remarks[61]—thereby completing a nearly perfect triple-trope. The Asian schoolchildren overstepped by being here in the first place—note the use of the slightly derogatory term "Oriental." Next, the Asian students had the effrontery to apply themselves at school, thereby imposing on the prerogative of the native-born to take things easy and still get good grades—witness the use of the word "normal" to imply that the Asian children were strange. Finally, the media overstepped by reporting the representative's remarks, thereby invading his prerogative to put the foreigners in their place without drawing attention.

Words That Impugn the Outsider's Motives

Imposition language can also cast reformers or an outsider group in a negative light because of their supposed bad motives or unstated agenda. The outsider is not looking for social justice but spoiling for a fight, has a chip on his or her shoulder. Or the outsider has an impermissible motive—is advancing social claims to win funding, acclaim, or power he or she does not deserve.

Supreme Court Opinions. A line of recent cases, including the one mentioned earlier, illustrates the first approach. Courts have been rejecting prisoners' writs brusquely, sometimes implying that prisoners write them because they are bored and have too much time on their hands. Sometimes, they imply bad character in other ways as well. The plurality opinion of Justice Sandra Day O'Connor in *J.A. Croson Co. v. City of Richmond*, the construction contractor case discussed earlier, warned of the danger of acceding to "a politics of racial hostility." In doing so she implied that the backers of the Richmond program that would have increased the number of minority contractors were themselves racially hostile, were prepared to be unfair to innocent whites.[62] The opinion echoed earlier Supreme Court cases that also saw black demands as hypersensitivity. In 1883, in the *Civil Rights Cases*, the Court struck down a federal civil rights statute, finding that Congress lacked the power to enact it. Although the grounds for invalidation are technical and narrow, the Court went on to chide the plaintiffs for having brought the suit in the first place, observing that what they seemed to want was not equal but special treatment. The cases all concerned access to public accommodations, such as inns and public conveyances. Yet to the Court, the demands seemed like a request for special aid. It was time for African-Americans to stop insisting on such treatment and to become "mere citizens."[63]

General Popular Discourse. Columnists and reviewers have been even less reticent about attributing base motives to reformers than has the Court. Recall, for example, the Kaus article that depicted a well-known advocate for children's rights as concerned mainly with her own funding. Similarly, detractors criticized Representative Maxine Waters for her role in the wake of the Los Angeles insurrection. Waters spoke to reporters about the causes of the L.A. riots, including black poverty and the unresponsiveness of the city's bureaucracy, only to have her accusers charge her with cynically exploiting the tragedy of the riots.[64] In a note on street hassling, the editors of *The New Republic* ridiculed a theory pioneered in a *Harvard Law Review* article, urging that women who are subjected to leers, whistles, and unwanted remarks on the streets should have legal recourse. The note suggests that those who support this movement are petty and vindictive, that being hassled is "a hazard of existence," and that the author is advocating a violation of the constitutional rights of men.[65]

Words That Find Imposition
in Particular Forms of Behavior

In a third variant the speaker does not impeach reformers or their motives but rather their actions. These accusations tend to be less harsh than the first kind. Nevertheless, they hold that the reformer is doing something wrong—is either demanding something that by its very nature constitutes imposition, or is going about things the wrong way, for example, by trying to vault to the head of the line.

Legal and Supreme Court Discourse. Civil rights measures for blacks invariably strike some commentators as troublesome. For example, the Civil
Rights Act of 1964, enacted in the wake of John F. Kennedy's assassination
and Martin Luther King's marches in southern cities, today is regarded as
a moderate mainstay of legal protection for minorities. When it was proposed, however, U.S. Senator Barry Goldwater and Alabama Governor
George Wallace argued that it might take the creation of a police state to
enforce the measure.[66] In *Regents of the University of California v. Bakke*, the
university instituted a program that gave blacks certain priorities in admission to medical school. In striking it down, Justice Powell highlighted
the way in which the program, although aimed at increasing diversity,
nevertheless operated unfairly against "innocent persons in respondent's
position."[67] This "innocent whites" concern has been appearing more and
more frequently in judicial opinions rejecting black demands. The judge
notices that a complicated job program, for example, increases the number of jobs for blacks but decreases or holds constant those for whites. He
or she fixates on the latter, finds a causal connection, and holds that no
program of racial justice can come at the expense of nonminorities not
personally responsible for African-Americans' predicament.[68]

In *McClesky v. Kemp,* the Georgia death penalty case, the Court
highlighted the potentially unlimited scope of the remedy the challengers
had requested. If the legal system accepted the idea that statistical disparities in jury outcomes along racial lines warranted relief in death penalty
cases, things might not stop there. Challengers might be able to show
class, race, and sex-based disparities in other types of sentencing as well,
placing the integrity of our entire jury system in question. The Court displayed some thinly veiled exasperation with McClesky and the attorneys
who had brought the case, describing McClesky's earlier motion for a new
trial as "extraordinary," calling the study upon which the case was based
"clearly insufficient," and referring to McClesky's arguments as "wide-
ranging."[69]

General Public Discourse. Nonlegal writers also see many forms of behavior and advocacy as encroachment. For example, some conservative
writers describe gays and lesbians as *pushing* themselves into the mainstream or *pressing* their sexuality upon the rest of us. The physical images
evoked are striking, if unconscious—the efforts of gay activists to resist
discrimination are seen as a kind of aggression verging on rape.[70] Writers
advocating immigration restraints use similar, if less colorful, language.
The illegal alien is said to sneak into the United States, insinuate himself
into our midst, hide, remain without asking permission.[71] The language of
overstepping and introjection is both literal and unmistakable. Finally,
feminists seeking to regulate hardcore pornography and civil rights activists attempting to control hate speech often evoke charges of censorship.
Commentators ranging from moderate liberals to archconservatives often

focus exclusively on the restraint of speech, overlooking the equally serious harms to equality and dignity the reformers are trying to redress.[72] The reformers' behavior is judged according to the one standard alone—that of freedom of speech—and found wanting.

Imposition Through Effects or Implications

A final approach portrays a reform movement as threatening encroachment through its effects or symbolic impact.

Supreme Court Opinions. Courts seem to employ the *reductio ad absurdum* and the "where would you draw the line?" arguments in law reform cases more than anywhere else. As we shall describe later, these approaches can also be used when we do not want to take the reformers' request seriously but are merely entertaining or toying with it. But at other times we deploy these arguments with a vengeance—when we have decided to confront the reformers' demands squarely and reject them.

For example, in *Harris v. McRae*, the Supreme Court ridiculed the plaintiff's effort to establish a state's obligation to pay for abortions. If such an obligation were recognized, the Court reasoned, would things stop there? The next case might request that the state pay to send someone's child to a private school. In language reminiscent of *Bradwell v. Illinois*, the Court described the plaintiff's request as "extraordinary."[73]

A Florida school board's policy protected minority teachers in cases of layoff. In *Wygant v. Jackson Board of Education*, the Supreme Court struck down the policy, reserving especially scathing treatment for the teacher-as-role-model argument. Although social scientists had testified that the presence of minority teachers improves minority students' accomplishments, the Court spurned the argument. It would justify anything, could lead to separate rules for black and white teachers, and might even end up limiting the number of African-American teachers in districts that had few black students.[74] That these dangers were theoretical, almost farfetched, did not seem to trouble the Court. The role model argument threatened to restructure classrooms, a sensitive area. By its very nature that seemed to usher in imposition.

General Public Discourse. Popular writers have wielded the "drawing the line" or "where will it all stop?" arguments with a frequency and fervor almost equal to those of courts. Dinesh D'Souza, for example, in *Illiberal Education* and a number of articles warns that giving in to the demands of campus radicals could eventually spell the end of the university as we know it. He depicts minority students' demands for meeting places, theme houses, and dormitories as steps toward the Balkanization and politicization of university life. For D'Souza this first wave of requests is not so much dangerous in itself as for what it portends: a university in which knowledge is not unitary but shifting and contestable, a community that contains not one voice but many.[75]

Mainstream columnists writing about gay rights also raise the "where will it all stop?" specter, sometimes going on to supply their own answer: "truculent tribalism." One likens gay activists to "guerillas moving down from the hills to attack the cities."[76] Another warns that giving in to one group increases the chances that "other(s) ... will ... emerge demanding that their preferences or orientations receive similar treatment. If the barrier against ... homosexuality falls, there will be no other that can stand. ... Men have forgotten God."[77]

The Narrative's Efficacy and Attraction

As we have seen, the narrative of imposition appears at predictable periods in history, namely, when reform has gained momentum and appears poised to produce changes that make us uneasy. When so deployed, it seems to have real bite. What accounts for its persistence and power?

Efficacy and the Role of Subnarratives

Our research disclosed a veritable landscape of imposition-types, corresponding to a series of basic, almost innate, subnarratives, ranging from "Who are you, anyway?" to "Nobody talks about me anymore." Perhaps the most basic subnarrative of all is that of the bully. Everyone recalls childhood games and activities in which one of the opponents did not play fair—relied on force, broke the rules, or insisted on special treatment. In adult life, things are almost never so simple. Most reformers are not seeking to break the rules but change the game entirely. But we carry images from these early experiences and apply them to situations where they may or may not fit.

Baselines and Tipping Points—"The way things are." Recently a columnist complained that all the recent books seemed to be about women. It turned out that the writer was referring to a small group of books, mostly written by women, and dealing with such issues as child care, divorce reform, spousal battery, and menopause. In any literal sense, the reviewer was wildly inaccurate. Every year thousands of nonfiction books are published, a considerable majority of them dealing with subjects such as war, sports, mechanics, and power politics predominantly of interest to men. To the reviewer, however, these did not seem like men's books but just books. The current distribution, in other words, seemed fair and equal; the small group of new books about women unbalanced things all out of proportion.[78] With minority hiring, according to Derrick Bell, much the same happens.[79] We think this is true in general. The reformer seems to be seeking special treatment, asking for a departure from a situation we have come to regard as neutral and fair. We fail to notice how the current situation itself reflects a particular distribution of power and authority, arrived at long ago. (See, for example, Chapter 6.) But we do notice changes and proposals for change. These stand out starkly, seem like departures, and require justification.

The Rule and the Exception—"What's so special about you?" In a related mechanism, we view outsiders as seeking an exemption from universal rules that all of us must obey. For example, in the Oregon peyote decision, *Employment Division, Dept. of Human Resources v. Smith*, the Supreme Court portrayed the small group of Indians as requesting to be excused from a uniform criminal law.[80] Demands associated with multiculturalism often trigger the same response—why should we excuse the new writers and curricula from the same test of time we apply to Shakespeare, Milton, and Mark Twain?

Our preference for rules over ad hoc treatment gives this argument some initial plausibility. The difficulty is that there are rules and there are *rules*. For example, one could argue in the Oregon peyote case that the applicable rule is toleration for diverse cultures. Then, Oregon's law would be seen as an exception, an imposition on the Indians. Everything thus depends on the choice of rule that one declares central: the criminal prohibition, according to which taking mild drugs is illegal, or the principle of tolerance according to which Oregon was overstepping, imposing on the Indians who were merely trying to practice their religion.

Recall also Justice Brown's approach in *Plessy v. Ferguson*, in which he found blacks guilty of imposing on the other riders by demanding to ride in the same railroad cars as whites. Viewed in that light, the Negroes were imposing on the whites' customary rule—separate but equal. Of course, if one declared that the relevant norm was the contrary one, the one that the Supreme Court adopted in *Brown v. Board of Education*—namely, that citizens are entitled to public services regardless of color—then the railroad, which had a contrary rule, would be seen as imposing on the blacks.

"If you give them an inch ... " As we have seen, many deployments of the imposition figure rest on a fear of the floodgates. Because the first request strikes us as extreme, the possibility of others raises real fears. Giving in could set a precedent, start us down a path at the end of which is a world we might not even recognize. This in turn taps a related narrative—fear of the unfamiliar, fear of loss of control.

Fear of Loss of Control—"I know what they really want." All of us derive part of our self-definition from the wider society. Thus, on some level we understand that radical changes in our surroundings could change us as persons. Changes in our city government, the curriculum or teachers in our children's schools, or in the composition of our neighborhood could require us to adjust, to give up something, to become different. In time our very identities might change, a prospect that of course discomfits. Anyone who makes this fear seem plausible commands our instant attention.

The Reformer as Ingrate—"After all we have done for them." Part of that identity is an image of ourselves as a tolerant and generous society. Reformers, however, are suggesting that we have not lived up to our national ideals—that all men are not brothers, all immigrants not welcome, and so on. This cannot be true; the reformer must be wrong for even having raised the idea. The imposition trope neatly enables us to accomplish both objectives. We get to reaffirm that society is as we think, and that the outsider transgresses by suggesting that the contrary may be true.

The Usual and the Aberrant—"They're standing the world on its head." Most of us believe that the United States is a fair and just society. We prefer to think of racism, sexism, and homophobia as exceptions, occasional mistakes that with diligence can be reduced, if not eliminated entirely. Reformers, however, often seem to be saying the opposite—that injustice is the norm and fairness the exception. This view seems to turn the world on its head, to insist that night is day, and day night.

Evasion of Responsibility, the Role of Denial—"It's not my fault." Avoidance of blame and responsibility are universal human tendencies. No one likes to believe that he or she may be responsible for serious continuing injustice. Yet the outsider seems to be saying just that. Declaring him misguided or an opportunist eliminates any need for soul-searching or admission of error.

The Ordinary and the Extraordinary—"I have problems too." The reformer's plea demands attention and possibly reallocation of resources. But everyone has problems—What about mine? If we can characterize the outsider group's complaints as unexceptionable and ordinary, any urgency in addressing them dissipates. One may even discover that one's own problems are more interesting, more gripping, more subtle than those of the outsider group. The other group is imposing, monopolizing attention that we deserve as well.

The Metaphor's Seeming Legitimacy:
Its Manifest Content and Why It Rings True

As we have seen, courts and other articulators of cultural wisdom find the imposition-narrative natural and attractive. They deploy it freely, enthusiastically, unapologetically, and with considerable effect. We have also seen how the metaphor taps a variety of existing subnarratives ranging from "I know what they really want" to "no special treatment" to denial of responsibility. A final question concerns the metaphor's manifest content. A narrative might be powerful but unattractive on its face for some reason—

for example, white supremacy, or the idea that men should be women's protectors. In short, a rhetorical device must appear right and true, must enable the speaker to use it and still maintain his or her self-image as a moral actor.

The imposition narrative performs these tasks admirably. First, we typically apply it only to a group that bears a preexisting stigma. When such a group mobilizes to make demands on us, it is easy to attach a further element to its stereotype: Now, in addition to being shiftless, hapless, immoral, and so forth, it is overstepping and pushy. The new element seems to stand in a logical relation to the ones we have already assigned it. The attachment causes few qualms; indeed seems self-evidently correct. The group's very demandingness verifies the accusation. It shows what we think of them is true.

Characterizing the outsider group as imposing allows us to feel justified in rejecting their claim. They are the ones metaphorically throwing the first blow. As victims, we are entitled not only to deny their demands but to tell the world how unfair and unprincipled they are. Many writers who employ imposition language do so with a kind of relish and zeal. They expect no rebuttal, for none is possible. Indeed, the background against which they deliver their message assures them that the rest of us will nod assent. Of course, that group is overstepping. That is what they do.

Reform: Natural History and Lessons for Its Proponents

How Our Society Treats Most Reform Movements

Underlying many uses of the imposition metaphor is nonreflexivity, the quite natural tendency to believe that one's own way of seeing and doing things is natural and universal. Upon hearing one's most settled beliefs impugned by an outsider, the nonreflexive person immediately thinks that the outsider must be wrong. By a kind of backward reasoning we conclude that since the individual is questioning what we believe, he or she must be mistaken and probably operating from base motives as well.

The natural path of most reform movements, then, takes something like the following form. At early stages, the culture responds generously. We are curious, interested in the new things the reformers are saying. We invite them to our homes, read their books, discuss their theories and ideas. Behaving in this fashion reaffirms our self-image as an open, sharing people. Little seems to be at stake, indeed, our lives appear to be enriched by the reform movement—there is a new piquancy at parties, some welcome variety to talk in the faculty lounge.

Later, the reality of what the reformers are asking for starts to sink in. Our attitudes change. We begin to wonder whether the reformers can actually be asking for *that*. We question the reformers' factual predicate or description of the world as containing much injustice. We ask is there not another possible account? Could not the lack of blacks in the construction industry be due to some reason other than discrimination? We question the necessity or plausibility of their story. Or we shrink from the substance of their demands, retreating into proceduralism. We profess not to understand their claim or ask questions demanding greater specificity. If we heeded your request, what other things would we have to do?

At this stage of incipient denial, we also question the remedy the reformers might be requesting. In our view, racism or other injustices are aberrations, hence any remedy would naturally have to be short-lived and bounded. But this group's appears to go on forever—how can that be? We express concern, ask for clarification, pretend not fully to understand what the outsiders are demanding. Derision creeps in.

Each of these replies is a kind of shrinking from substance, a fear of the earth shifting, of what might happen if it turns out that structural change in fact is in order. Notice the metaphors of earth-movement or washing away: "parade of horribles," "flood of litigation," "drawing the line," "opening the floodgates," and so on. The *Croson* Court said, in effect, another minority might come along and make the same claim—say, an Aleut, or an Eskimo, or an Alsatian, or a ... and then what would happen?—and so dismissed the case.[81] Something similar happened in *McClesky v. Kemp*, the Georgia death penalty decision, which dismissed a challenge based on statistical evidence because this approach could lead to "too much justice."[82]

At later stages, of course, we put procedure behind us. We tell the reformer: All right, we will reach the merits of your claim. We understand full well what you are saying, its implications, whom it will affect, who has standing. And we find your claim illegitimate, unprincipled, and wrong.

What a Reformer Can Do: Dealing with Scorn or the Imposition-Narrative

The issue arises, then: What can a reform movement do when it finds scorn or imposition-language being used against it? Ultimately, we fear, very little. Society deploys the imposition metaphor only when a broad consensus is forming that reform has gone too far. The reformers are no longer in favor; we have decided that they are taxing our patience, imposing on our good natures. The point of designating someone guilty of imposition is to declare that no excuses are possible. From this point forward we need not listen to what he or she has to say: We have heard enough.

The same is true of language of scorn: We laugh or poke fun only when we know it is safe, feel confident others will join in.

Nevertheless, there are a few measures that reformers can take, including simply naming and calling attention to the strategy being deployed against them. With imposition one can also question the premise underlying the charge. Is not the status quo itself unfair, an imposition, an affront to minorities? Does it not reflect a centuries-old distribution of resources and power that should be open to question? (See, for example, Chapter 8.)

Outsiders can counterdeploy the metaphor of the bully to depict their critics as unsympathetic and overbearing. In our culture one is supposed to be generous to underdogs. One who scorns or too early declares them *non grata* runs the risk of being seen as uncharitable. Another approach—cultural nationalism—is sometimes available. This strategy ignores the way mainstream writers characterize one's movement, focusing instead on strengthening the group's own sense of itself and its own institutions. The hope is that by strategic retreat the group will avoid expending energy in nonproductive struggles over its own identity and legitimacy.

Another strategy is to remind the violator of the historical fate of similar actors. Holmes's remark about three generations of imbeciles is now notorious and mars an otherwise illustrious career. Recall also Marie Antoinette's famous remark, Reagan's observation about redwood trees, and Justice Brown's comment about the injury of being forced to ride in a segregated railroad car. Pointing out that history has not been kind to those who treat others cavalierly can sometimes cause one's adversary to reconsider a course of conduct. This may be particularly so with judges; it is akin to being reversed.

A final strategy is the preemptive strike. As soon as one notices that opinion is changing, seize the initiative. Write a book like Martin Luther King's *Why We Can't Wait*.[83] Explain why the movement is not imposing or not worthy of scorn—but has been long-suffering and patient. We are skeptical that measures like these will provide more than temporary benefit. Society has a built-in homeostat: The status quo appears natural, reform unnatural. The burden is always on the reformer. And when he or she tries to shoulder that burden the reformer finds that all the presumptions, all the prevailing narratives and expectations, cut the other way.

Our social situation is always, at some level, continuous with our selves. It seems natural, forms part of the baseline from which we reason. The current regime will always strike us as legitimate and justified. Reformers who are trying radically to restructure that regime invariably strike us as dangerous and extreme. The paradox of reform is that we seem doomed to resist it until it essentially is too late—has already taken place or has lost its power to transform us.

Conclusion

If one lesson emerged from our study, it is that the task of social reform is more difficult than we like to think. Our imaginative capacities are often not up to the task of visualizing a better world. Our very language and tools of thought stand in the way, preventing us from hearing or appreciating what an outsider group is saying. We overlook evidence in front of us or translate claims into safer, tamer versions. When reform begins to seem necessary, we embrace moderate saviors espousing moderate solutions rather than persevere until we find more sweeping, long-lasting ones. We disparage reformers, condemning them as opportunistic, painting their demands as encroachments on our own justified prerogatives.

What can we conclude from the portrait of frustrated reforms and blocked progress we have drawn? In the final sections of many of the chapters, we put forward a number of suggestions. We can act decisively in cases of racism, sexism, or other forms of injustice that we do see, treating them in effect as proxies for those we know are hidden—hidden because they occur out of our view or because a failure of empathy prevents us from seeing them. We can use past rather than present injustice, which is much more difficult to notice or acknowledge, in designing social programs. We can distrust the ability of free-market solutions, including the marketplace of ideas, to dispel systemic social ills, at the same time empowering minority speakers and actors so that they can play more active roles in that market. We can pay particular attention to what our mavericks and reformers are saying, even those whose demands strike us as harsh and extreme.

We can remind ourselves how failure to act may bring condemnation in history's judgment. We can attempt to understand how seemingly fair, "objective" social and legal rules favor the powerful and remind ourselves to make the gestalt switch that can enable us to detect the power dimension of social rules and practices. We can refuse to join in derision aimed at the poor and outcast.

Will these strategies enable us to accomplish much? We have our doubts. If our review of social reform movement histories shows anything, it is that American society is deeply ambivalent about change. We desire and fear it, wish for a better world and shrink from it at the same time. Reform is always a partial obliteration of who we are, a discontinuity, a kind of death. We embrace it only much later, after the reformist wave has subsided and we no longer see it as radical or novel.

In the meantime, we place the cost of social adjustment on the reform group, seeing to it that they are misunderstood, resisted, and portrayed as unreasonable. Prophets are not only without favor in their own countries. A somber theme that emerged is that they are almost always, everywhere, denied honor in their own times.

Epilogue

On the Relation Between Hope and Struggle: A Concluding Message for the Young Lawyer

Earlier, we mentioned that this book is written for reformers. Yet, over the last nine chapters we have been showing how difficult reform is, how failures of imagination, perception, and will cause most movements to founder, to achieve less than what their advocates hoped. Law reform is no different, indeed confronts special obstacles of its own.

Why struggle, then, the reader may ask, why push on if dashed hopes and unfulfilled promises are the reformer's more usual fate? We believe one must go on, but the reasons for doing so require seeing the relationship of hope, perseverance, and realism in a slightly different light from the one in which we usually see them.

To see this, consider the career path of many young lawyers. We have spent much of our lives teaching and working with law students. It is important to us that they not see this book as a counsel of despair, for that is not how it is intended. Many of our students come to law school imbued with the desire to work for the public good. They are idealistic and reform-minded. They want to make bureaucracy more responsive, schools more integrated, prisons more humane. They want to represent consumers injured by shoddy products, want to defend the poor and homeless. They want to champion unpopular causes, persons accused of crime.

The young idealist soon learns that the way is rocky, however. Society despises criminals. Their friends ask how they can represent such people. They encounter rude, racist judges, and clients who lie to them. Cases that should win, lose. Many leave public interest practice after a few years, disillusioned and burned out.

It turns out, then, that hope, realism, and despair are more delicately balanced than we sometimes acknowledge. Hope is, of course, necessary for any long and difficult struggle. But equally important is an understanding of how society works. An individual who understands the ways near-universal forces resist change is better armored against self-blame. He or she realizes that failure is not always the result of lack of skill or nerve, that the real question is often not, Why go on? but, Why quit?

Hope, unaccompanied by a comprehensive critique of social institutions, can be a formula for premature capitulation and defeat; paradoxically, the person who counsels simplistic, hopeful philosophies can end up being the real nihilist. Sometimes a stone-cold understanding of the forces and mechanisms arrayed against one is what one needs when "the path is long and the night dark."

Notes

Chapter 1

1. See, e.g., Mari J. Matsuda, Charles R. Lawrence III, Richard Delgado, and Kimberlè Williams Crenshaw, *Words That Wound: Critical Race Theory, Assaultive Speech, and the First Amendment* (Boulder, Colo.: Westview Press, 1993) and Catharine A. MacKinnon, "Not A Moral Issue," *Yale Law & Policy Review* 2 (1984): 321.

2. See, e.g., Derrick Bell and Preeta Bansal, "The Republican Revival and Racial Politics," *Yale Law Journal* 97 (1988): 1609; Richard Delgado, "Zero-Based Racial Politics and an Infinity-Based Response: Will Endless Talking Cure America's Racial Ills?" *Georgetown Law Journal* 80 (1992): 1879; Robert Justin Lipkin, "Kibitzers, Fuzzies, and Apes Without Tails: Pragmatism and the Art of Conversation in Legal Theory," *Tulane Law Review* 66 (1991): 69.

3. We have identified the following: Alternative Museum, New York City, *Prisoners of Image: Ethnic and Gender Stereotypes*, curated by Robbin Henderson and Geno Rodriguez (1989); The Balch Institute for Ethnic Studies, Philadelphia, *Ethnic Images in Advertising* (1984), *Ethnic Images in Comics* (1986), *Ethnic Images in World War I Posters* (1988), *Ethnic Images in Toys and Games* (1990); Berkeley Art Center, Berkeley, *Ethnic Notions: Black Images in the White Mind, The Janette Faulkner Collection of Stereotypes and Caricature of Afro-Americans* (1982); Galeria de la Raza, San Francisco, *Cactus Hearts/Barbed Wire Dreams: Media, Myths, and Mexicans*, curated by Yolanda Lopez (1988) (Telephone interviews with Phyllis Bischof, Librarian for African and African American Collections, U.C. at Berkeley; Jan Faulkner, Collector and Clinical Professor, Psychiatry, U.C.S.F.; Robbin Henderson, Director, Berkeley Art Center [Feb. 1992]). See also Jessie Smith, *Images of Blacks in American Culture: Reference Guide to Information Sources* (New York: Greenwood Press, 1988), p. 289 (listing collections of Black Americana).

For a recent film addressing these issues, see Marlon Riggs's *Ethnic Notions* (P.B.S. 1986). By the same filmmaker, see also *Color Adjustment*, a TV documentary on racial images of the last forty years on prime time television.

4. See Robert Jay Lifton, *The Nazi Doctors* (New York: Basic Books, 1986) (pointing out that German administrators and physicians who carried out atrocities were highly educated); Elie Wiesel, *Against Silence* (New York: Holocaust Library, 1985).

5. Of course, it is possible that consciousness will not progress but regress or remain at the same level—i.e., we may never condemn David Duke or the Willie Horton commercial. David Duke is a former white supremacist who campaigned for state and national office in the late 1980s and early 1990s. The Willie Horton

commercial featured a black recidivist; its purpose was to imply that Democrats are soft on crime.

6. The term, as well as the fallacy it names, is our own invention.

7. For the earliest known discussion of this fallacy, see John Ruskin, vol. 3 of *Modern Paintings* (New York: Wiley, 1885), p. 152; see also William K. Wimsatt, Jr., and Monroe C. Beardsley, "The Affective Fallacy," *Sewanee Review* 57 (1949): 31 (further discussion of literary fallacies); Josephine Miles, *Pathetic Fallacy in the Nineteenth Century* (New York: Octagon Books, 1965), pp. 10–56 (giving examples, from prominent poets, of nature weeping, smiling, groaning, all in sympathy with humans).

8. Some of the works we found particularly helpful are the following: Arthur G. Pettit, *Images of the Mexican American in Fiction and Film* (College Station: Texas A & M University Press, 1980); Catherine Silk and John Silk, *Racism and Anti-Racism in American Popular Culture* (New York: Manchester University Press, 1990); Raymond W. Stedman, *Shadows of the Indian: Stereotypes in American Culture* (Norman: University of Oklahoma Press, 1982); Eugene Wong, *On Visual Media Racism: Asians in the American Motion Picture* (New York: Arno Press, 1978); Ronald Takaki, ed., *From Different Shores: Perspectives on Race and Ethnicity in America* (New York: Oxford University Press, 1987); Jannette L. Dates and William Barlow, eds., *Split Image: African Americans in the Mass Media* (Washington: Howard University Press, 1990).

For examples of sexist images concerning women, see Tama Starr, *The "Natural Inferiority" of Women: Outrageous Pronouncements by Misguided Males* (New York: Poseidon Press, 1991). For a discussion of other minority groups and their role in U.S. civil rights history, see Stetson Kennedy, *Jim Crow Guide: The Way It Was* (Boca Raton: Florida Atlantic University Press, 1990), pp. 26–46.

9. Lerone Bennett, Jr., *Before the Mayflower: A History of the Negro in America, 1619–1964*, rev. ed. (Baltimore: Penguin Books, 1966), p. 373.

10. Silk and Silk, *Racism and Anti-Racism*, p. 4.

11. See Dates and Barlow, *Split Image*, p. 6. On black characters and types generally in U.S. literature, see Sterling Brown, *The Negro in American Fiction* (New York: Argosy-Antiquarian, 1969) (detailing recurring caricatures, such as the contented slave, wretched freedman, tragic mulatto, brute Negro, entertaining clown, etc.).

12. Dates and Barlow, *Split Image*, pp. 5–6.

13. Id., p. 7.

14. George Frederickson, Interview in *Ethnic Notions*.

15. The dandified image (the "coon") showed the folly of the North's policy concerning freedom, while that of the happy Southern slave reassured whites that blacks were happiest in "their natural condition." See Dates and Barlow, *Split Image*, p. 7. The dandified urban "coon" image, played by white actors, reappeared in the 1920s and continued until the 1950s in the phenomenally popular radio serial "Amos 'N' Andy." See Melvin Ely, *The Adventures of Amos 'N' Andy: A Social History of an American Phenomenon* (New York: Free Press, 1991).

16. See Henry Gates, ed., *The Classic Slave Narratives* (New York: New American Library, 1987); Dates and Barlow, *Split Image*, p. 10.

17. See Dates and Barlow, *Split Image*, p. 8; William L. Van DeBurg, *Slavery and Race in American Popular Culture* (Madison: University of Wisconsin Press, 1984),

pp. 35–36 (arguing that Uncle Tom's character was but a slight improvement over previous stereotypes).

18. Dates and Barlow, *Split Image*, p. 11; Silk and Silk, *Racism and Anti-Racism*, p. 142.

19. Dates and Barlow, *Split Image*, pp. 12–24.

20. Silk and Silk, *Racism and Anti-Racism*, p. 139; Van DeBurg, *Slavery*, p. 43.

21. See Dates and Barlow, *Split Image*, p. 11. This obsession with matters sexual dates back to Puritan times in Massachusetts and has surfaced in similar stereotyping of the four major racial groups in the United States. See Stedman, *Shadows*, p. 81; Van DeBurg, *Slavery*, pp. 122–125 (on recurring image of the Negro as beast).

22. See Silk and Silk, *Racism and Anti-Racism*, pp. 48–49; see also Allen W. Trelease, *White Terror: The Ku Klux Klan Conspiracy and Southern Reconstruction* (New York: Harper & Row, 1971).

23. Silk and Silk, *Racism and Anti-Racism*, p. 39

24. Id. p. 49.

25. Id., p. 50; see Russell Merritt, "D. W. Griffith's *The Birth of a Nation*: Going After Little Sister," in *Close Viewings: An Anthology of New Film Criticism* (Tallahassee: Florida State University Press, 1990), p. 215.

26. Silk and Silk, *Racism and Anti-Racism*, p. 50.

27. *The Leopard's Spots* (New York: Doubleday, Page & Co., 1902).

28. Dates and Barlow, *Split Image*, p. 135; Silk and Silk, *Racism and Anti-Racism*, pp. 121, 127 (Wilson's comment probably was intended as praise, for he added: "[O]ne of my regrets is that it is so horribly true.").

29. See Silk and Silk, *Racism and Anti-Racism*, p. 128.

30. Id., pp. 31–32.

31. Id., p. 45; Dates and Barlow, *Split Image*, pp. 11–12, Van DeBurg, *Slavery*, pp. 100–102. On the status of the Negro at that time, see Rayford W. Logan, *The Negro in America Life and Thought: The Nadir, 1877–1901* (New York: Dial Press, 1954).

32. Silk and Silk, *Racism and Anti-Racism*, p. 46.

33. 163 U.S. 543 (1896).

34. See Silk and Silk, *Racism and Anti-Racism*, pp. 61–62.

35. Bennett, *Mayflower*, p. 288.

36. David L. Lewis, *When Harlem Was in Vogue* (New York: Knopf, 1981); Van DeBurg, *Slavery*, pp. 120–121, 202–203.

37. Silk and Silk, *Racism and Anti-Racism*, pp. 63, 135; see also *Ethnic Notions* (detailing roles of entertainers such as Paul Robeson and Burt Williams during this period).

38. Van DeBurg, *Slavery*, pp. 121–122.

39. See "The Congo," in Harriet Monroe, ed., *The New Poetry* (New York: The Macmillan Co., 1932), p. 291.

40. Richard A. Hope, *Racial Strife in the U.S. Military: Toward the Elimination of Discrimination* (New York: Praeger, 1979).

41. Derrick A. Bell, Jr., "*Brown v. Board of Education* and the Interest-Convergence Dilemma," *Harvard Law Review* 93 (1980): 524; Mary Dudziak, "Desegregation as a Cold War Imperative," *Stanford Law Review* 41 (1989): 71–73.

42. See *Color Adjustment* (describing last forty years of media depiction and noting, among other things, the resemblance between current shows featuring sani-

tized, myth-making Rhodes Scholar, super-Negroes and previous images); see also Dates and Barlow, *Split Image,* pp. 254–280; George Zinkhan et al., "Changes in Stereotypes: Blacks and Whites in Magazine Advertisements," *Journalism Quarterly* 63 (Autumn 1986): 568.

43. Stedman, *Shadows,* p. 253 (noting descriptions that explorers Christopher Columbus and Amerigo Vespucci gave). For further writings on Columbus and his early impressions, see J. M. Cohen, trans. & ed., *The Four Voyages of Christopher Columbus* (Baltimore: Penguin Books, 1969).

44. Dee Brown, *Bury My Heart at Wounded Knee* (New York: Holt, Rinehart & Winston, 1972), pp. 2–5; Fairfax Downey, *Indian Wars of the U.S. Army (1776–1865)* (Garden City, New York: Doubleday, 1963); Robert A. Williams, *The American Indian in Western Legal Thought* (New York: Oxford University Press, 1990).

45. Stedman, *Shadows,* pp. 17–41; see John Bowman, *Powhatan's Daughter* (New York: Viking Press, 1973).

46. Stedman, *Shadows,* pp. 42–57.

47. William Shakespeare, *The Tempest* (1611; reprint, New York: Oxford University Press, 1987).

48. James Fenimore Cooper, *The Last of the Mohicans* (1826; reprint, Boston: Houghton Mifflin, 1958).

49. Stedman, *Shadows,* pp. 50–51; see Jenni Calder, *There Must Be a Lone Ranger* (London: Hamilton, 1974).

50. Mary Rowlandson, *The Sovereignty & Goodness of God, Together with the Faithfulness of His Promises Displayed: Being a Narrative of the Captivity and Restoration of Mrs. Mary Rowlandson* (1682; microfilm, Ann Arbor, MI: University Microfilms, 1971).

51. Stephen Osborne, "Indian-Hating in American Literature 1682–1859," *Dissertation Abstracts International* 50(10) (1990): 3228A; Stedman, *Shadows,* pp. 77–78 (historian Richard Drinnon has referred to this literature as "violence pornography").

52. Stedman, *Shadows,* p. 78.

53. Id., p. 75; see Perry Miller, *The New England Mind: The Seventeenth Century* (New York: The Macmillan Co., 1939) (providing a full exposition of "the anatomy of the Puritan mind").

54. Stedman, *Shadows,* pp. 75, 81; see Jean Ehly, "Horrifying Story of an Indian Captive," *Western Frontier Annual* (1975): 26.

55. Stedman, *Shadows,* p. 120. This stereotype occurred with blacks as well.

56. Id., p. 121.

57. Id., p. 123. For a treatment of the cannibal concept, see Michael Harner and Alfred Meyer, *Cannibal* (New York: Morrow, 1979); Marvin Harris, *Cannibals and Kings: The Origins of Cultures* (New York: Random House, 1977).

58. Stedman, *Shadows,* p. 125.

59. Id., p. 124; see Roy H. Pearce, *Savagism and Civilization: A Study of the Indian and the American Mind,* rev. ed. (Berkeley: University of California Press, 1988); Robert Keller, "Hostile Language: Bias in Historical Writing About American Indian Resistance," *Journal of American Culture* 9 (Winter 1986): 9.

60. Stedman, *Shadows,* p. 126. Vine Deloria, Jr., wrote "[W]e were never slaves. We gave up land instead of life and labor. Because the Negro labored, he was con-

sidered a draft animal. Because the Indian occupied large areas of land, he was considered a wild animal." Vine Deloria, Jr., *Custer Died for Your Sins* (New York: The Macmillan Co., 1969), pp. 7–8.

61. On Indian films, see Jon Tuska, *The Filming of the West* (Garden City, New York: Doubleday, 1976); John E. O'Connor, *The Hollywood Indian: Stereotypes of Native Americans in Films* (Trenton: New Jersey State Museum, 1980).

62. Stedman, *Shadows*, p. 108.

63. During this period, some of the titles, in themselves, tell the story: e.g., *On the Warpath* (1909), *The Flaming Arrows* (1911), *Poisoned Arrows* (1911), *Incendiary Indians* (1911), *The Indian Raiders* (1910), *The Cheyenne Raiders* (1910), *Attack by Arapahoes* (1910), *The Dumb Half-Breed's Defense* (1910), *Saved from the Redmen* (1910), *Love in a Tepee* (1911), *The Hair Restorer and the Indian* (a "comedy" of 1911).

64. Similarly, stereotypes in adult fiction are replicated in juvenile literature. See Magda Lewis, "Are Indians Nicer Now? What Children Learn From Books About Native North Americans," in Betty Bacon, ed., *How Much Truth Do We Tell The Children? The Politics of Children's Literature* (Minneapolis: MEP Publications, 1988).

65. Stedman, *Shadows*, pp. 206–209, 218–220.

66. Id., p. 58.

67. Id., p. 62.

68. Id., pp. 62–63; see Alber C. Myers, ed., *William Penn's Own Account of the Lenni Lenape or Delaware Indians* (Somerset, N.J.: Middle Atlantic Press, 1970).

69. See Vine Deloria, Jr., "Identity and Culture," in Ronald Takaki, ed., *From Different Shores: Perspectives on Race and Ethnicity in America* (New York: Oxford University Press, 1987), pp. 94, 102. Indian talk that matched an even harsher racial stereotype of the mid-nineteenth century was created in Robert Montgomery Bird, *Nick of the Woods: Or, The Jibbenainosay* (1837; reprint, New York: Vanguard Press, 1928). For discussion of Bird and his influence on American culture, see Ronald Takaki, "The Metaphysics of Civilization: Indians and the Age of Jackson," in Takaki, *From Different Shores*, pp. 61–75.

70. See Alexander Saxton, *The Indispensable Enemy: Labor and the Anti-Chinese Movement in California* (Berkeley: University of California Press, 1971), pp. 19–45.

71. For a history of this period, see Ping Chiu, *Chinese Labor in California, 1850–80: An Economic Study* (Madison: State Historical Society of Wisconsin, 1963).

72. Saxton, *Indispensable Enemy*, pp. 19–45.

73. Rubin Weston, *Racism in U.S. Imperialism: The Influence of Racial Assumptions on American Foreign Policy, 1893–1946* (Columbia: University of South Carolina Press, 1972) (reviewing history of immigration quotas and policies). For a general treatment of anti-Asian sentiment, see Stuart Creighton Miller, *The Unwelcome Immigrant: The American Image of the Chinese, 1785–1882* (Berkeley: University of California Press, 1969).

74. Donald Hata, *"Undesirables": Early Immigrants and the Anti-Japanese Movement in San Francisco, 1892–1893* (New York: Arno Press, 1978).

75. See Richard A. Thompson, *The Yellow Peril, 1890–1924* (New York: Arno Press, 1978).

76. See *Chae Chan Ping v. United States*, 130 U.S. 581 (1889); see also Shin S. Tsai, *The Chinese Experience in America* (Bloomington: Indiana University Press, 1986), pp. 56–81.

77. E.g., Wong, *Visual Media Racism*, pp. 25, 72–74; see Ronald Takaki, *Strangers from a Different Shore* (Boston: Little, Brown & Co., 1989) (detailing resistance to Asian immigrants).

78. Id., pp. 29, 124–128; see Peter Irons, *Justice at War* (New York: Oxford University Press, 1983), pp. 52–73.

79. Takaki, *Strangers;* Wong, *Visual Media Racism*, pp. 3, 108.

80. Wong, *Visual Media Racism*, pp. 34–38, 55–103.

81. Id., p. 74 (much in the manner that Hollywood created the "generic Indian" with either whites or Indians of any convenient tribe assigned to play the part).

82. Id., pp. 88–92, 93.

83. Id., pp. 111–114, 124–128; see R. A. Maynard, ed., *Propaganda on Film: A Nation at War* (Rochelle Park, NJ: Hayden Book Co., 1975).

84. See Richard Griffith and Arthur Mayer, *The Movies*, rev. ed. (New York: Simon & Schuster, 1970), p. 108.

85. Wong, *Visual Media Racism*, pp. 136–138; see Joe Morella and Edward Epstein, *The Films of World War II* (Secaucus, NJ: Citadel Press, 1973); Lewis Jacobs, "World War II and the American Film," *Cinema Journal* 7 (1967–68).

86. Irons, *Justice* (describing events that led up to and followed this tragic chapter in our history). For two Supreme Court cases upholding curfews placed on Japanese-Americans, see *Hirabayashi v. United States,* 320 U.S. 81 (1943) and *Korematsu v. United States,* 323 U.S. 214 (1944).

87. Bill Hosokawa, *Nisei: The Quiet Americans* (New York: Morrow, 1969), p. 348; see Maisie Conrat and Richard Conrat, *Executive Order 9066: The Internment of 110,000 Japanese Americans* (San Francisco: California Historical Society, 1972).

88. Hosokawa, *Nisei,* pp. 292–301; see generally Irons, *Justice* (internment a product of war hysteria and military alarmism).

89. Jim Carrier, "Japanese-Americans Relive Days of Shame: Bashing Binge Bringing Back Scars of Racism," *Denver Post,* March 22, 1992, p. 1A; Lance Morrow, "Japan in the Mind of America," *Time,* February 10, 1992, pp. 16, 19–20, 23–24.

90. Petit, *Images of the Mexican American* (cataloging and describing the evolution of these and related images). For treatments of Mexicans in popular and high literature, see Cecil Robinson, *With the Ears of Strangers: The Mexican in American Literature* (Tucson: University of Arizona Press, 1963); Cecil Robinson, "Mexico and the Hispanic Southwest," in *American Literature* (Tucson: University of Arizona Press, 1977); Carl Allsup, "Who Done It? The Theft of Mexican American History," *Journal of Popular Culture* 17 (Winter 1983): 50.

91. Delgado, "Words that Wound," p. 137 (summarizing sources on how stereotyping accomplishes this); see Pierre L. van den Berghe, *Race and Racism: A Comparative Perspective,* 2d ed. (New York: Wiley, 1978). On the efficacy of racial images and their cultural encoding in our very ideas and vocabulary, see Patricia Williams, *The Alchemy of Race and Rights* (Cambridge: Harvard University Press, 1991).

92. Petit, *Images of the Mexican American,* pp. 32–40. These images naturally tended to justify U.S. expansion. See generally Rodolfo Acuna, *Occupied America: A History of the Chicano,* 3d ed. (New York: Harper & Row, 1988).

93. Petit, *Images of the Mexican American,* pp. xiv–xvii; see Juan Garcia, "Americanization and the Mexican Immigrant," in Takaki, *Different Shores,* pp. 69–70.

94. Petit, *Images of the Mexican American*, pp. xix–xx; Garcia, "Americanization," in Takaki, *Different Shores*, pp. 69–71. For a background and treatment of cultural relations between the two groups, see Angel del Rio, *The Clash and Attraction of Two Cultures: The Hispanic and the Anglo Saxon Worlds in America*, J. Shearer trans. & ed. (Baton Rouge: Louisiana State University Press, 1965).

95. Petit, *Images of the Mexican American*, pp. 22–25; see also Robinson, *Ears of Strangers* (tracing this and other Latin stereotypes).

96. Petit, *Images of the Mexican American*, p. 137.

97. Id., pp. 84, 154–157; Garcia, "Americanization," in Takaki, *Different Shores*.

98. See Petit, *Images of the Mexican American*, pp. 84–85.

99. See id., pp. 85–104; see also Albert Johannsen, *The House of Beadle and Adams and Its Dime and Nickel Novels: The Story of a Vanished Literature* (Norman: University of Oklahoma Press, 1950).

100. See Petit, *Images of the Mexican American*, pp. 112–114, 123–126, 128–131; Blaine Lamb, "The Convenient Villain: The Early Cinema Views the Mexican-American," *Journal of the West* 14 (1975): 75.

101. See Petit, *Images of the Mexican American*, p. 131; for a filmography see id., pp. 264–269.

102. Petit, *Images of the Mexican American*; see Juan Garcia, "Hollywood and the West: Mexican Images in American Films," in Jody Nolte Lensink, ed., *Old Southwest/New Southwest* (Tucson: Tucson Public Library, 1987), p. 75.

103. See Petit, *Images of the Mexican American*, pp. 137–145; see also George Roeder, Jr., *Mexicans in the Movies: The Images of Mexicans in American Films, 1894–1947* (1971) (unpublished manuscript, on file with University of Wisconsin). For another treatment of Mexican women, see Beverly Trulio, "Anglo-American Attitudes Toward New Mexican Women," *Journal of the West* 12 (1973): 229.

104. Petit, *Images of the Mexican American*, p. 155.

105. Id., pp. 224–231, 237–245.

106. See also Stanley Fish, *Is There a Text in This Class? The Authority of Interpretive Communities* (Cambridge: Harvard University Press, 1980) (the background of assumptions that make up the dominant worldview in any era limits how we see the world, but is always contingent, never necessary); Steven Lukes, *Power: A Radical View* (London: Macmillan, 1974), pp. 21–25 (powerful groups manipulate discourse to prevent others from appreciating how things work); Adam Smith, "Lectures on Jurisprudence," in R. Meek et al., eds., vol. 5 of *The Glasgow Edition of the Works and Correspondence of Adam Smith* (Oxford: Clarendon Press, 1978) (commercial interests determine law and culture).

107. For the view that speech may serve this counter-hegemonic function, see Stephen M. Feldman, "Whose Common Good? Racism in the Political Community," *Georgetown Law Journal* 80 (1992): 1835; Ed Sparer, "Fundamental Human Rights, Legal Entitlements, and the Social Struggle: A Friendly Critique of the Critical Legal Studies Movement," *Stanford Law Review* 36 (1984): 509.

108. For classic works on dialogism or the Republican revival, see Robert M. Cover, "Foreword: Nomos and Narrative," *Harvard Law Review* 97 (1983): 4; Frank I. Michelman, "Foreword: Traces of Self-Government," *Harvard Law Review* 100 (1986): 4; Cass R. Sunstein, "Naked Preferences and the Constitution," *Columbia Law Review* 84 (1984): 1689.

109. See Richard Delgado, "Campus Antiracism Rules: Constitutional Narratives in Collision," *Northwestern University Law Review* 85 (1991): 358–361.

110. For an exposition of these and related arguments, see Nadine Strossen, "Regulating Racist Speech on Campus: A Modest Proposal?" *Duke Law Journal* (1990): 484.

111. Derrick Bell, *And We Are Not Saved: The Elusive Quest for Racial Justice* (New York: Basic Books, 1987) (noting that racism is ubiquitous and discouragingly difficult to eradicate).

112. See "Symposium, Legal Storytelling," *Michigan Law Review* 87 (1989): 2073 (including articles by Ball, Bell, Delgado, Matsuda, and Williams on race and narrative).

113. In *Plessy v. Ferguson*, 163 U.S. 537, 550–51 (1896), the Court failed to see any difference between requiring blacks to sit in a separate railroad car and a similar imposition on whites. For Justice Taney, if blacks found that requirement demeaning, it was only because they chose to put that construction on it; the cars were equal, and the races had similar accommodations. See also Herbert Wechsler, "Toward Neutral Principles of Constitutional Law," *Harvard Law Review* 73 (1959): 1 (making similar criticism of *Brown v. Board of Education*: Whites forced to associate with blacks were mistreated just as seriously as blacks denied the right to associate with whites—both were denied freedom of action).

In the campus-speech controversy, some argue that the right of a racist to hurl an ethnic insult must be balanced against the right of a person of color not to receive it. Who is to say which right (to speak or not to be spoken to) is superior? Denying one right strengthens the other, but only at the expense of the first.

114. See Milner Ball, *Lying Down Together: Law, Metaphor and Theology* (Madison: University of Wisconsin Press, 1985), p. 135; Paul Ricoeur, *Time and Narrative* (Chicago: University of Chicago Press, 1984–85). For modernist/postmodernist expositions of this view, see, e.g., Peter L. Berger and Thomas Luckmann, *Social Construction of Reality* (Garden City, NY: Anchor Books, 1967); Nelson Goodman, *Ways of Worldmaking* (Indianapolis: Hackett Publishing Co., 1978).

115. Wayne C. Booth, *The Company We Keep: An Ethics of Fiction* (Berkeley: University of California Press, 1988), p. 40 (minds we use in judging and interpreting stories have been formed, in large part, by those very stories).

116. E.g., Charles Chesnutt, *The Conjure Woman* (Boston: Houghton, Mifflin and Co., 1898); Zora Neale Hurston, *Their Eyes Were Watching God* (Philadelphia: J. B. Lippincott Co., 1937).

117. For an earlier exposition of this view, see Richard Delgado, "Critical Legal Studies and the Realities of Race—Does the Contradiction Have a Corollary?" *Harvard Civil Rights-Civil Liberties Law Review* 23 (1988): 407–408; Williams, *Alchemy* (detailing extent of racism's inscription in minds of most individuals).

118. Alan David Freeman, "Legitimizing Racial Discrimination Through Antidiscrimination Law: A Critical Review of Supreme Court Doctrine," *Minnesota Law Review* 62 (1978): 1049 (arguing that racism is endemic and law is often impotent to redress it).

119. Delgado, "Fundamental Contradiction," p. 408; see Derrick Bell, "Racism: A Prophecy for the Year 2000," *Rutgers Law Review* 42 (1989): 93 (implying whites place saving the environment and reducing pollution above justice for blacks).

120. See Randall L. Kennedy, "Racial Critiques of Legal Academia," *Harvard Law Review* 102 (1989): 1809–1810.

121. See Franz Kafka, *The Metamorphosis,* Willa Muir and Edwin Muir, trans. (New York: Schocken Books, 1968). One could see a parallel between the predicament of the insect-man protagonist of Kafka's novel and that of blacks forced to accept an alien view that denies their own reality. That is, both are compelled by outside forces to live life in a fashion other than the one they would otherwise choose.

122. On the "subtle" or latter-day variety of racism, see Thomas Pettigrew, "New Patterns of Racism: The Different Worlds of 1984 and 1964," *Rutgers Law Review* 37 (1985): 673; see also David O. Sears, "Symbolic Racism," in Phyllis A. Katz and Dalmas A. Taylor, eds., *Eliminating Racism* (New York: Plenum Press, 1988), p. 53.

123. *City of Richmond v. J. A. Croson, Co.,* 488 U.S. 469, 499–506 (1988); Thomas Ross, "The Richmond Narratives," *Texas Law Review* 68 (1989): 381 (criticizing *Croson* Court for refusing to see racism in governmental history that to others spoke loudly).

124. Lawrence, "If He Hollers," pp. 466–467 (pointing out that courts construed First Amendment law narrowly, so as to uphold convictions of peaceful civil rights protestors; citing cases).

125. On the tort of defamation in general, see Joel D. Eaton, "The American Law of Defamation Through *Gertz v. Robert Welch, Inc.,* and Beyond," *Virginia Law Review* 61 (1975): 1349. Of course, an impecunious plaintiff may sue for defamation just as a wealthy person may. But the poor individual is likely to have less of a property interest in his or her reputation and so will find suit less attractive than one with a higher standing and profile.

126. *Harper & Row Publishers, Inc. v. Nation Enterprises,* 471 U.S. 539 (1985). As with libel, intellectual property law can be employed by middle-income persons who nevertheless somehow have managed to secure a property interest worth protecting and who can afford the high cost of litigation. See, e.g., *Zacchini v. Scripps-Howard Broadcasting Co.,* 433 U.S. 562 (1977).

127. See, e.g., *Snepp v. United States,* 444 U.S. 507 (1988) (per curium); *United States v. Progressive, Inc.,* 467 F. Supp. 999 (W.D. Wis. 1979).

128. See, e.g., *Bethel School Dist. v. Fraser,* 478 U.S. 675 (1986); *Toledo Newspaper Co. v. United States,* 247 U.S. 402 (1918).

129. See Rollin M. Perkins and Ronald N. Boyce, *Criminal Law,* 3d ed. (Mineola, NY: Foundation Press, 1982), pp. 304–308, 1048.

130. *Zurcher v. Stanford Daily,* 436 U.S. 547 (1978) (criminal conspiracy); Lawrence Sullivan, *Handbook of the Law of Antitrust* (St. Paul: West Publishing Co., 1977), pp. 29–30, 132–134 (price-fixing conspiracies).

131. See, e.g., *Chaplinsky v. New Hampshire,* 315 U.S. 568 (1942) (fighting words); *Schenk v. United States,* 249 U.S. 47, 52 (1919) (dictum) (discussing shouting fire in a crowded theater).

132. See Edward Cleary, *McCormick on Evidence,* 3d ed. (St. Paul: West Publishing Co., 1984), pp. 544–548.

133. See Lee C. Bollinger, *The Tolerant Society* (New York: Oxford University Press, 1986) (racist speech must be protected—part of the price "we" pay for living in a free society); Benno Schmidt, professor of law and president, Yale University,

remarks at campus speech, panel discussion and program, Yale Law School (Oct. 11, 1991); Strossen, "Modest Proposal."

134. On "triumphalism"—the view that conquerors always construct history so that they appear to have won fairly through superior thought and culture rather than by force of arms—see Richard Delgado, "Norms and Normal Science: Toward a Critique of Normativity in Legal Thought," *University of Pennsylvania Law Review* 139 (1991): 933; Martin, "College Curriculum Scrutinized in 'Politically Correct' Spotlight," *Denver Post*, January 25, 1992. For the view that many Enlightenment figures were genteel or not-so-genteel cultural supremists, see Bell, *And We Are Not Saved*, pp. 26–51 (pointing out that the U.S. Constitution's Framers calculatedly sold out the interests of African-Americans in establishing a union of free propertied white males).

135. Delgado, "Campus Antiracism Rules," p. 379; Delgado, "Words that Wound," pp. 137, 139–140.

136. See *Buckley v. Valeo*, 424 U.S. 1, 17–19 (1976).

137. This "economic determinist" view is associated with Derrick Bell, and earlier with Charles Beard.

138. The American Civil Liberties Union, for example, follows a policy of challenging virtually every campus speech code as soon as it is enacted. See, e.g., *Doe v. University of Michigan*, 721 F. Supp. 852 (E.D. Mich. 1989); *U. W. M. Post, Inc. v. Regents, University of Wisconsin*, 774 F. Supp. 1163 (E.D. Wis. 1991).

139. Derrick Bell, "Racial Realism," *Connecticut Law Review* 24 (1992): 363; Derrick Bell, *Faces at the Bottom of the Well* (New York: Basic Books, 1992).

140. This casts doubt on Professor Sullivan's thesis that we should not focus on the past but devise racial remedies based on today's conditions and perceptions. Kathleen M. Sullivan, "Sins of Discrimination: Last Term's Affirmative Action Cases," *Harvard Law Review* 100 (1986): 78.

141. Except, of course, where the racism of the past (lynchings, beatings, use of long-condemned words and images) appears today—in which case we of course seize on and denounce it roundly.

142. But will the majority listen? See Duncan Kennedy, "A Cultural Pluralist Case for Affirmative Action in Legal Academia," *Duke Law Journal* (1991): 705 (proposing empowerment of minority spokespersons through race-conscious affirmative action).

143. Our candidates for items that today seem innocuous or only mildly troublesome (warranting, perhaps, the "Oh, come on!" reaction)—but that history will declare unspeakable ("How could they?")—include the following:

- The English-only movement
- Black super-stud films
- The Willie Horton commercial
- "Political correctness," when used as a put-down for someone trying to redress racism or diversify the academy
- Code words such as "articulate (or qualified) black," "those people," "welfare mothers," and "inner-city crime"
- Portraying affirmative action as carried out at the expense of "innocent whites"

- Refusal to recognize Indian treaty rights
- TV programs and films that feature cowboys and Indians (still), blacks solely in the role of domestic workers, or minorities or foreigners speaking in funny accents
- Maintaining that the right of the racist to hurl a racist epithet trumps or is equally balanced with the right of the victim not to have it addressed to him or her
- Immigration quotas and policies aimed at excluding people from developing nations but allowing virtually unlimited entry to propertied Europeans
- Sports teams with racist names (Redskins) or stereotypical logos

144. E.g., Richard Rodriguez, *Hunger of Memory* (Boston: Godine, 1982) (each author stating that race plays a much less important role today); see also Steven Carter, *Confessions of an Affirmative Action Baby* (New York: Basic Books, 1991) (rejecting less extreme statement of same position); Thomas Sowell, *Civil Rights: Rhetoric or Reality?* (New York: William Morrow, 1984); Shelby Steele, *The Content of Our Character: A New Vision of Race in America* (New York: St. Martin's Press, 1990).

145. On the debate about "essentialism" and whether the minority community contains one or many voices, see Angela P. Harris, "Race and Essentialism in Feminist Legal Theory," *Stanford Law Review* 42 (1990): 581; Kennedy, "Racial Critiques."

Chapter 2

1. We are not the first to write of such matters. See, e.g., Robert Cover, *Justice Accused: Anti-Slavery and the Judicial Process* (New Haven: Yale University Press, 1975) (discussing the dilemma of the antislavery judge in choosing between his conscience and the era's accepted legal principles regarding slavery); Peter Irons, *Justice at War* (New York: Oxford University Press, 1983) (examining the tragedy of the Japanese-American wartime cases).

2. The law and literature movement is diverse and includes many claims: (1) literature can supply insight into the nature and origins of law; (2) understanding literature helps us to understand a traditional legal subject; (3) the study of law and literature yields a broader perspective on law and culture, expands the lawyer's creative mind, furthers the development of values and an understanding of the human condition, and enriches understanding of literature steeped in law; (4) law and literature contributes to a better understanding of constitutional values and analogies, promotes a better grasp of professional responsibility, and improves legal writing. See Richard Posner, *Law and Literature: A Misunderstood Relation* (Cambridge: Harvard University Press, 1988); Harold Leventhal, "Law and Literature: A Preface," *Rutgers Law Review* 32 (1979): 603; John Denvir, "Comic Relief," *Tulane Law Review* 63 (1989): 1423; Richard Weisberg, "Coming of Age Some More: 'Law and Literature' Beyond the Cradle," *Nova Law Review* 13 (1988): 107; Jay Wishingrad, "Why Law and Literature?" *New York Law Journal*, June 23, 1986, p. 2; William H. Page, "The Place of Law and Literature," *Vanderbilt Law Review* 39 (1986): 391.

3. 60 U.S. 393 (1856).

4. 163 U.S. 537 (1896).

5. *Dred Scott*, 60 U.S. at 407.

6. Id. at 410.

7. Id. at 405.

8. Harriet Beecher Stowe, *Uncle Tom's Cabin* (1852; reprint, New York: Harper & Row, 1965).

9. Frederick Douglass, "Narrative of the Life of Frederick Douglass, An African Slave," in Henry Gates, ed., *The Classic Slave Narratives* (New York: New American Library, 1987). Douglass's book sold 11,000 copies between 1845 and 1847.

10. Douglass, *Narrative*, p. 256.

11. Id., pp. 256–257.

12. Id., p. 258.

13. Only Justices McLean and Curtis dissented. See *Dred Scott*, 60 U.S. at 529 (McLean, J., dissenting); id. at 564 (Curtis, J., dissenting).

14. *Plessy*, 163 U.S. at 543.

15. Id. at 544, 551, 552.

16. Id. at 556, 557, 559, 563.

17. See, e.g., Philip Foner, ed., *The Voice of Black America: Major Speeches by Negroes in the United States, 1797–1971* (New York: Simon and Schuster, 1972), pp. 249–595.

18. See Martin Dann, ed., *The Black Press 1827–1890: The Quest for National Identity* (New York: Putnam, 1971), pp. 168, 174.

19. See Frank Webb, *The Garies and Their Friends* (1857; reprint, New York: Arno Press, 1969); Frances E. W. Harper, *Iola Leroy, or Shadows Uplifted* (1893; reprint, New York: Oxford University Press, 1988); Sutton Griggs, *Imperium in Imperio* (1899; reprint, New York: Arno Press, 1969); Charles Chesnutt, *The Conjure Woman* (1899; reprint, Ridgewood, NJ: Gregg Press, 1968); Paul Dunbar, *Folks from Dixie* (New York: Dodd, Mead, 1898).

20. In a telling passage from *The Garies*, Frank Webb describes a railroad trip from North Carolina to New York taken by his protagonist, Charlie Ellis, and Ellis's guardian, Mrs. Bird. Shortly after they boarded the train and found their seats, the conductor roughly shook Charlie, who was ill and sleeping, and ordered him and Mrs. Bird out of the white car. After an argument between the conductor and the car's passengers, eventually Mrs. Bird and the child acquiesced to group pressure and moved to the colored section of the train. Webb, *Garies*, pp. 110–112. See Robert A. Bone, *The Negro Novel in America*, rev. ed. (New Haven: Yale University Press, 1965), pp. 13–18.

21. Bone, *Negro Novel*, p. 18.

22. On the historical and theoretical foundations of Indian law, see Vine DeLoria, Jr., and Clifford M. Lytle, *American Indians, American Justice* (Austin: University of Texas Press, 1983); Charles Wilkinson, *American Indians, Time, and the Law: Native Societies in a Modern Constitutional Democracy* (New Haven: Yale University Press, 1987), pp. 7–14. See also Robert A. Williams, *The American Indian in Western Legal Thought: The Discourses of Conquest* (New York: Oxford University Press, 1990) (discussing how various European philosophies affected colonists' perceptions of Native Americans).

23. 21 U.S. 543 (1823).

24. Id. at 574.

25. Id.

26. Id. at 590.

27. Id.

28. Id.

29. 31 U.S. 515 (1832).

30. E.g., *Oliphant v. Suquamish Indian Tribe*, 435 U.S. 191, 194–196 (1978) (Rehnquist, J.).

31. See Robert L. Cord, *Separation of Church and State: Historical Fact and Current Fiction* (New York: Lambeth Press, 1982), pp. 42–43 (describing early American propagation of the gospel among the "heathen").

32. See Robert A. Williams, "Documents of Barbarism: The Contemporary Legacy of European Racism and Colonialism in the Narrative Traditions of Federal Indian Law," *Arizona Law Review* 31 (1989): 244–245, 248–258 (noting that breaches of treaties were often justified on the grounds that Indians were savage, barbaric, and unconcerned about civilization, land use, and economic development).

33. Isabel Kelsay, *Joseph Brant, 1743–1807: Man of Two Worlds* (Syracuse, NY: Syracuse University Press, 1984), p. 342.

34. Shirley Witt and Stan Steiner, eds., *The Way: An Anthology of American Indian Literature* (New York: Knopf, 1972), pp. 5–7.

35. 130 U.S. 581 (1889).

36. Id. at 595–596.

37. Shih–shan Henry Tsai, *The Chinese Experience in America* (Bloomington: Indiana University Press, 1986), pp. 56–81 (discussing American exclusion of the Chinese); Stanford M. Lyman, *Chinese Americans* (New York: Random House, 1974), pp. 54–85 (discussing the anti-Chinese movement in America between 1885 and 1910). For treatments of this and other embarrassing chapters of our history, see Irons, *Justice*, p. 65, and Ronald Takaki, *Strangers from a Different Shore* (Boston: Little, Brown & Co., 1989).

38. Takaki, *Strangers*, pp. 84, 88, 89, 91, 98.

39. Otis Gibson, *The Chinese in America* (1877; reprint, New York: Arno Press, 1978), pp. 4, 97–99. (In particular, Gibson addresses claims that Chinese labor damages the American economy.)

40. Id., pp. 13–23, 241, 249–250, 257.

41. Yan Phou Lee, *When I Was a Boy in China* (Boston: D. Lothrop Company, 1887).

42. See Elaine H. Kim, *Asian American Literature: An Introduction to the Writings and Their Social Context* (Philadelphia: Temple University Press, 1982), p. 25.

43. See Bill Hosokawa, *Nisei: The Quiet Americans* (New York: W. Morrow, 1969), pp. 292–301, 348 (discrediting every argument given for Japanese internment).

44. 320 U.S. 81 (1943).

45. 323 U.S. 214 (1944).

46. See *Hirabayashi*, 320 U.S. at 90–91, 95–98 (accusing the Japanese community of fifth column activity, pro-Japan propaganda dissemination, and a failure to as-

similate into the white population); *Korematsu*, 323 U.S. at 218–219 (noting Japanese residents' ties to Japan and disloyalty to the United States).

47. *Korematsu*, 323 U.S. at 236, 237, 239, 240, 241–242.

48. Etsu Sugimoto, *A Daughter of the Samurai* (New York: Doubleday, Page & Company, 1925).

49. Id., p. v.

50. See Kim, *Literature*, p. 27; "Contemporary Chivalry of the Samurai," *New York Times*, January 10, 1926, Book Review Section, p. 2.

51. *Bradwell v. Illinois*, 83 U.S. 130, 141 (1872).

52. Id. at 141–142.

53. See Mary Wollstonecraft, *A Vindication of the Rights of Women*, 2d rev. ed. (London: Printed for J. Johnson, 1792); Sojourner Truth, "Ain't I a Woman?" in Sandra M. Gilbert and Susan Gubar, eds., *The Norton Anthology of Literature by Women* (New York: Norton, 1985), p. 253; Elizabeth Cady Stanton, "Address to the New York State Legislature," reprinted in id., p. 344.

54. Margaret Fuller, "Women in the Nineteenth Century," in Gilbert and Gubar, eds., *Norton*, pp. 295, 306.

55. Id., p. 308.

56. Id., p. 297.

57. *Buck v. Bell*, 274 U.S. 200 (1927).

58. See Michael H. Shapiro and Roy G. Spece, Jr., *Cases, Materials, and Problems on Bioethics & Law* (St. Paul: West Publishing Co., 1981), pp. 404–405.

59. See *Buck*, 274 U.S. at 207 (comparing sterilization with compulsory vaccination in times of epidemic).

60. Id.

61. Id. at 208.

62. Id.

63. See Stephen Jay Gould, *The Mismeasure of Man* (New York: W. W. Norton, 1981), pp. 32, 335–336 (mentioning Holmes's belief that breeding between Native Americans and Europeans was an aesthetically unpleasing idea); Oliver Wendell Holmes, "Law and Social Reform," in Max Lerner, ed., *The Mind and Faith of Justice Holmes* (Boston: Little, Brown & Co., 1943), pp. 399, 400–401. ("I can understand better legislation that aims rather to improve the quality than to increase the quantity of the population.")

64. For a discussion of the American advent of a hereditarian theory of I.Q., see Gould, *Mismeasure*, pp. 21–23, 146–320. For a discussion of the ways government can regulate immigration in response to eugenics concerns, see Harry H. Laughlin, *Immigration and Conquest* (New York: Chamber of Commerce, Special Committee on Immigration and Naturalization, 1939).

65. *Encyclopedia Britannica*, 11th ed., s.v. "heredity."

66. For a description of this early controversy, see Daniel J. Kevles, *In the Name of Eugenics* (New York: Knopf, 1985), pp. 118–128; Kenneth M. Ludmerer, *Genetics and American Society* (Baltimore: Johns Hopkins University Press, 1972), pp. 121–124.

67. *Bowers v. Hardwick*, 478 U.S. 186, 190–195 (1986).

68. For a description of how the emerging doctrine of freedom of intimate association spans a constitutional spectrum including the right to privacy and to free-

dom of association, see Kenneth Karst, "The Freedom of Intimate Association," *Yale Law Journal* 89 (1980): 624.

69. 388 U.S. 1 (1967).

70. 381 U.S. 479 (1965).

71. 410 U.S. 113 (1973).

72. *Bowers,* 478 U.S. at 190–191.

73. Id. at 195–196.

74. See, e.g., John C. Hayes, "The Tradition of Prejudice Versus the Principle of Equality: Homosexuals and Heightened Equal Protection Scrutiny After *Bowers v. Hardwick,*" *Boston College Law Review* 31 (1990): 375; Sylvia Law, "Homosexuality and the Social Meaning of Gender," *Wisconsin Law Review* 1988 (1988): 187; David A. J. Richards, "Constitutional Legitimacy and Constitutional Privacy," *New York University Law Review* 61 (1986): 800; Thomas B. Stoddard, "*Bowers v. Hardwick*: Precedent by Personal Predilection," *University of Chicago Law Review* 54 (1987): 648; Julia Sullens, "Thus Far and No Further: The Supreme Court Draws the Outer Boundary of the Right to Privacy," *Tulane Law Review* 61 (1987): 907.

75. Anand Agneshwar, "Ex-Justice Says He May Have Been Wrong," *National Law Journal,* November 5, 1990, p. 3 (describing Justice Powell's doubts that the opinion was consistent with his stance in *Roe v. Wade*).

76. For examples of such literary works, see W. H. Auden, "Heavy Date," in W. H. Auden, *The Collected Poetry of W. H. Auden* (New York: Random House, 1945), pp. 105–108; W. H. Auden, "The Lesson," in id., pp. 116–117; W. H. Auden, "What's the Matter," in id., pp. 143–144; James Baldwin, *Giovanni's Room* (New York: Dial Press, 1956); E. M. Forster, *Maurice* (New York: Norton, 1971); Christopher Isherwood, *A Single Man* (London: Methuen, 1964); Walt Whitman, *Leaves of Grass* (1855; reprint, New York: Penguin, 1959). For an account of Auden's relationship with Chester Kallman, see Dorothy J. Farnan, *Auden in Love* (New York: Simon and Schuster, 1984).

77. Forster, *Maurice,* p. 64.

78. Baldwin, *Giovanni's Room,* p. 121.

79. On the debate over "the canon" and what should be included in it, see Sandra Gilbert and Susan Gubar, "A New Anthology of Literature by Women: Does It Define a Canon or Merely 'Baptize a Kangaroo?'" *Chronicle of Higher Education,* November 22, 1989, p. B-1; Adam Begley, "Henry Louis Gates, Jr., Black Studies' New Star," *New York Times,* April 1, 1990, Magazine Section, p. 25. See generally Allan Bloom, *The Closing of the American Mind* (New York: Simon and Schuster, 1987) (discussing the fall from favor of the Great Books approach in many academic circles).

80. For a discussion of the current academic trend of revising or rejecting the traditional literary canon, see James Atlas, "The Battle of the Books," *New York Times,* June 5, 1988, Magazine Section, p. 24. For the anthologists' dilemma, see Howell Raines, "Getting to the Heart of Dixie," *New York Times,* September 17, 1989, Book Review Section, p. 3.

81. See Hans-Georg Gadamer, *Truth and Method* (New York: Seabury Press, 1975) (exploding the myth that tradition and reason are antithetical but explaining that each actor's perception is limited by his milieu); Stanley Fish, "Is There a Text in This Class?" in Stanley Fish, *Is There a Text in This Class: The Authority of Interpre-*

tive Communities (Cambridge: Harvard University Press, 1980), pp. 303–304 (claiming that communication can only occur when people live in the same intellectual universe); Wayne Booth, *The Company We Keep* (Berkeley: University of California Press, 1988), p. 40 (asserting that a clear "circularity ... springs from the obvious fact that the minds we use in judging stories have been constituted [at least in part] by the stories we judge").

More optimistic views exist. See James B. White, *Justice as Translation* (Chicago: University of Chicago Press, 1990), pp. 35–36 (arguing that language necessarily takes on private meaning based upon each person's prior experiences, but that the communication of the language itself may form part of that experience that colors the private meaning); Clifford Geertz, *Local Knowledge* (New York: Basic Books, 1983), p. 1 (stating that "[t]he reshaping of categories ... so that they can reach beyond the contexts in which they originally arose" is a necessary part of anthropology).

82. William H. Davenport, "A Bibliography: Readings in Legal Literature," *American Bar Association Journal* 41 (1955): 939; William H. Davenport, "Readings in Legal Literature: A Bibliographical Supplement," *American Bar Association Journal* 43 (1957): 813; James B. White, *The Legal Imagination* (Boston: Little, Brown & Co., 1973); Richard Weisberg and Karen Kretschman, "Wigmore's 'Legal Novels' Expanded: A Collaborative Effort," *Maryland Legal Forum* 7 (June 1977): 94; Elizabeth Gemmette, "Law and Literature: An Unnecessarily Suspect Class in the Liberal Arts Component of the Law School Curriculum," *Valparaiso Law Review* 23 (1989): 267.

83. Richard Posner, "Law and Literature: A Relation Reargued," *Virginia Law Review* 72 (1986): 1374.

84. See id., pp. 1374, 1387–1388.

85. Posner, *Law and Literature Misunderstood*, pp. 13–14.

86. Michel Foucault coined the term. See Michel Foucault, *Power/Knowledge: Selected Interviews and Other Writings, 1972–1977* (New York: Pantheon Books, 1980), p. 233.

87. For a discussion of the importance of language to attaining knowledge, see Peter Berger and Thomas Luckmann, *The Social Construction of Reality* (Garden City, NY: Anchor Books, 1967), pp. 34–46.

88. See Booth, *Company*, p. 223.

89. See Richard Delgado, "Legal Storytelling for Oppositionists and Others: A Plea for Narrative," *Michigan Law Review* 87 (1989): 2425–2426 (detailing how the deconstructionist process can work). There are several current myths and dominant narratives in the law: *Cinderella* is the myth that justice and the right will ultimately always prevail; as applied to law, it is the myth that our common law and constitutional jurisprudence are evolving toward higher and higher reaches of moral sensitivity and refinement. *Fair fight* is the myth that our current methods for sifting out and identifying merit and justice are fair and equitable. *Just deserts* is the myth that the winner in any competitive struggle or marketplace deserved to win and is superior. *Do what your mother tells you* is the myth that regularity and following precedent are valuable in themselves.

90. Notice, for example, how today we canonize and tame the political writings of Locke, Hobbes, Paine, and Thoreau. These writers were true revolutionaries

who believed in the right to overthrow any oppressive government. We conveniently neglect to consider that they might also have been writing for our times, not just that of kings.

91. Of course, fear of tomorrow's judgment may only induce perseveration—that is, digging in and trying even more desperately to justify the harm one does today by writing an even more normative—or literary—opinion. For the view that fear is not necessarily redemptive, see Richard Delgado, "Norms and Narratives: Toward a Critique of Normativity in Legal Thought," *University of Pennsylvania Law Review* 139 (1991): 935. See also Milner Ball, "Stories of Origin and Constitutional Possibilities," *Michigan Law Review* 87 (1989): 2280.

Chapter 3

1. See Martin Mayer, *The Lawyers* (New York: Harper & Row, 1967), p. 431 (West Publishing Company shapes law by establishing headnotes); Robert Stevens, *Law School: Legal Education in America from the 1850s to the 1980s* (Chapel Hill: University of North Carolina Press, 1983), pp. 132–133 (West's headnote system encourages mechanical, atheoretical scholarship); Robert C. Berring, "Full-Text Databases and Legal Research: Backing into the Future," *High Technology Law Journal* 1 (1986): 35–36 (lawyers learn to think according to West headnotes). See also Karl N. Llewellyn, *Jurisprudence: Realism in Theory and Practice* (Chicago: University of Chicago Press, 1962), p. 82 ("threat of the available").

2. The very rules of structure that enable editors and indexers to place an article or case into particular categories are themselves matters of interpretation, custom, and ultimately politics, which in time have come to seem natural and inevitable. See Steven M. Barkan, "Deconstructing Legal Research: A Law Librarian's Commentary on Critical Legal Studies," *Law Library Journal* 79 (1987): 632–634; see also Basil B. Bernstein, "On the Classification and Framing of Educational Knowledge," in Basil B. Bernstein, *Class, Codes, and Control: Towards a Sociology of Language* (London: Routledge and Kegan Paul, 1971), p. 202 (the way society selects and classifies public knowledge "reflects both the distribution of power and the principles of social control"); Duncan Kennedy, "The Structure of Blackstone's Commentaries," *Buffalo Law Review* 28 (1979): 215–216 (all legal categories are essentially lies, artificial constructs designed to make things seem more orderly than they are, and yet, paradoxically, we cannot live without them).

3. See Barkan, "Deconstructing Legal Research"; Robert C. Berring, "Legal Research and Legal Concepts: Where Form Molds Substance," *California Law Review* 75 (1987): 15; Virginia Wise, "Of Lizards, Intersubjective Zap, and Trashing: Critical Legal Studies and the Librarian," *Legal Reference Services Quarterly* 8, nos. 1/2 (1988): 7; Jim Dwyer, "Alternative Perspectives: A Conversation with Sandy Berman," *Technicalities* (Oct. 1986): 3.

Minnesota's Hennepin County Library and its spokesperson, Sanford Berman, have served as leaders in urging the Library of Congress to eliminate white Western bias and insulting or reactionary headings. See, e.g., Sanford Berman, *Prejudices and Antipathies: A Tract on the LC Subject Heads Concerning People* (Metuchen, NJ: Scarecrow Press, 1971).

4. *Library of Congress Subject Headings*, 15th ed. (Washington: Library of Congress Cataloging Distribution Service, 1992), pp. vii–viii; see also Library of Congress Subject Cataloging Division, *Subject Cataloging Manual: Subject Headings*, 4th ed. (Washington: Library of Congress Cataloging Distribution Service, 1991), pp. H-187, H-202:1, 3.

5. William E. Studwell, "The 1990s: Decade of Subject Access," *American Libraries* 18 (1987): 960 (Library of Congress's Subject Cataloging Division, the only organization substantially engaged in developing Library of Congress subject headings, works slowly); Monika Kirtland and Pauline Cochrane, "Critical Views of LCSH—A Bibliographic and Bibliometric Essay," *Cataloging & Classification Quarterly* 1, nos. 2/3 (1982): 71; Sanford Berman, "Out of the Kitchen—But Not Into the Catalog," *Technical Services Quarterly* 2 (1984): 167 (focusing on biases against women).

6. See, e.g., "Library of Congress Response to 'Library of Congress Subject Headings: Is Euthanasia the Answer?'" *Cataloging & Classification Quarterly* 8, no. 1 (1987): 7; William Mischo, "Library of Congress Subject Headings: A Review of the Problems, and Prospects for Improved Subject Access," *Cataloging & Classification Quarterly* 1, nos. 2/3 (1982): 105.

7. Richard Leiter, "A History of Legal Periodical Indexing," *Legal Reference Services Quarterly* 7, no. 1 (1987): 35–46. Among the chief objections to the older version of the Index was that it "was based on an inadequate thesaurus, one that contained too few subject headings to represent the topics covered by its collection." Daniel P. Dabney, "The Curse of Thamus: An Analysis of Full-Text Legal Document Retrieval," *Law Library Journal* 78 (1986): 12 n.9.

8. Leiter, "Legal Periodical," p. 46; see also Howard A. Hood, "Review of Current Law Index," *International Journal of Legal Information* 16 (1988): 123.

9. *Index to Legal Periodicals: Thesaurus* (New York: H. W. Wilson, 1988), p. iv.

10. *Current Law Index* 8 (1987): iii; Kent C. Olson and Robert C. Berring, *Practical Approaches to Legal Research* (New York: Haworth Press, 1988), p. 92 ("*CLI* uses Library of Congress subject headings instead of the more general Wilson headings").

11. Peter Enyingi, Melody Busse Lembke, and Rhonda Lawrence Mittán, *Cataloging Legal Literature: A Manual on AACR2 and Library of Congress Subject Headings for Legal Materials*, 2nd ed. (Littleton, CO: F. B. Rothman, 1988), p. 370.

12. Circularities are also rampant within particular systems. A 1988 search on LEGALTRAC of the term "sexual orientation" provided a "see also" reference to "sexual deviation," which carried a "see" reference from "sexual perversion." Under "sexual deviation" was a "see also" reference to "sexual masochism." The University of San Francisco Law Library notified Information Access of these peculiarities, and the headings have since been revised. See generally Mary Dykstra, "Can Subject Headings Be Saved?" *Library Journal*, Sept. 15, 1988, p. 55; Mary Dykstra, "LC Subject Headings Disguised as a Thesaurus," *Library Journal*, March 1, 1988, pp. 42, 44–46.

13. There was, however, lively debate in a number of law reviews over how law should be classified. See William Marvin, *West Publishing Company: Origin, Growth, Leadership* (St. Paul: West Publishing Co., 1969), p. 67; Thomas Woxland, "'Forever Associated with the Practice of Law': The Early Years of the West Publishing Com-

pany," *Legal Reference Services Quarterly* 5, no. 1 (1985): 116; see also Berring, "Legal Concepts," pp. 21–25.

14. See, e.g., Albert Kocourek, "Classification of Law," *New York University Law Quarterly Review* 11 (1934): 319; Roscoe Pound, "Classification of Law," *Harvard Law Review* 37 (1924): 933; Henry T. Terry, "Arrangement of the Law," *University of Illinois Law Review* 15 (1920): 61; Charles C. Ulrich, "A Proposed Plan of Classification for the Law," *Michigan Law Review* 34 (1935): 226.

15. Terry, "Arrangement," p. 61.

16. Woxland, "Forever," p. 123.

17. *Law Finder* (St. Paul: West Publishing Co., 1988), p. 5. West's success spelled secondary status for the English model of selective reporting, carried on chiefly by *American Law Reports*, and for attempts to simplify and codify American case law, such as the *Restatement*. The West model of "comprehensive reporting of all decisions, no matter how boring or stupid," is entrenched; each year over 65,000 decisions are added to the National Reporter System, along with a simliar number of memorandum decisions. Berring, "Legal Concepts," pp. 21–23 & n.38.

18. Tom Woxland, "My Favorite Headnotes," *Legal Reference Services Quarterly* 6, nos. 1/2 (1986): 120 (historical); Jill Abramson, John Kennedy, and Ellen Joan Pollock, "Inside the West Empire: They Define American Jurisprudence—and Make Millions in the Process. Can They Keep It Up?" *American Lawyer*, Oct. 1983, p. 90 (current). But see Berring, "Legal Concepts," p. 23 n.38 (reporting slightly larger current figure).

19. See Marvin, *Origin*, p. 74.

20. See Berring, "Full-Text Databases," pp. 33–36; Ulrich, "Proposed Plan," p. 226.

21. Abramson, Kennedy, and Pollock, "West Empire," pp. 94–95.

22. See, e.g., Derrick Bell, *And We Are Not Saved* (New York: Basic Books, 1987), pp. 51–74, 140–161; Derrick Bell, *Race, Racism and American Law*, 2d ed. (Boston: Little, Brown, and Company, 1980), pp. 40–44, 51–74; Kimberlè Williams Crenshaw, "Race, Reform, and Retrenchment: Transformation and Legitimation in Antidiscrimination Law," *Harvard Law Review* 101 (1988): 1331; Richard Delgado, "The Imperial Scholar: Reflections on a Review of Civil Rights Literature," *University of Pennsylvania Law Review* 132 (1984): 561; Alan David Freeman, "Legitimizing Racial Discrimination Through Antidiscrimination Law: A Critical Review of Supreme Court Doctrine," *Minnesota Law Review* 62 (1978): 1049; Charles R. Lawrence III, "The Id, the Ego, and Equal Protection: Reckoning with Unconscious Racism," *Stanford Law Review* 39 (1987): 317; Mari J. Matsuda, "Looking to the Bottom: Critical Legal Studies and Reparations," *Harvard Civil Rights–Civil Liberties Law Review* 22 (1987): 323; Patricia J. Williams, "Alchemical Notes: Reconstructing Ideals from Deconstructed Rights," *Harvard Civil Rights–Civil Liberties Law Review* 22 (1987): 401; Robert A. Williams, Jr., "Taking Rights Aggressively: The Perils and Promise of Critical Legal Theory for Peoples of Color," *Law & Inequality* 5 (1987): 103.

23. See Kimberlè Crenshaw, "Demarginalizing the Intersection of Race and Sex: A Black Feminist Critique of Antidiscrimination Doctrine, Feminist Theory and Antiracist Politics," *Chicago Legal Forum* (1989): 152.

24. For a case dealing with concepts that are not referred to by name, see *United States v. Berrigan*, 283 F. Supp. 336 (D. Md. 1968), aff'd sub nom., *United States v. Moylan*, 417 F.2d 1002 (4th Cir. 1969) (Catholic priest convicted of dousing Selective Service files with blood in protest against Vietnam War, but the district court does not refer to civil disobedience by name). For articles dealing with concepts that are not referred to by name, see Berring, "Full-Text Databases," p. 48 ("The fact is that law involves ideas, and ideas are not directly correlated with particular words."); Steven Childress, "The Hazards of Computer-Assisted Research to the Legal Profession," *Oklahoma Bar Journal* 55 (1984): 1533 (computers' focus on words grounds searches in language, rather than content, of an opinion).

Studies by the Norwegian Research Center for Computers and Law showed that 15 percent to 25 percent of failures to retrieve relevant documents were due to the fact that no single word or set of synonyms represented the idea sought by the researcher. Jon Bing, "Performance of Legal Text Retrieval Systems: The Curse of Boole," *Law Library Journal* 79 (1987): 193. For a discussion of articles and cases dealing with concepts that are referred to by name but are not included in standard legal databases, see Wise, "Intersubjective Zap" (early critical legal studies materials often absent from databases).

25. Professor J. Myron Jacobstein stumped demonstrators of the new LEXIS system at a 1975 convention with a challenge to find a certain case concerning a child. Jacobstein knew, but the demonstrators did not, that the judge had consistently called the child an "infant." Berring, "Full-Text Databases," pp. 38–39.

26. See id., p. 39 (databases can only retrieve exact terms); Margaret F. Stieg and Joan L. Atkinson, "Librarianship Online: Old Problems, New Solutions," *Library Journal*, Oct. 1, 1988, pp. 48, 51, 56 (decisions to include or exclude material in databases often irrational).

27. See Richard Delgado, "Legal Storytelling for Oppositionists and Others: A Plea for Narrative," *Michigan Law Review* 87 (1989): 2411 (on role of peripheral groups in reforming law through telling of "counterstories").

28. See Bell, *Not Saved* (using narrative and parables to challenge racial myths); Bell, *Race, Racism*; Derrick Bell, "*Brown v. Board of Education* and the Interest-Convergence Dilemma," *Harvard Law Review* 93 (1980): 518 (asserting that interests of blacks are accommodated only where they converge with interests of whites); Derrick Bell, "The Supreme Court, 1984 Term—Foreword: The Civil Rights Chronicles," *Harvard Law Review* 99 (1985): 4.

29. Richard K. Sherwin, "A Matter of Voice and Plot: Belief and Suspicion in Storytelling," *Michigan Law Review* 87 (1988): 550–552 (noting necessity of balancing rhetoricians' search for belief and community with deconstructionists' suspicion).

30. W. E. Burghardt DuBois, *The Souls of Black Folk* (Greenwich, CT: Fawcett Publications, 1961), p. 16.

31. For example, current law practice has increased the pressure to generate billable hours and to specialize. Megafirms are replacing smaller ones, and much of law practice is becoming routinized.

32. Compare this approach with that suggested by Kennedy, "Blackstone's Commentaries," pp. 210–211 (using Blackstone's famous work as template to lay out and analyze structure of traditional Western thought: "Blackstone serves both

as a convenient starting point for the substantive history of American legal thought and as a relatively easy object for the method of discovering hidden political intentions beneath the surface of legal exposition"). See also William E. Benemann, "American Graffiti, Library-Style," *American Libraries* 18 (1987): 650 ("the [subject heading] lists provide a window on American society ... that may tell us more about ourselves than we could learn from 21 linear feet of statistical data").

33. Cf. Mary Ellen S. Capek, ed., *A Women's Thesaurus* (New York: Harper & Row, 1987), p. viii (indexing and classification systems lack vocabulary suited to retrieve many items of concern to feminists; these issues tend to be lumped together under "women" or other broad terms, e.g., lesbian issues categorized under sexuality, although many are nonsexual issues).

34. Most progressive librarians are quick to recognize and condemn *active* censorship. See Ron Seely, "Censors Take More Liberty in Banning Books," *Wisconsin State Journal*, Sept. 25, 1988, p. 1 (discussing campaign to remove controversial books). But the kind of unconscious self-censorship we have been describing is much more difficult to deter and counter. The categories we use to screen and interpret reality seem natural and inevitable. We rarely question their adequacy or fairness.

Chapter 4

1. Richard Delgado, "The Imperial Scholar: Reflections on a Review of Civil Rights Literature," *University of Pennsylvania Law Review* 132 (1984): 561.

2. Jon Weiner, "Law Profs Fight the Power," *Nation*, September 4, 1989, p. 246 (quoting Derrick Bell).

3. Richard Delgado, "Imperial Scholar," pp. 562, n.3, 563, 567, 573–578.

4. An example is the assertion that perspective matters—who is writing may be as important as what is written. See, e.g., "Symposium, Excluded Voices: Realities in Law and Law Reform," *University of Miami Law Review* 42 (1987): 1 (describing the symposium as being "about how differences in opinions, motivation, and language can construct social and political ideas that may form the basis for law reform"); "Symposium, Legal Storytelling," *Michigan Law Review* 87 (1989): 2073 (containing articles by Milner S. Ball, Derrick Bell, Richard Delgado, Mari J. Matsuda, Patricia Williams, and Steven L. Winter on the place of voice and perspective in legal scholarship).

5. See, e.g., Randall L. Kennedy, "Racial Critiques of Legal Academia," *Harvard Law Review* 102 (1989): 1745 (commending critical race theorists for their intellectual contributions to academia but taking issue with the manner in which they present their arguments).

6. For coverage of critical race theorists, see Charles Rothfeld, "Minority Critic Stirs Debate on Minority Writing," *New York Times*, January 5, 1990, p. B9 (describing the controversy created by Randall Kennedy's critique of critical race studies); Weiner, "Law Profs." For an example of coverage of radical feminism, see Fred Strebeigh, "Defining Law on the Feminist Frontier," *New York Times*, October 6, 1991, Magazine Section, p. 29 (describing the work of Catharine MacKinnon).

7. For discussion of the historical roots of CLS, see Mark Kelman, *Guide to Critical Legal Studies* (Cambridge: Harvard University Press, 1989); "Symposium, Critical Legal Studies," *Stanford Law Review* 36 (1984): 1 (collection of articles on CLS history, tenets, and subdivisions within movement); Roberto Unger, "The Critical Legal Studies Movement," *Harvard Law Review* 96 (1984): 561; David Kairys, ed., *The Politics of Law,* 2d ed. (New York: Pantheon Books, 1990).

On the origins of contemporary critical thought in these and other disciplines, see, e.g., Roberto Unger, *Knowledge and Politics* (New York: Free Press, 1975); Martin Jay, *The Dialectical Imagination: A History of the Frankfurt School and The Institute of Social Research, 1923–1950* (Boston: Little, Brown, 1973); Hans-Georg Gadamer, *Truth and Method* (New York: Seabury Press, 1975).

8. For an introduction to feminist thought, see Cass R. Sunstein, ed., *Feminism and Political Theory* (Chicago: University of Chicago Press, 1990); Catharine MacKinnon, *Feminism Unmodified* (Cambridge: Harvard University Press, 1987).

9. See Richard Delgado, "Brewer's Plea: Critical Thoughts on Common Cause," *Vanderbilt Law Review* 44 (1990): 1; Colloquy, "Responses to Randall Kennedy's Racial Critique of Legal Academia," *Harvard Law Review* 103 (1990): 184; Richard Delgado and Jean Stefancic, "Critical Race Theory: An Annotated Bibliography," *Virginia Law Review* 79 (1993): 461.

10. Friederich Schleiermacher, *Hermeneutics: The Handwritten Manuscripts* (Missoula, MT: Scholars Press for the American Academy of Religion, 1978); Stanley Fish, *Is There a Text in This Class?* (Cambridge: Harvard University Press, 1980); Art Berman, *From the New Criticism to Deconstruction: The Reception of Structuralism and Post-Structuralism* (Urbana: University of Illinois Press, 1988).

11. Duncan Kennedy and Peter Gabel, "Roll Over Beethoven," *Stanford Law Review* 36 (1984): 1. For early exposition of law's indeterminacy from a leading legal realist, see Karl Llewellyn, *The Bramble Bush* (1926; reprint, New York: Oceana Publications, 1951).

12. Duncan Kennedy, "The Structure of Blackstone's Commentaries," *Buffalo Law Review* 28 (1979): 205.

13. For discussion of the idea of patriarchy—that law, like most social institutions, reflects male norms and values—see Robin West, "Jurisprudence and Gender," *University of Chicago Law Review* 55 (1988): 1; MacKinnon, *Feminism Unmodified*.

14. Catharine MacKinnon, "Pornography, Civil Rights and Speech," *Harvard Civil Rights–Civil Liberties Law Review* 20 (1985): 920.

15. Fran Olsen, "The Family and the Market," *Harvard Law Review* 96 (1983): 1497.

16. Catharine MacKinnon, *Sexual Harassment of Working Women: A Case of Sex Discrimination* (New Haven: Yale University Press, 1979).

17. Martha Minow and Elizabeth Spelman, "In Context," *Southern California Law Review* 63 (1991): 1597. See "Symposium, Excluded Voices: Realities in Law and Law Reform," *University of Miami Law Review* 42 (1987): 1.

18. E.g., Carrie Menkel-Meadow, "Portia in a Different Voice: Speculations on a Women's Lawyering Process," *Berkeley Women's Law Journal* 1 (1985): 39; Nadine Taub and Elizabeth Schneider, "Perspectives on Women's Subordination," in Kairys, ed. *The Politics of Law,* p. 117.

19. E.g., Stephanie Wildman, "Integration in the 1980s: The Dream of Diversity and the Cycle of Exclusion," *Tulane Law Review* 64 (1990): 1625.

20. Clare Dalton, "An Essay on the Deconstruction of Contract Doctrine," *Yale Law Journal* 94 (1985): 999; Mary Jo Frug, "Rereading Contracts: A Feminist Analysis of a Contracts Casebook," *American University Law Review* 34 (1985): 1065.

21. Katherine Bartlett, "Feminist Methods," *Harvard Law Review* 103 (1990): 829; Herma Hill Kay, "Models of Equality," *University of Illinois Law Review* 1985 (1985): 39.

22. E.g., Martha Fineman, "Challenging Law, Establishing Differences: The Future of Feminist Legal Scholarship," *Florida Law Review* 42 (1990): 24; Angela Harris, "Race and Essentialism in Feminist Legal Theory," *Stanford Law Review* 42 (1990): 581.

23. Harris, "Race and Essentialism"; Kimberlè Crenshaw, "Demarginalizing the Intersection of Race and Sex: A Black Feminist Critique of Antidiscrimination Doctrine, Feminist Theory and Antiracist Politics," *University of Chicago Legal Forum* 1989 (1989): 139.

24. Fineman, "Challenging Law"; Harris, "Race and Essentialism"; Crenshaw, "Demarginalizing the Intersection of Race and Sex"; Judy Scales-Trent, "Commonalities: On Being Black and White, Different and the Same," *Yale Journal of Law and Feminism* 2 (1990): 305.

25. Crenshaw, "Demarginalizing the Intersection of Race and Sex"; Kimberlè Crenshaw, "Race, Reform and Retrenchment," *Harvard Law Review* 101 (1988): 1331; Mari Matsuda, "Affirmative Action and Legal Knowledge: Planting Seeds in Plowed-Up Ground," *Harvard Women's Law Journal* 11 (1988): 1; Mari Matsuda, "Public Response to Racist Speech: Considering the Victim's Story," *Michigan Law Review* 87 (1989): 2320; Leslie Espinoza, "Masks and Other Disguises," *Harvard Law Review* 103 (1990): 1878.

26. For histories of the critical race theory movement, see Delgado, "Brewer's Plea," p. 6; Richard Delgado, "When a Story Is Just a Story: Does Voice Really Matter?" *Virginia Law Review* 76 (1990): 95.

27. Derrick Bell, "*Brown v. Board of Education* and the Interest-Convergence Dilemma," *Harvard Law Review* 93 (1980): 518.

28. Derrick Bell, *And We Are Not Saved* (New York: Basic Books, 1987); Richard Delgado, "Derrick Bell and the Ideology of Racial Reform: Will We Ever Be Saved?" *Yale Law Journal* 97 (1988): 923–924.

29. Robert A. Williams, "Documents of Barbarism," *Arizona Law Review* 31 (1989): 237.

30. Mari Matsuda, "Looking to the Bottom: Critical Legal Studies and Reparation," *Harvard Civil Rights–Civil Liberties Law Review* 22 (1987): 323.

31. Matsuda, "Planting Seeds"; Charles R. Lawrence, III, "If He Hollers, Let Him Go," *Duke Law Journal* 1990 (1990): 431.

32. Michael Olivas, "The Chronicles, My Grandfather's Stories, and Immigration Law," *St. Louis University Law Journal* 34 (1990): 425; Rachel Moran, "Bilingual Education as a Status Conflict," *California Law Review* 75 (1987): 321.

33. Randall Kennedy, "*McClesky v. Kemp*: Race, Capital Punishment, and the Supreme Court," *Harvard Law Review* 101 (1988): 1388.

34. Richard Delgado, "Fairness and Formality: Minimizing the Risk of Prejudice in Alternative Dispute Resolution," *Wisconsin Law Review* 1985 (1985): 1359; Trina Grillo, "The Mediation Alternative: Process Dangers for Women," *Yale Law Journal* 100 (1991): 1545.

35. Bell, *And We Are Not Saved;* Patricia Williams, "Alchemical Notes: Reconstructing Ideals from Deconstructed Rights," *Harvard Civil Rights–Civil Liberties Law Review* 22 (1987): 401; Richard Delgado, "Storytelling for Oppositionists and Others: A Plea for Narrative," *Michigan Law Review* 87 (1989): 2412–2414.

36. Association of American Law Schools, *A Time for Sharing: Speaking Difference, Sharing Strength* (Washington, D.C., 1990) (program of annual meeting).

37. Outsiders currently have a substantial presence in elite law reviews. Of the articles on civil rights published in three top journals, the *Harvard Law Review,* the *Yale Law Journal,* and the *University of Pennsylvania Law Review,* between 1985 and 1990, nearly three-fourths were written by women or people of color.

38. *Western Addition Community Org. v. NLRB,* 485 F.2d 917, 940 (D.C. Cir. 1973) (Wyzanski, J., dissenting), reviewed sub nom., *Emporium Capwell Co. v. Western Addition Co.,* 420 U.S. 50 (1975).

39. See William Van Alstyne, "Closing the Circle of Constitutional Review from *Griswold v. Connecticut* to *Roe v. Wade*: An Outline of a Decision Merely Overruling Roe," *Duke Law Journal* 1989 (1989): 1677 n.1, 1681 n.15, 1679–1682, 1685, 1688.

40. See Laurence H. Tribe, *American Constitutional Law,* 2d ed. (Mineola, NY: Foundation Press, 1988), p. 13 n.9 (citing only Mark V. Tushnet, "A Note on the Revival of Textualism in Constitutional Theory," *Southern California Law Review* 58 [1985]: 685, for the idea of constitutional indeterminacy); Laurence H. Tribe, "On Reading the Constitution," *Utah Law Review* 1988 (1988): 762, 770 (citing Mark V. Tushnet, "Diatribe," *Michigan Law Review* 78 [1980]: 694, and Mark V. Tushnet, "The Dilemmas of Liberal Constitutionalism," *Ohio State Law Journal* 42 [1981]: 411, for same).

Several sections of Tribe's *American Constitutional Law* that call out for citation to a critical minority or radical feminist writer are notably devoid of them. Tribe's treatment of *Brown v. Board of Education,* 347 U.S. 483 (1954), includes no reference to his colleague Derrick Bell's pathbreaking article, *"Brown v. Board of Education* and the Interest-Convergence Dilemma," *Harvard Law Review* 93 (1980): 523–526, in which Bell argues that *Brown* was decided not so much as a matter of conscience by the white establishment but rather to forward economic and Cold War imperatives important to our ruling elite. See Laurence Tribe, *American Constitutional Law,* pp. 1475–1480, 1488–1490, 1499, 1514. Tribe's section on pornography and feminism mentions only Catharine MacKinnon and Susan Estrich among legal feminists; Cass Sunstein (a man) is cited more often. See id. pp. 920–928. Tribe also fails to mention the idea that the Constitution was an antiblack instrument, an idea put forward by Bell and Thurgood Marshall among others, and the thesis by Olsen, MacKinnon, and others, that the law is inherently antifemale.

This treatment stands in marked contrast to those who argue that racism affects our entire political and legal systems and hence antiracist thought and commentary should be brought into every area of constitutional discussion, not just equal protection. See T. Alexander Aleinikoff, "The Constitution in Context," *Colorado Law Review* 63 (1992): 325; Stephen M. Feldman, "Whose Common Good? Racism in the Political Community," *Georgetown Law Journal* 80 (1992): 1835. *American Constitutional Law* contains no index entries for legitimation, critical race theory, patriarchy, hierarchy, hegemony, indeterminacy, or deconstruction. Gramsci, Foucault, Jurgen Habermas, Herbert Marcuse, and Marx are not mentioned at all.

41. Derrick Bell, for example, argues that our system of antidiscrimination laws and rules is not only manipulable and prone to backsliding but also designed to operate that way. See Bell, *And We Are Not Saved*. Catharine MacKinnon argues that the legal system is inherently biased against women and that applying sex-neutral and race-neutral concepts of fairness and equal protection will only exacerbate the law's biases. See MacKinnon, *Feminism Unmodified*, pp. 104–105, 164–166; MacKinnon, *Toward a Feminist Theory of the State*.

42. See Theodore Eisenberg, *Civil Rights Legislation*, 3d ed. (Charlottesville, VA: Michie Co., 1991), p. 1027. The 1,700-page casebook contains hundreds of references to works by white men, including several by the author himself. But the section on sexual harassment of women in the workplace lacks any reference to MacKinnon's groundbreaking work, *Sexual Harassment of Working Women*. See Eisenberg, *Civil Rights Legislation*, pp. 893–900. The sole treatment of discrimination against Mexican-Americans is an excerpt from a relatively old article by two white men, Gary A. Greenfield and Don B. Kates, Jr., "Mexican Americans, Racial Discrimination, and the Civil Rights Act of 1866," *California Law Review* 63 (1975): 662. See Eisenberg, *Civil Rights Legislation*, p. 104.

43. See Joanna Russ, *How to Suppress Women's Writing* (Austin: University of Texas Press, 1983) (examining the techniques literary scholars have used throughout the nineteenth and twentieth centuries to belittle literature by women).

44. See, e.g., Bruce Ackerman, "Constitutional Politics/Constitutional Law," *Yale Law Journal* 99 (1989): 466, n.23. In the main text Ackerman uses Owen Fiss as an example of a collectivist who stresses the rights of disadvantaged groups to equal treatment. But in his footnote to Owen Fiss, Ackerman mentions that Catharine MacKinnon has "more recently developed and deepened this group-oriented perspective in *Sexual Harassment of Working Women* (1979), and *Toward a Feminist Theory of the State* (1989)." Ackerman, "Constitutional Politics," p. 466, n.23. Why, then, is MacKinnon not in the main text in place of or alongside Owen Fiss? Patricia Cain argues that citation to feminists is altogether dismissive, trivializing, and absent. See Patricia A. Cain, "Feminist Legal Scholarship," *Iowa Law Review* 77 (1991): 19.

45. See, e.g., Boris I. Bittker, "The Bicentennial of the Jurisprudence of Original Intent: The Recent Past," *California Law Review* 77 (1989): 257 (dismissing Unger by making light of his "CLS shock troops," who began to preach original intent when they discovered the Declaration of Independence, causing conservatives to leave by the rear door after first pronouncing themselves "*Original* Original Intentionalists"); Paul D. Carrington, "Of Law and the River," *Journal of Legal Education* 34 (1984): 227 (stating that critical legal studies writers are preaching antilaw and that to be consistent with their own premises, they should leave the legal academy); Lino A. Graglia, "Permissible and Impermissible Content-Based Restrictions on Freedom of Speech," *Harvard Journal of Law and Public Policy* 10 (1987): 71–72 (arguing that MacKinnon's work is little more than feminist propaganda and

that its adoption by two cities is "the best argument against democracy I have heard in some time").

46. See, e.g., Carrington, "Of Law and the River" (stating that CLS writers are impassioned and audacious but not really doing law, are poor influences on their students, and should consider transferring to other university departments).

47. See, e.g., Paul Brest, "Affirmative Action and the Constitution: Three Theories," *Iowa Law Review* 72 (1987): 281 n.2 (citing no minority scholar or woman and only one criticalist, Alan Freeman, in an article about a racially based and gender-based policy). Although Alan Freeman advanced and documented the astonishing proposition that Supreme Court antidiscrimination law injures and suppresses persons of color (see Alan D. Freeman, "Legitimizing Racial Discrimination Through Antidiscrimination Law: A Critical Review of Supreme Court Doctrine," *Minnesota Law Review* 62 (1978): 1052–1119), Brest cites Freeman for the obscure proposition that "fault" theories of racial justice are in question. See Brest, "Affirmative Action," p. 281 n.2. In Brest's discussion of theories justifying affirmative action, he does not cite writers of color, such as Bell, who have expressed grave misgivings over the doctrine, its footing, and its intentions. See Bell, *And We Are Not Saved*, pp. 146–161.

48. See Edward W. Cleary, ed., *McCormick on Evidence*, 3d ed. Supp. (St. Paul: West Publishing Co., 1987), p. 83 n.92 (citing article by Massaro on rape trauma syndrome; otherwise, feminists are not much in evidence).

49. See, e.g., Kenneth L. Karst, "Boundaries and Reasons: Freedom of Expression and the Subordination of Groups," *University of Illinois Law Review* 1990 (1990): 114 n.73 (citing Derrick Bell, Kimberlè Crenshaw, and Charles Lawrence as authority for various propositions having to do with the continuing menace of racism).

50. See, e.g., Karst, "Boundaries and Reasons," p. 114 (agreeing with outsiders that racism still exists and is a current issue); Alan Freeman, "Racism, Rights and the Quest for Equality of Opportunity: A Critical Legal Essay," *Harvard Civil Rights–Civil Liberties Law Review* 23 (1988): 331, and n.94 (mentioning Mari Matsuda in the main text of his article and also detailing in the footnote why he disagrees with her proposition that real experiences cannot be paradoxical).

51. See, e.g., Aleinikoff, "The Constitution in Context"; Freeman, "Racism, Rights and the Quest for Equality of Opportunity"; Duncan Kennedy, "A Cultural Pluralist Case for Affirmative Action in Legal Academia," *Duke Law Journal* 1990 (1990): 705; Gary Peller, "Race Consciousness," *Duke Law Journal* 1990 (1990): 758; see also Cain, "Feminist Legal Scholarship" (listing Sunstein, Tobias, Chused, Karst, Michelman, and Posner as men who have taken women's writing seriously).

52. See, e.g., Edward Rubin, "The Concept of Law and the New Public Law Scholarship," *Michigan Law Review* 89 (1991): 811 n.55.

53. See J. M. Balkin, "Ideology as Constraint," *Stanford Law Review* 43 (1991): 1148 n.59, 1149 nn.61–62 (book review).

54. See Lea S. VanderVelde, "The Labor Vision of the Thirteenth Amendment," *University of Pennsylvania Law Review* 138 (1989): 497 n.267.

55. See A. Leon Higginbotham, Jr., *In the Matter of Color: Race and the American Legal Process: The Colonial Period* (New York: Oxford University Press, 1978).

56. See David Rosenberg, "Class Actions for Mass Torts: Doing Individual Justice by Collective Means," *Indiana Law Journal* 62 (1987): 562 n.5.

57. For examples of such early-page citation, see Neal Devins, "Gender Justice and Its Critics," *California Law Review* 76 (1988): 1382 n.27, 1385 n.36, 1389 n.62, 1390 nn.63 and 65 (book review) (citing early passages of MacKinnon's and Minow's works); Suzanna Sherry, "Civic Virtue and the Feminine Voice in Constitutional Adjudication," *Virginia Law Review* 72 (1986): 565 n.98, 586 n.182 (citing to Fran Olsen's work in its entirety or to its early pages).

58. See, e.g., Deborah Tannen, *You Just Don't Understand: Women and Men in Conversation* (New York: William Morrow and Co., 1990) (detailing the use and the perception of interruptions by men and women).

59. See Tribe, *American Constitutional Law,* pp. 920–925 (approaching MacKinnon's Indianapolis ordinance as a First Amendment problem); Cass Sunstein, "Pornography and the First Amendment," *Duke Law Journal* 1986 (1986): 589–627 (analyzing antipornography legislation under the First Amendment and concluding that it is constitutional if narrowly aimed at immediate harms to women). See also Kingsley R. Browne, "Title VII as Censorship: Hostile-Environment Harassment and the First Amendment," *Ohio State Law Journal* 52 (1991): 481 (treating various proposals to regulate hate speech as First Amendment problems exclusively).

60. See Derrick Bell and Richard Delgado, "Minority Law Professors' Lives: The Bell-Delgado Survey," *Harvard Civil Rights–Civil Liberties Law Review* 24 (1989): 357–358 (discussing selective forgetfulness).

61. See, e.g., Alexander Aleinikoff, "The Constitution in Context" (citing Steve Smith with regard to feminism—a rare lapse because the author cites Matsuda, Olsen, Guinier, and MacKinnon elsewhere in the article); Alex M. Johnson, Jr., "The New Voice of Color," *Yale Law Journal* 100 (1991): 2023 (an otherwise excellent article says: "According to Sunstein, the difference strand of Critical Feminist Theory is …"); Laurence H. Tribe, "The Curvature of Constitutional Space," *Harvard Law Review* 103 (1989): 15 n.60 (citing Sunstein for the principle of difference, which is commonly associated with feminist authors).

62. For a sparkling treatment of this issue, see Trina Grillo and Stephanie M. Wildman, "Obscuring the Importance of Race: The Imposition of Making Comparisons Between Racism and Sexism (or other -isms)," *Duke Law Journal* 1991 (1991): 401–412.

63. See Nadine Strossen, "Regulating Racist Speech on Campus: A Modest Proposal?" *Duke Law Journal* 1990 (1990): 537 (deploying the trite "no exceptions" argument with the statement that "[t]o attempt to craft free speech exceptions only for racist speech would create a significant risk of a slide down the proverbial 'slippery slope'").

64. Joanna Russ discusses false categorizing as a mechanism to diminish women's writing. See Russ, *Women's Writing*, pp. 49–61.

65. See the following reviews of Derrick Bell's book, *And We Are Not Saved*: Kevin E. Kennedy, Book Review, *Michigan Law Review* 86 (1988): 1131 (using terms "stirring" and "poignant" to describe Bell's book); Peter M. Yu, Book Review, *Harvard Civil Rights–Civil Liberties Law Review* 23 (1988): 289 (using terms such as "embellished by the speculation of fiction," "poignan[t]," and "potent"); see also

Wendy Kaminer, "Citizens of the Supermarket State," *New York Times*, May 26, 1991, Book Review Section, p. 10 (reviewing Patricia J. Williams, *The Alchemy of Race and Rights*, and stating that Williams writes with "eloquence" and "passion"). There is nothing wrong with writing powerfully or with praising writing that is clean or graphic, but we must not allow our fascination with the vividness of a passage to distract us from the author's meaning, as some do with critical race theory scholarship.

66. See Mark Kelman, "Concepts of Discrimination in 'General Ability' Job Testing," *Harvard Law Review* 104 (1991): 1233–1234 (stating that informality increases risk of prejudice, as various critical race theory writers have argued, but "[o]f course, this position has long been taken by some white male critical legal studies scholars as well"); see also Cain, "Feminist Legal Scholarship" (describing the "what's new" response to feminist writers, in which the author points out that a feminist's work is like other radical theory or contains nothing original); Martha Minow, "Beyond Universality," *University of Chicago Legal Forum* 1989 (1989): 129 (same observation).

67. For an example of this type of dismissiveness, see Kaminer, "Supermarket State," p. 10 (implying that Williams uses fancy vocabulary and arcane language to reiterate the obvious: that racism is bad).

68. See, e.g., Stephen M. Feldman, "Exposing Sunstein's Naked Preferences," *Duke Law Journal* 1989 (1989): 1353 n.87, 1354 n. 93, 1355 n.97, 1356 n.99 (citing to Derrick Bell and Richard Delgado for one predictable work each); Linda R. Hirshman, "Brontë, Bloom, and Bork: An Essay on the Moral Education of Judges," *University of Pennsylvania Law Review* 137 (1988): 202 n.160, 205 n.178, 217 n.240, 222 n.272, 224 n.285 (citing MacKinnon for one predictable work); James S. Liebman, "Implementing *Brown* in the Nineties: Political Reconstruction, Liberal Recollection, and Litigatively Enforced Legislative Reform," *Virginia Law Review* 76 (1990): 356 n.37, 359 n.51 (citing Bell for one predictable work).

69. See Russ, *Women's Writing*, pp. 62–75 (Chapter 7—Isolation) (describing a similar phenomenon in women's literature—"she wrote it, but she only wrote one of it"; also describing the phenomenon of women being categorized as something other than writers or else as occasional labored imposters).

70. See Michael Rosenfeld, "Decoding *Richmond*: Affirmative Action and the Elusive Meaning of Constitutional Equality," *Michigan Law Review* 87 (1989): 1729, 1768 n.183 (citing familiar standbys, including Fiss, Bickel, Dworkin, and Ely, and bringing in Kimberlè Crenshaw as though by afterthought: "Thus, for example, if the racist portrays blacks as being lazy and irresponsible ..."). Id., p. 1768 n.183 (citing Crenshaw). Surely the talented Crenshaw had something more vital to say about our system of white-over-black subordination than that racists often portray blacks as lazy and irresponsible. Also, one would presume that more than one minority scholar has something relevant and significant to say about affirmative action.

71. For examples of the hostility critical race theory has generated, see Rothfeld, "Minority Critic"; Wiener, "Law Profs"; Micaela diLeonardo and Adolph L. Reed, Jr., "Academic Poverty Pimping," *The Nation*, October 23, 1989, p. 442 (categorizing certain African-American scholarship as "muddle-headed, self-aggrandizing slop"). But see Rothfeld, "Minority Critic," p. B6 (describing the remarks of

Kenneth Karst, a professor who was singled out as an inner-circle member, who called the new movement "inevitable" and "a kind of growth"); Wiener, "Law Profs," praising the new scholarship.

72. For descriptions of narrative theory, see W.J.T. Mitchell, ed., *On Narrative* (Chicago: University of Chicago Press, 1981); Paul Ricoeur, *Time and Narrative* (Evanston, IL: Northwestern University Press, 1984); Robin West, "Jurisprudence as Narrative: An Aesthetic Analysis of Modern Legal Theory," *New York University Law Review* 60 (1985): 145. For a treatment of some of these theories in the legal arena, see Steven L. Winter, "Contingency and Community in Normative Practice," *University of Pennsylvania Law Review* 139 (1991): 971–1002 (arguing that structures of legal thought often determine content).

73. See, e.g., Derrick Bell, "The Price and Pain of Racial Perspective," *Stanford Law School Journal*, May 8, 1986, p. 5 (discussing a reaction by some Stanford Law School faculty to Bell's teaching of constitutional law; faculty members offered supplemental classes to Bell's students); see also Delgado, "Storytelling," pp. 2413–2416, 2435–2438 (arguing that internalized stories determine beliefs).

Chapter 5

1. See "Symposium of Law Publishers," *American Law Review* 23 (1889): 396. Before this time few law reviews existed. See Robert Stevens, *Law School: Legal Education in America from the 1850s to the 1980s* (Chapel Hill: University of North Carolina Press, 1983), p. 127 n.34; Erwin C. Surrency, *A History of American Law Publishing* (New York: Oceana Publications, 1990).

2. Ted Peters, *Futures—Human and Divine* (Atlanta: John Knox Press, 1978); Hillel Schwartz, *Century's End: A Cultural History of the Fin-de-Siècle—From the 990s Through the 1990s* (New York: Doubleday, 1990); Timothy P. Weber, *Living in the Shadow of the Second Coming*, Enlarged ed. (Grand Rapids: Academie Books, 1983).

3. Kenneth Lasson, "Scholarship Amok: Excesses in the Pursuit of Truth and Tenure," *Harvard Law Review* 103 (1990): 926.

4. Plato, "The Symposium," in *The Dialogues of Plato*, v. 1, B. Jowett, trans. (New York: Random House, 1937), p. 301.

5. *Oxford English Dictionary*, 2d ed., v. 17 (Oxford: Oxford University Press, 1989), p. 464.

6. See Symposium, "Methods of Legal Education," *Yale Law Journal* 1 (1892): 139, including articles by Edward J. Phelps, William A. Keener, Christopher G. Tiedman, and John C. Gray.

7. Edward Q. Keasby, "Restrictions upon the Use of Land," *Harvard Law Review* 6 (1893): 280; H. W. Chaplin, "Record Title to Land," id.: 302; Joseph H. Beale, "Registration of Title to Land," id.: 369; F. V. Balch, "Land Transfer—A Different Point of View," id.: 410; James R. Carret, "Land Transfer—A Reply to Criticisms of the Torrens System," *Harvard Law Review* 7 (1893): 24.

8. "Editor's Foreword," *Law and Contemporary Problems* 48 (1933): 1.

9. Robert C. Post, "The Constitutional Concept of Public Discourse: Outrageous Opinion, Democratic Deliberation and *Hustler Magazine v. Falwell*," *Harvard Law Review* 103 (1990): 645.

10. "Editor's Introduction," *Texas Law Review* 60 (1982): i.

11. "President's Page," *Stanford Law Review* 36 (1984): i.

12. Christopher D. Stone, "Introduction: Interpreting the Symposium," *Southern California Law Review* 58 (1985): 7.

13. Stephen F. Rhode, "Introduction," *Western Legal History* 3 (1990): 177–178.

14. Richard G. Singer, "Foreword," *Rutgers Law Journal* 19 (1988): 520.

15. Alexander D. Brooks and Bruce J. Winick, "Foreword: Mental Disability Comes of Age," *Rutgers Law Review* 39 (1987): 238.

16. John Kaplan, "Foreword," *Law and Contemporary Problems* 49 (1986): 3.

17. Martha Layne Collins, "Introduction," *Kentucky Law Journal* 74 (1986): 690.

18. Dale D. Goble, "Introduction to the Symposium on Legal Structures for Managing the Pacific Northwest Salmon and Steelhead: The Biological and Historical Context," *Idaho Law Review* 22 (1986): 418, 420.

19. See, e.g., Kim Lane Schepple, "Foreword: Telling Stories," *Michigan Law Review* 87 (1989): 2073 (law review received letter from two outside authors proposing topic).

20. "Colloquy: Tax Transitions," *Harvard Law Review* 98 (1985): 1809 (two articles and a reply).

21. "Local Government Law Symposium," *Stetson Law Review* 15 (1986): 649.

22. Telephone interview with Kathy Grove, American Bar Association (November 25, 1991). By 1990 the figure had grown to 25 percent.

23. See, e.g., "Symposium: New Directions in Family Law," *UCLA Law Review* 28 (1981): 1125 (all five articles authored by women).

24. "Interpretation Symposium," *Southern California Law Review* 58 (1985): 1.

25. "Symposium, Critical Legal Studies," *Stanford Law Review* 36 (1984): 1; "A Symposium of Critical Legal Studies," *American University Law Review* 34 (1985): 927; "Symposium of Critical Legal Studies," *Cardozo Law Review* 6 (1985): 691; "Professing Law: A Colloquy on Critical Legal Studies," *St. Louis University Law Review* 31 (1986): 1; "Constitutional Law from a Critical Legal Perspective," *Buffalo Law Review* 36 (1987): 211.

26. "A Bicentennial Symposium—The Constitution and Human Values: The Unfinished Agenda," *Georgia Law Review* 20 (1986): 811.

27. See "Chicago-Kent Law Review Faculty Scholarship Survey," *Chicago-Kent Law Review* 65 (1989): 204.

28. For examples of the growing literature on this subject see Ted Peters, *Futures;* Hillel Schwartz, *Century's End;* Timothy P. Weber, *Living in the Shadow.* See also William M. Johnston, *Celebrations: The Cult of Anniversaries in Europe and the United States Today* (New Brunswick, NJ: Transaction Publishers, 1991) (studies the impact of the bimillennium by examining the cultural anniversaries that will precede it).

29. "Reason, Passion, and Justice Brennan: A Symposium," *Cardozo Law Review* 10 (1988): 1.

30. "Symposium: Law and Literature," *Mercer Law Review* 39 (1988): 739.

31. "Symposium: Law and Social Theory," *Northwestern University Law Review* 83 (1988): 1.

32. "Symposium: The Fiftieth Anniversary of the Federal Rules of Civil Procedure," *Notre Dame Law Review* 63 (1988): 597.

33. The pull of community is limited, however, to what we call "strong second-tier reviews." Although there are a few exceptions, few top authors seem to write below this level.

34. Many other measures are possible. For example, a symposium on the rights of the institutionalized (prisoners), or marginalized (the homeless), may attract relatively few citations but nevertheless may have a substantial impact on the welfare or morale of members of these groups. We chose citation count mainly because of its easy quantifiability. In so doing we do not mean to minimize the importance of other more intangible factors. See Fred S. Shapiro, "The Most-Cited Law Review Articles," *California Law Review* 73 (1985): 1540–1544; Fred S. Shapiro, "The Most-Cited Law Review Articles from the *Yale Law Journal*," *Yale Law Journal* 100 (1991): 1453–1458 (both discussing the rationale of citation analysis); Edward L. Rubin, "On Beyond Truth: A Theory of Evaluating Legal Scholarship," *California Law Review* 80 (1992): 889 (proposing that the legal community evaluate scholarship according to normative clarity, significance, applicability, and persuasiveness—and that divergent or insurgent scholarship be evaluated according to its ability to engender doubt and anxiety).

35. Richard Delgado, "The Imperial Scholar: Reflections on a Review of Civil Rights Literature," *University of Pennsylvania Law Review* 132 (1984): 561.

36. "Symposium on Efficiency as a Legal Concern," *Hofstra Law Review* 8 (1980): 485; "Symposium: Constitutional Adjudication and Democratic Theory," *New York University Law Review* 56 (1981): 259; "Symposium: Judicial Review Versus Democracy," *Ohio State Law Journal* 42 (1981): 1; "Symposium on Legal Scholarship: Its Nature and Purposes," *Yale Law Journal* 90 (1981): 955; "Symposium on the Legacy of the New Deal: Problems and Possibilities in the Administrative State; Part 1–2," *Yale Law Journal* 92 (1983): 1083; "Symposium: The Conceptual Foundations of Labor Law," *University of Chicago Law Review* 51 (1984): 945; "Interpretation Symposium," *Southern California Law Review* 58 (1985): 1; "[Symposium] Religion and the State," *William and Mary Law Review* 27 (1986): 833; "The Federalist Society Symposium: Federalism and Constitutional Checks and Balances: A Safeguard of Minority and Individual Rights," *Brigham Young University Law Review* 1987 (1987): 719; "[Symposium] 1787: The Constitution in Perspective," *William and Mary Law Review* 29 (1987): 1; "The Federalist Society Sixth Annual Symposium on Law and Public Policy: The Crisis in Legal Theory and the Revival of Classical Jurisprudence," *Cornell Law Review* 73 (1988): 281; "Symposium on Judicial Election, Selection and Accountability," *Southern California Law Review* 61 (1988): 1555; "Symposium: The Republican Civic Tradition," *Yale Law Journal* 97 (1988): 1493; "[Symposium] Contractual Freedom in Corporate Law," *Columbia Law Review* 89 (1989): 1395; "[Symposium] Conceptions of Democracy: The Case of Voting Rights," *Florida Law Review* 41 (1989): 409; "Symposium: Michael J. Perry's Morality, Politics, and Law," *Tulane Law Review* 63 (1989): 1283.

37. See "Critical Legal Studies Symposium," *Stanford Law Review* 36 (1984): 1.

38. "Symposium: Excluded Voices, Realities in Law and Law Reform," *University of Miami Law Review* 42 (1987): 1.

39. "Symposium: The Critique of Normativity," *University of Pennsylvania Law Review* 139 (1991): 801.

40. "Symposium: The Legal System and Homosexuality—Approbation, Accommodation, or Reprobation," *University of Dayton Law Review* 10 (1985): 445.

41. "Symposium: Law and Literature," *Mercer Law Review* 39 (1988): 739.

Chapter 6

1. There is a vast literature on the social construction of sex roles. For example, see Catharine MacKinnon, *Toward a Feminist Theory of the State* (Cambridge: Harvard University Press, 1989); Catharine MacKinnon, *Feminism Unmodified: Discourses on Life and the Law* (Cambridge: Harvard University Press, 1987); Catharine MacKinnon, *Sexual Harassment of Working Women: A Case of Sex Discrimination* (New Haven: Yale University Press, 1979); Catharine MacKinnon, "Pornography as Sex Discrimination," *Law & Inequality Journal* 4 (1986): 38; and Catharine MacKinnon, "Feminism, Marxism, Method, and the State: Toward Feminist Jurisprudence," *Signs* 8 (1983): 635. For a discussion that women begin to challenge these roles, see Andrea Dworkin and Catharine MacKinnon, *Pornography and Civil Rights: A New Day for Women's Equality* (Minneapolis: Organizing Against Pornography, 1988). For a thorough account focusing on the sexuality of women, see Judith Laws and Pepper Schwartz, *Sexual Scripts: The Social Construction of Female Sexuality* (Hinsdale, IL: Dryden Press, 1977). See also Carol Gilligan, *In a Different Voice* (Cambridge: Harvard University Press, 1982). On the special issues of black women, see bell hooks, *Ain't I a Woman: Black Women and Feminism* (Boston: South End Press, 1981). On the construction of the social world in general, see Peter L. Berger and Thomas Luckmann, *The Social Construction of Reality* (Garden City, NY: Anchor Books, 1967).

2. For an excellent historical treatment, see Sara M. Evans, *Born for Liberty: A History of Women in America* (New York: Free Press, 1989) pp. 27–34 (life on hardscrabble farms and settlements). See also Rosalyn Baxandall et al., eds., *America's Working Women* (New York: Vintage, 1976) (classic discussion of various periods in the history of the United States, including analysis of women's role, imagery, and treatment under the law).

3. For a treatment of this period and others in the history of the United States, see Angela G. Dorenkamp et al., eds., *Images of Women in Popular Culture* (San Diego: Harcourt Brace, 1985). See also Janet James, *Changing Ideas About Women in the United States, 1776–1825* (New York: Garland Publishing, 1981), pp. 6–30; Mary Ryan, *Womanhood in America*, 3rd ed. (New York: F. Watts, 1983), pp. 20–21, 24 (idea of women as derived from Adam's rib). But see June Sochen, *Enduring Values: Women in Popular Culture* (New York: Praeger, 1987), p. xiv (Eve, temptress figure, surfaces at other times). For a bibliography of media depiction of women, see Leslie J. Friedman, *Sex Role Stereotyping in the Mass Media: An Annotated Bibliography* (New York: Garland Publishing, 1977).

4. See Joan Swallow Reiter, *The Women* (Alexandria, VA: Time-Life Books, 1978), pp. 22–23.

5. James, *Changing Ideas*, pp. 40–49, 55–57; Sochen, *Enduring Values*, p. xiv; Evans, *Liberty*, p. 35.

6. "Health and Beauty," *Godey's Lady's Book* (August 1848), reprinted in Dorenkamp, ed., *Popular Culture*, p. 129.

7. Sochen, *Enduring Values*, pp. xiv, 9–10. Of course, men wrote in this vein as well. Evans, *Liberty*, pp. 68–69.

8. Evans, *Liberty*, pp. 31–37; James, *Changing Ideas*, pp. 57–63; Baxandall et al., *Working Women*, pp. 41–63, 85–125.

9. Sochen, *Enduring Values*, pp. 15–18; Baxandall et al., *Working Women*, pp. 78–80, 83. American feminism's roots can be traced to the American and French revolutions, when Abigail Adams and Mary Wollstonecraft wrote of women's rights and liberty. See, e.g., Evans, *Liberty*, pp. 45–66; James, *Changing Ideas*, pp. 65–119. On the trials of early feminists, see Evans, *Liberty*, pp. 119–143, 156–172.

10. James Gordon Bennett, "Women's Rights Convention," in *History of Woman Suffrage* 1 (1881), p. 805, reprinted in Dorenkamp, *Popular Culture*, p. 418.

11. Sochen, *Enduring Values*, pp. 3–4.

12. Id., pp. xii, 25–38, 95–102; Baxandall et al., *Working Women*, pp. 241–251, 284–298. On women's status during this period, see Evans, *Liberty*, pp. 198–204, 219–229.

13. For example, in the popular movie *Since You Went Away*, the heroine Anne Hilton is initially sheltered from the war effort and restricted to home, family, church, and social affairs. As the movie progresses, however, she makes a series of sacrifices, from giving up her maid to taking in a boarder, and in the end makes the ultimate sacrifice by becoming a welder in the shipyard. She receives male approval, affirming "not only the housewife-heroine's willingness to get a war job, but her conduct through the war (especially [her] loyalty to [her husband])." M. Joyce Baker, *Images of Women in Film: The War Years, 1941–1945* (Ann Arbor, MI: UMI Research Press, 1980), pp. 96–110.

14. Evans, *Liberty*, pp. 243–250 (development of "feminine mystique" idea); Sochen, *Enduring Values*, pp. 35–38; Baxandall et al., *Working Women*, pp. 299–313.

15. Susan Brownmiller, "Confessions: 'He Made Me Do It!'" in *Against Our Will: Men, Women, and Rape*, p. 381, reprinted in Dorenkamp, *Popular Culture*, p. 152.

16. Sochen, *Enduring Values*, pp. 19–20.

17. Id., pp. 61–74.

18. For a cultural history of pornography, see Walter Kendrick, *The Secret Museum: Pornography in Modern Culture* (New York: Viking Press, 1987). See also Richard Kyle-Keith, *The High Price of Pornography* (Washington: Public Affairs Press, 1961).

19. Kyle-Keith, *High Price*, pp. 27–30. The nation's first antiobscenity law was passed on March 3, 1865, making it a federal offense to mail matter of an obscene nature.

20. Kendrick, *Museum*, pp. 129–130. Earlier, *Adventures of Huckleberry Finn* had been banned from the library at Concord, Massachusetts, when Louisa May Alcott wrote that Mr. Clemens (Mark Twain) should have better things to write about. Kyle-Keith, *High Price*, p. 32.

21. Kendrick, *Museum*, pp. 67, 188–189. See Ronald J. Berger et al., *Feminism and Pornography* (New York: Praeger, 1991), pp. 7–9.

22. Kyle-Keith, *High Price*, pp. 31–34; Dan Brown and Jennings Bryant, "The Manifest Content of Pornography," in Dolf Zillman and Jennings Bryant, eds., *Pornography: Research Advances and Policy Considerations* (Hillsdale, NJ: L. Erlbaum Associates, 1989), pp. 4–7; Berger et al., *Feminism*, p. 44.

23. Brown and Bryant, "Manifest Content," in Zillman and Bryant, *Research Advances*, pp. 9, 14–20; Judith Hill, "Pornography and Degradation," in Robert M. Baird and Stuart E. Rosenbaum, eds., *Pornography: Private Right or Public Menace?* (Buffalo: Prometheus Books, 1991), pp. 62, 70 ($7 billion-a-year business); William A. Linsley, "The Case Against Censorship of Pornography," in Baird and Rosenbaum, *Private Right*, p. 138; Linda Williams, *Hard Core: Power, Pleasure and the "Frenzy of the Visible"* (Berkeley: University of California Press, 1989), pp. 96–100.

24. E.g., Berger et al., *Feminism*, pp. 7–8, 17–20, 25–26; Kyle-Keith, *High Price*, pp. 212–220.

25. Dworkin and MacKinnon, *New Day*, pp. 31–57 (explaining particular provisions of ordinance), p. 99 (Appendix A: The Minneapolis Ordinance). The ordinance also appears in Catharine A. MacKinnon, "Pornography, Civil Rights and Speech," *Harvard Civil Rights–Civil Liberties Law Review* 20 (1985): 1–2 n.1.

26. See Nan D. Hunter and Sylvia A. Law, "Brief Amici Curiae of Feminist Anti-Censorship Taskforce, et al.," in *American Booksellers Association v. Hudnut, University of Michigan Journal of Law Reform* 21 (1988): 70, 89 (describing FACT organization).

27. *American Booksellers, Inc. v. Hudnut*, 771 F.2d 323 (7th Cir. 1985), aff'd, 475 U.S. 1001 (1986) (civil rights antipornography ordinance found to violate First Amendment).

28. Dworkin and MacKinnon, *New Day*, pp. 76–81, 84.

29. Hunter and Law, "Brief Amici Curiae," pp. 71–75, 112–118, 125–132. Elson, "Passions over Pornography," *Time*, March 30, 1992, pp. 52–53.

30. Dworkin and MacKinnon, *New Day*, pp. 76–81, 84.

31. See *Regina v. Butler*, 89 D.L.R.4th 449 (1992).

32. Cynthia Tucker, "Rape Does Hurt Somebody," *San Francisco Chronicle*, April 6, 1992, p. A16.

33. Nancy Gibbs, "When Is It Rape?" *Time*, June 3, 1991, p. 54. Another example, in a different context, occurred when Japanese Prime Minister Kiichi Miyazawa commented that American workers struck him as lazy and unproductive and "may lack a work ethic," a charge that made national headlines. On questioning, it appeared that the basis of his observation lay in the finding of Kabun Moto, former Japanese Minister of International Trade and Industry, that American workers worked essentially a three-day week, being consumed by their weekend plans on Friday and recovering from the weekend on Monday. Americans were outraged; to Americans this behavior seemed normal, whereas the Japanese pattern of behavior seemed unhuman and robotic. See David E. Sanger, "Japan Premier Critical of Americans' Work Habits," *New York Times*, February 4, 1992, p. A1. But see Steven R. Weisman, "More Japanese Demanding Shorter Hours and Less Hectic Work," *New York Times*, March 3, 1992, p. A8 (commenting that Americans work fewer hours but more intensely).

34. Anthony D'Amato, "A New Political Truth: Exposure to Sexually Violent Materials Causes Sexual Violence," *William & Mary Law Review* 31 (1990): 576–585.

35. Larry Baron and Murray A. Straus, *Four Theories of Rape in American Society* (New Haven: Yale University Press, 1989), pp. 95–124; D'Amato, "Political Truth," pp. 585, 588–590; Hunter and Law, "Brief Amici Curiae," pp. 113, 115–117; Thelma McCormack, "Making Sense of the Research on Pornography," in Varda Burstyn et al., ed., *Women Against Censorship* (Vancouver: Douglas & McIntyre, 1985), pp. 183, 192.

36. MacKinnon, "Civil Rights and Speech," pp. 16–18, 22, 27; Andrea Dworkin, "Pornography and Grief," in Laura Lederer, *Take Back the Night: Women on Pornography* (New York: Morrow, 1980), pp. 286–288; Hill, "Pornography and Degradation," pp. 62–66.

37. See Alan Soble, "Defamation and the Endorsement of Pornography," in Baird and Rosenbaum, *Private Right*, pp. 96, 99–101 (degradation in eye of beholder; no empirical proof it occurs broadly). For a different "translation," see Kendrick, *Museum*, p. 232 (male author translates MacKinnon's *per se* degradation-social construction of women thesis into one *about men*: "I don't feel degraded").

38. MacKinnon, "Civil Rights and Speech," pp. 16–17, 53–55. On the teaching function of pornography, see Edward Dinnerstein and Leonard Berkowitz, "Victim Reactions in Aggressive Erotic Films as a Factor in Violence Against Women," *Journal of Personality & Social Psychology* 41 (October 1981): 710; Doug McKenzie-Mohr and Marla P. Zanna, "Treating Women as Sexual Objects: Look to the (Gender Schematic) Male Who Has Viewed Pornography," *Personality and Social Psychology* 16 (June 1990): 296; Robin Morgan, "Theory and Practice: Pornography and Rape," in Lederer, *Take Back the Night*, pp. 134, 139 (arguing that pornography is the theory, rape the practice).

39. See, e.g., *Columbia University Seminars on Media and Society: Safe Speech, Free Speech, and the University* (PBS television broadcast, June 1991) (American Civil Liberties Union president Nadine Strossen describing leering and whistling at women postulated in moderator's hypothetical as [a] inoffensive and [b] protected speech); Brown and Bryant, "Manifest Content," in Zillman and Bryant, *Research Advances*, pp. 3–4.

40. Compare MacKinnon, "Civil Rights and Speech," pp. 1, 8, 16–18, 22, 27 (social construction of women; desensitization thesis) and Chapter 2 (noting similar response to ethnic depiction) with Henry J. Reske, "Stroh's Ads Targeted," *American Bar Association Journal*, February 1992, p. 20. On these issues, see also F. H. Christensen, "Elicitation of Violence: The Evidence," in Baird and Rosenbaum, *Private Right*, pp. 221, 222–223 (correlation complex), pp. 233–235 (violent depiction does seem to trigger much "low level" aggression against women).

41. See Dworkin and MacKinnon, *New Day*, pp. 34–35; Elson, "Passions," p. 52 (discussing copycat sexual violence carried out by men who consumed pornography). In the early 1970s, a nine-year-old girl was the victim of a brutal bottle rape perpetrated by neighborhood youths. Subsequently, a suit was filed against NBC alleging that a made-for-television movie, *Born Innocent*, served as the catalyst for the attack. The prime-time movie graphically depicted reformatory schoolgirls raping a classmate with the handle of a plunger. Morton Mintz, "Worries About

TV Violence Persistent: Suit Against NBC Raised Question, Jury Never Got a Chance to Decide," *Washington Post*, August 14, 1978, p. A2.

42. E.g., Hunter and Law, "Brief Amici Curiae," pp. 113, 127–128 (dismissing incident as exceptional or idiosyncratic; "men are not attack dogs").

43. Further, considerable evidence suggests that exposure to sexually violent or degrading materials correlates with an increase in the likelihood of aggression in general and in particular greater acceptance of the rape myth—that women enjoy being coerced into sexual activity, that they enjoy being physically hurt in a sexual context, and that as a result a man who forces himself on a woman sexually is merely acceding to the "real" wishes of the woman. E.g., Baird and Rosenbaum, *Private Right*, pp. 41–42 (reprinting portions of the Attorney General's Commission on Pornography: Final Report [1986]).

44. Hunter and Law, "Brief Amici Curiae," pp. 102–105 (ordinance reinforces "double standard" according to which women are prim, frail, and in need of protection); 13–31 (deprives women of choice to express their sexuality in this way); see Susan Brownmiller, "Women Fight Back," in Baird and Rosenbaum, *Private Right*, p. 39 (reformers like herself accused of being square or prissy); Barbara Dority, "Feminist Moralism, 'Pornography,' and Censorship," in Baird and Rosenbaum, *Private Right*, pp. 111–116 (accusing proregulation feminists of being moralistic, antisex, and Victorian in their attitudes and program of reform).

45. Susan Brownmiller, *Against Our Will: Men, Women, and Rape* (New York: Simon & Schuster, 1975); Andrea Dworkin, *Intercourse* (New York: Free Press, 1987) (both arguing that systematic sexual violence against women is tacitly permitted or encouraged by men and that much intercourse is not fully consensual on the woman's part and could therefore be seen as rape).

Chapter 7

1. Joseph Sax, "The Public Trust Doctrine in Natural Resource Law: Effective Judicial Intervention," *Michigan Law Review* 68 (1970): 474–489, 553–561. The doctrine satisfies three simple criteria for a theory of environmental protection. It provides a legal right in the public; it is enforceable against the government; and it is likely to protect current standards of environmental quality. Sax's later work includes: Joseph Sax, "Liberating the Public Trust Doctrine from Its Historical Shackles," *University of California at Davis Law Review* 14 (1980): 185; Joseph Sax, *Mountains Without Handrails* (Ann Arbor: University of Michigan Press, 1980); Joseph Sax, "The Limits of Private Rights in Public Waters," *Environmental Law* 19 (1989): 473.

2. For a general history of the period, see Samuel P. Hays, *Beauty, Health and Permanence: Environmental Politics in the United States, 1955–1985* (New York: Cambridge University Press, 1987). The early 1970s culminated in a famous debate about plastic trees and the theoretical bases for environmental protection. See, e.g., Krieger, "What's Wrong with Plastic Trees?" *Science* 179 (1973): 446; Laurence Tribe, "Ways Not to Think About Plastic Trees: New Foundations for Environmental Law," *Yale Law Journal* 83 (1974): 1315; Christopher D. Stone, "Should Trees Have Standing?—Toward Legal Rights for Natural Objects," *Southern California*

Law Review 45 (1972): 450; Timothy O'Riordan, *Environmentalism* (London: Pion, 1976); John Passmore, *Man's Responsibility for Nature* (London: Duckworth, 1974); Charles J. Meyers, "An Introduction to Environmental Thought: Some Sources and Some Criticisms," *Indiana Law Journal* 50 (1975): 426; White, "The Historical Roots of Our Ecological Crisis," *Science* 155 (1967): 1203; Rachel Carson, *Silent Spring* (Boston: Houghton Mifflin, 1962) (presaging 1970s activism); Stewart L. Udall, *The Quiet Crisis* (New York: Holt, Rinehart and Winston, 1963).

3. Sax, "Public Trust," pp. 484, 490, 560.

4. 42 U.S.C. §§ 4321–4370a (National Environmental Policy Act). The Act first passed Congress and has been amended a number of times. On the Act's history and interpretation, see Frederick R. Anderson, Daniel R. Mandelker, and A. Dan Tarlock, *Environmental Protection: Law and Policy*, 2d ed. (Boston: Little, Brown, 1990), pp. 781–840; George Cameron Coggins and Charles F. Wilkinson, *Federal Public Land and Resources Law*, 2d ed. (Westbury, NY: Foundation Press, 1986), pp. 321–356.

5. See, e.g., *West Indian Co. v. Government of Virgin Islands*, 844 F.2d 1007, 1019 (3d Cir.), cert. denied sub. nom.; *Gressing v. West Indian Co.*, 488 U.S. 802 (1988); *District of Columbia v. Air Florida, Inc.*, 750 F.2d 1077, 1083 (D.C. Cir. 1984); *Sierra Club v. Block*, 622 F. Supp. 842, 866, n. 15 (D. Colo. 1985); *Commonwealth of Puerto Rico v. S. S. Zoe Colocotroni*, 456 F. Supp. 1327, 1337 (D.P.R. 1978), aff'd in part & vacated in part, 628 F.2d 652 (1st Cir. 1980), cert. denied, 450 U.S. 912 (1981).

6. Sax, "Public Trust," pp. 475–476, 485–491. Early Supreme Court cases that cite trust language include *Illinois Central R.R. v. Illinois*, 146 U.S. 387, 451–463 (1892); *Martin v. Waddell*, 41 U.S. 367 (1842).

7. Charles F. Wilkinson, "The Headwaters of the Public Trust: Some Thoughts on the Source and Scope of the Traditional Doctrine," *Environmental Law* 19 (1989): 465–466. See also Michael C. Blumm, "Public Property and the Democratization of Water Law: A Modern View of the Public Trust Doctrine," *Environmental Law* 19 (1989): 574–575; Scott W. Reed, "The Public Trust Doctrine: Is It Amphibious?" *Journal of Environmental Law and Litigation* 1 (1986): 107.

8. See Gary D. Meyers, "Variations on a Theme: Expanding the Public Trust Doctrine to Include Protection of Wildlife," *Environmental Law* 19 (1989): 724–731 (arguing that all ecosystems are related, so trust theory, although it originated in the area of water rights, now is being extended logically to land and forests); Wilkinson, "Headwaters," p. 466; Charles Wilkinson, "The Public Trust Doctrine in Public Land Law," *University of California at Davis Law Review* 14 (1980): 298.

9. 42 U.S.C.A. §§ 4321–4370a. See also *Kieppe v. Sierra Club*, 427 U.S. 390, 409–411 (1976) (requiring that an executive agency take a "hard look" at adverse environmental impacts); Coggins and Wilkinson, *Federal Public*, pp. 355–356.

10. 33 U.S.C. §§ 1251(5), 1344 (1988).

11. 16 U.S.C. §§ 1531–1542 (1988). Of course, some serious environmentalists regard these statutes as corrupt and ineffectual almost by design. For them, Sax's role in setting them up is not an honor but the opposite.

12. Jan S. Stevens, "The Public Trust and In-Stream Uses," *Environmental Law* 19 (1989): 638; Wilkinson, "Headwaters," pp. 465–466 (listing statutes); Wilkinson, "Public Trust," pp. 269–278.

13. James L. Huffman, "A Fish Out of Water: The Public Trust Doctrine in a Constitutional Democracy," *Environmental Law* 19 (1989): 527; Richard Lazarus, "Changing Conceptions of Property and Sovereignty in Natural Resources: Questioning the Public Trust Doctrine," *Iowa Law Review* 71 (1986): 631.

14. James P. Karp, "Aldo Leopold's Land Ethic: Is an Ecological Conscience Evolving in Land Development Law?" *Environmental Law* 19 (1989): 738–749; Donald Scherer, "Anthropocentrism, Atomism, and Environmental Ethics," in Donald Scherer and Thomas Attig, eds., *Ethics and the Environment*, 2d ed. (Englewood Cliffs, NJ: Prentice-Hall, 1983), p. 73.

15. George T. Bogert, *Trusts*, 6th ed. (St. Paul: West Publishing Co., 1987), Sec. 1 at 2–3, Secs. 2–3 at 7–10, and Secs. 8–11 at 19–25.

16. See, e.g., Christopher D. Stone, *Earth and Other Ethics: The Case for Moral Pluralism* (New York: Harper & Row, 1987); Paul W. Taylor, *Respect for Nature: A Theory of Environmental Ethics* (Princeton, NJ: Princeton University Press, 1986); Gary Goodpaster, "On Being Morally Considerable," in Scherer and Attig, *Ethics and the Environment*, p. 30.

17. Another view is that fewer women establish trusts than men because they lack the resources to do so or because men control estate planning. The very idea of a trust was developed by men, and not women, centuries ago when men's values and ideas predominated. Would it be so surprising if it served as a vehicle for advancing values and plans men hold dear?

18. See Homer, *The Odyssey*, R. Fitzgerald, trans. (Garden City, NY: Anchor Books, 1963). The sirens' song was so seductive it lured sailors from their course and shipwrecked them against the rocks. The mariners' standard solution was to stop their ears. Odysseus, however, wanted to hear the song, so he ordered his crew to stop their ears and sail through while he kept his ears open, his body strapped down to combat temptation. In this way he enjoyed the fruits of the song without paying the penalty; his crew, with their stopped ears, suffered the deprivation of the song for him. The parallels go further. In uncanny similarity, the resource-intensive industrialized world has strapped itself to the mast of the developing world, causing the developing world to suffer much of the environmental predation and degradation necessary to keep the ears of the industrial nations open to hear the song of their own rich lifestyle. A tale for our time.

19. Such values include consumerism and comfort over conservation; development over wilderness preservation; earth-belongs-to-man; what-is-best-for-us-is-best-for-the-world; and so on.

20. In this case, most "trustees" will be government bureaucrats—generally male, white, middle class, and with little passion or zeal for environmental innovation.

21. Some small gains, of course, may come about because, unlike us, the governmental agent (1) feels responsible; (2) knows he or she is accountable; and (3) learns from past errors—i.e., is a repeat player. See Marc Galanter, "Why the 'Haves' Come Out Ahead: Speculations on the Limits of Legal Change," *Law & Society Review* 9 (1974): 95.

22. Most experts believe air and water quality has improved little if at all, while the problem of toxic waste has worsened markedly over the last decade or so. See Paul R. Portney, "Air Pollution Policy," in Paul R. Portney, ed., *Public Policies for*

Environmental Protection (Washington: Resources for the Future, 1990), pp. 27, 49–52. Toxic waste problems also present a gloomy picture. See Roger C. Dower, "Hazardous Wastes," in Portney, *Public Policies*, pp. 151, 167 (stating that better-financed firms are beginning to shift production processes and inputs to reduce waste produced).

The Comprehensive Environmental Response, Compensation and Liability Act of 1980 (CERCLA), 42 U.S.C. §§ 9601–9657 (1988), was an attempt to clean up already existing toxic sites. It, too, has moved neither far nor fast. "After nearly 12 years, the Superfund program has cleaned up no more than 5 percent of the nearly 1200 sites listed on the national priorities list." From John T. Ronan III, "A Clean Sweep on Cleanup," *The Recorder*, September 30, 1992, p. 10.

This lack of progress on air and water quality and on hazardous waste problems is due in part to the sheer magnitude of any attempted cleanup. It, however, is also due in part to the inertia of preconceived, set ways of dealing with the problems.

23. Aldo Leopold, "A Sand County Almanac and Sketches Here and There," reprinted in *A Sand County Almanac with Other Essays on Conservation from Round River* (New York: Oxford University Press, 1966), p. 240.

24. Id., pp. 219–230.

25. Kenneth E. Boulding, "Economics of the Coming Spaceship Earth," in Henry Jarrett, ed., *Environmental Quality in a Growing Economy* (Baltimore: Johns Hopkins Press, 1966), p. 3.

26. For a collection of essays on Native American thought on nature and the environment, see Christopher T. Vecsey and Robert W. Venables, eds., *American Indian Environments: Ecological Issues in Native American History* (Syracuse: Syracuse University Press, 1980). Other writings include Rennard Strickland, "The Idea of Environment and the Ideal of the Indian," *Journal of American Indian Education* 10 (1970): 8; N. Scott Momaday, "An American Land Ethic," in John G. Mitchell, ed., *Ecotactics: The Sierra Club Handbook for Environmental Activists* (New York: Pocket Books, 1970), p. 97. For works on the general subject of Indians and the land, see, e.g. Vine Deloria, Jr., *We Talk, You Listen: New Tribes, New Truth* (New York: Macmillan, 1970), pp. 86, 194, 197; Wilbur R. Jacobs, *Dispossessing the American Indian* (New York: Scribners, 1972), pp. 19–30. See also David Getches, "A Philosophy of Permanence: The Indians' Legacy for the West," *Journal of the West* (July 1990), pp. 54–55, 64, 67. For the view that the Native American cultures did not attain a high level of environmental consciousness, see Calvin Martin, *Keepers of the Game* (Berkeley: University of California Press, 1978).

27. Seathe, "Dead, Did I Say? There Is No Death ... ," in Shirley Hill Witt and Stan Steiner, eds., *The Way: An Anthology of American Indian Literature* (New York: Knopf, 1972), pp. 28–29. Recently, the authenticity of this passage, although not its general content, has been drawn into question. See Jerry L. Clark, "Thus Spoke Chief Seattle: The Story of an Undocumented Speech," *Prologue* (Spring 1965): p. 58.

28. See, e.g., the collection of writings in *American Indian Environments*. Even the Supreme Court began to take note of the relationship between Native Americans and the land. In *Federal Power Comm'n v. Tuscarora Indian Nation*, 362 U.S. 99 (1960), J. Black in dissent stated:

It may be hard for us to understand why these Indians cling so tenaciously to their lands and traditional way of life. The record does not leave the impression that the lands ... are the most fertile, the landscape the most beautiful. ... But this is their home—ancestral home. There they, their children, and their forbears were born. They, too, have their memories and their loves. Some things are worth more than money.

Id. at 142 (Black, J., dissenting).

29. For a collection of essays, see Irene Diamond and Gloria Fenam Orenstein, eds., *Reweaving the World: The Emergence of Ecofeminism* (San Francisco: Sierra Club Books, 1990).

30. For more general discussions of feminism and feminist legal theory, see Katharine T. Bartlett, "Feminist Legal Methods," *Harvard Law Review* 103 (1990): 829; Ann C. Scales, "The Emergence of Feminist Jurisprudence: An Essay," *Yale Law Journal* 95 (1986): 1373; Robin West, "Jurisprudence and Gender," *University of Chicago Law Review* 55 (1988): 1. On patriarchy, see Diane Polan, "Toward a Theory of Love and Patriarchy," in David Kairys, ed., *The Politics of Law: A Progressive Critique* (New York: Pantheon Books, 1982), p. 294. On the connection between patriarchy (and men's values generally) and environmental despoliation, see Gloria Fenam Orenstein, *The Reflowering of the Goddess* (New York: Pergamon Press, 1990). For the view that law and legal culture are male in approach and mindset, see Carrie Menkel-Meadow, "Portia in a Different Voice: Speculations on a Woman's Lawyering Process," *Berkeley Women's Law Journal* 1 (1985): 39; Nadine Taub and Elizabeth M. Schneider, "Perspectives on Women's Subordination and the Role of Law," in *Politics of Law*, p. 117. See also "Ecofeminism: Healing Mother Earth," *Business Wire,* April 17, 1990, available in the on-line LEXIS Library, BWIRE File (reporting an interview with author G. Orenstein).

One of the themes missing from current environmental thought that ecofeminism provides is the notion of interconnectedness. Environmental problems of a global nature (e.g., overpopulation, the ozone hole, global warming) demand the realization not only that all humankind is interrelated and interdependent across national boundaries but that all things on this earth, alive and inert, are interrelated. More than this, the ecofeminists expand the feminist theories of domination of women to domination of the entire ecosystem. They thus are acutely aware of the damage that a hierarchical view of nature (with man—not merely humans—at the top) has done to our ability to understand and live with and within nature.

A seriously considered ecofeminism would reject the kind of environmental protection that protects the environment for someone (either for oneself or for future generations). The environment is protected because it is a part of us just as we are a part of it. Indeed, "interconnection" is almost too weak a word—what is necessary is a recognition of the essential unity between people and nature. Women share with nature the experience of being the other in a world dominated by men whose interests are often foreign, if not inimical, to their own. It is precisely this pattern of hierarchical separation and domination that has led us to the current environmental crisis. Only when our approach is supplanted by a more integrated, empathic, feminist one will we be able to address that crisis effectively.

31. On normativity in law and legal analysis and scholarship, see Symposium, "The Critique of Normativity," *University of Pennsylvania Law Review* 139 (1991): 801; Pierre Schlag, "Normative and Nowhere to Go," *Stanford Law Review* 43 (1991): 167. See also Richard Delgado, "Norms and Normal Science: Toward a Critique of Normativity in Legal Thought," *University of Pennsylvania Law Review* 139 (1991): 942–944; Pierre Schlag, "Normativity and the Politics of Form," *University of Pennsylvania Law Review* 139 (1991): 906–909.

32. E.g., Thomas S. Kuhn, *The Structure of Scientific Revolutions,* 2d ed. (Chicago: University of Chicago Press, 1970).

33. In feminism the individual who set the revolution on a softer, more acceptable course was Carol Gilligan. In critical race theory, Randall Kennedy both condemned and praised the old order. In critical legal studies Roberto Unger's scholarly writing and utopian vision made the movement acceptable to a wide audience.

34. On the notion that legal reform movements are often transformative and conservative at the same time, see Kimberlè Crenshaw, "Race, Reform and Retrenchment," *Harvard Law Review* 101 (1988): 1331.

35. Compare Richard Delgado, "Derrick Bell and the Ideology of Racial Reform: Will We Ever Be Saved?" *Yale Law Journal* 97 (1988): 923 (arguing that our broad system of civil rights laws comforts and assures us that blacks are no longer actively repressed, thereby enabling us to maintain an unfair and unjust racial status quo).

Chapter 8

1. See Richard Delgado, "Storytelling for Oppositionists and Others: A Plea for Narrative," *Michigan Law Review* 87 (1989): 2411; Pierre Schlag, "Normative and Nowhere to Go," *Stanford Law Review* 43 (1990): 167; Stephen L. Winter, "An Upside/Down View of the Countermajoritarian Difficulty," *Texas Law Review* 69 (1991): 1881. See also Maurice Merleau-Ponty, *Sense and Non-Sense* (Evanston, IL: Northwestern University Press, 1964).

2. See Schlag, "Normative"; see generally Symposium, "The Critique of Normativity," *University of Pennsylvania Law Review* 139 (1991): 801 (discussing ways in which the dominant forms of legal discourse mystify and misdirect our efforts). See also Richard Delgado, "Mindset and Metaphor," *Harvard Law Review* 103 (1990): 1872 (noting that the structures and metaphors of legal discourse mislead).

3. For an amusing treatment of these standoffs of legal and popular proverbs, see Jeremy Paul, "The Politics of Legal Semiotics," *Texas Law Review* 69 (1991): 1786, 1816.

4. William L. Prosser, *Handbook of the Law of Torts,* 4th ed. (St. Paul: West Publishing Co., 1971), pp. 149–150; John P. Calamari and Joseph M. Perillo, *Contracts,* 1st ed. (St. Paul: West Publishing Co., 1970), pp. 23–25, 118–123, 328–329.

5. 112 S. Ct. 2608 (1992).

6. See Richard Delgado and Helen Leskovac, "Informed Consent in Human Experimentation: Bridging the Gap Between Ethical Thought and Current Practice,"

UCLA Law Review 34 (1986): 67. See generally Jay Katz, *The Silent World of Doctor and Patient* (New York: Free Press, 1984) (discussing the doctor-patient relationship).

7. 502 P.2d 1, 11 (Cal. 1972).

8. Delgado and Leskovac, "Informed Consent." See also Robert A. Burt, *Taking Care of Strangers: The Rule of Law in Doctor-Patient Relations* (New York: Free Press, 1979) (proposing dialogic or partnership approach to doctor-patient interaction); Katz, *Silent* (proposing radical reform in way we think about the potential physician relationship).

9. N. Jan Almquist, "When the Truth Can Hurt: Patient-Mediated Informed Consent in Cancer Therapy," *UCLA-Alaska Law Review* 9 (1980): 143.

10. Nancy Gibbs, "When Is it Rape?" *Time,* June 3, 1991, p. 48; Philip Weiss, "The Second Revolution—Sexual Politics on Campus: A Case Study," *Harper's Magazine,* April 1991, p. 58.

11. See Gibbs, "Rape," p. 52 (discussing a rape charge as a second thought brought the morning after, or even a month after, the incident); Weiss, "Second Revolution," pp. 59–62, 66–67; Ellen Goodman, "He Says Date, She Says Rape," *Boulder Daily Camera* (Colorado), May 3, 1991, p. 10-A.

12. These are the standard arguments used to justify objective liability rules in general. See, e.g., Alice Kahn, " 'Date Rape' Studies Called Exaggerated," *San Francisco Chronicle,* May 31, 1991, p. A1 (activists "trivialize" rape by broadening its definition beyond reason, equating "sweet talk" with coercion, pressure with force, and a drink with intoxication).

13. For a discussion of the way in which elaborate scripts or arguments over "principle" often conceal something else, see Richard Delgado, "Norms and Normal Science: Toward a Critique of Normativity in Legal Thought," *University of Pennsylvania Law Review* 139 (1991): 933; Pierre Schlag, "Normativity and the Politics of Form, *University of Pennsylvania Law Review* 139 (1991): 801.

14. For a discussion of the connection between rules and power, see Mark Kelman, *A Guide to Critical Legal Studies* (Cambridge: Harvard University Press, 1987), pp. 15–63. See also the storm of criticism that followed the release of *Ellison v. Brady,* 924 F.2d 872 (9th Cir. 1991) ("reasonable woman" case); Lisa Stansky, "The Reasonable Jurist," *The Recorder,* November 20, 1991, p. 1.

15. See Peter L. Berger and Thomas Luckmann, *The Social Construction of Reality* (Garden City, NY: Anchor Books, 1967); Nelson Goodman, *Ways of Worldmaking* (Indianapolis: Hackett Publishing Co., 1978); Paul Ricoeur, *Time and Narrative* (Chicago: University of Chicago Press, 1984).

16. See Jean Stefancic and Richard Delgado, "Outsider Jurisprudence and the Electronic Revolution: Will Technology Help or Hinder the Cause of Law Reform?" *Ohio State Law Journal* 52 (1991): 847 (explaining the term "outsider jurisprudence" as applied to the oppositional writing of gays, lesbians, and persons of color, among others). On outsider jurisprudence, see generally Mari Matsuda, "Looking to the Bottom: Critical Legal Studies and Reparations," *Harvard Civil Rights–Civil Liberties Law Review* 22 (1987): 323.

17. For a discussion of the legal storytelling movement, see "Symposium, Legal Storytelling," *Michigan Law Review* 87 (1989): 2073.

18. See Michel Foucault, *Power/Knowledge: Selected Interviews and Other Writings, 1972–1977* (New York: Pantheon Books, 1980); Jacques Derrida, *Of Grammatology* (Baltimore: Johns Hopkins University Press, 1976); Antonio Gramsci, *Selections from the Prison Notebooks* (New York: International Publishers, 1971).

19. See Richard Delgado, "Derrick Bell and the Ideology of Racial Reform: Will We Ever Be Saved," *Yale Law Journal* 97 (1988): 931 (discussing the role of sincerity in the liberal's justification of the world as it is).

20. This is a classic but poor argument against subjective rules because it obscures the role of power.

21. For a discussion of the view that men construct women and women's role to suit their own interests, see Catharine A. MacKinnon, *Feminism Unmodified: Discourses on Life and Law* (Cambridge: Harvard University Press, 1987).

22. Id.; see also Andrea Dworkin, *Intercourse* (New York: Free Press, 1987); Gibbs, "Rape," p. 51.

23. See Delgado, "Oppositionists," pp. 2412–2414; Derrick Bell, *And We Are Not Saved: The Elusive Quest for Racial Justice* (New York: Basic Books, 1987) (telling series of "Chronicles" aimed at exposing mean or self-serving nature of majoritarian law and beliefs regarding civil rights and racial justice); Patricia J. Williams, *The Alchemy of Race and Rights* (Cambridge: Harvard University Press, 1991) (discourse of law perpetuates white-over-black injustice).

24. Robin West is the prime advocate of the view that women must tell and retell their stories of patriarchy and sexual oppression. See Robin West, "Authority, Autonomy, and Choice: The Role of Consent in the Moral and Political Visions of Franz Kafka and Richard Posner," *Harvard Law Review* 99 (1985): 384. See also Patricia Meisol, "A New Genre of Legal Scholarship: Storytelling Feminist Takes on the Fundamentals of Law," *Los Angeles Times*, October 7, 1988, p. V8 ("We need to flood the market with our stories until we get one simple point across").

25. Charles R. Lawrence III, "The Id, the Ego, and Equal Protection: Reckoning with Unconscious Racism," *Stanford Law Review* 39 (1987): 317.

26. Id., pp. 317–339, 351–374.

27. See Darryl Brown, "Racism and Race Relations in the University," *Virginia Law Review* 76 (1990): 295; Richard Delgado, "Recasting the American Race Problem," *California Law Review* 79 (1991): 1389.

28. We are grateful to Steven Winter for this metaphor.

Chapter 9

1. Joseph T. Shipley, *The Origins of English Words* (Baltimore: Johns Hopkins University Press, 1984), p. 441; see also Charles T. Onions, ed., *Oxford Dictionary of English Etymology* (New York: Oxford University Press, 1966), p. 45.

2. *United States v. Carolene Products, Inc.*, 304 U.S. 144, 152 n.4 (1938).

3. Voltaire, *Candide and Other Writings* (1759; reprint, New York: Modern Library, 1956). For further discussion of Voltaire and his work, see Peter Gay, *Voltaire's Politics: The Poet as Realist* (New Haven: Yale University Press, 1988); Theodore Besterman, *Voltaire*, 3d ed. (Oxford: Blackwell, 1976).

4. Jonathan Swift, *Gulliver's Travels* (1726; reprint, Indianapolis: Bobbs Merrill, 1963).

5. "Let them eat cake," attributed to the soon-to-be-beheaded queen on the occasion of being informed that her subjects were hungry and lacked bread. *The Oxford Dictionary of Quotations*, 2d ed. (New York: Oxford University Press, 1953).

6. Robin Sowerby, ed., *Alexander Pope, Selected Poetry and Prose* (New York: Routledge, 1988). See particularly *Epistle to Miss Blount with the Works of Boiture* (1712), p. 55; *To Miss M.B. on Her Birthday* (1724), p. 149; *Epistle to a Lady: Of the Characters of Women* (1735), p. 158.

7. Sigmund Freud, *Jokes and Their Relation to the Unconscious* (1905; reprint, New York: Norton, 1963), p. 200; Leonard Feinberg, *Introduction to Satire* (Ames: Iowa State University Press, 1967), pp. 6, 10, 30, 206–209, 220–221; Wayne Booth, *A Rhetoric of Irony* (Chicago: University of Chicago Press, 1974), pp. 47–86. See also D. C. Muecke, *The Compass of Irony* (London: Methuen, 1969).

8. John Warrington, ed., *Juvenal's Satires I* (1802; reprint, New York: Dutton, 1954), p. ix.

9. Jean Baptiste Poquelin de Molière, *Tartuffe* act I, scene 5 (1664; reprint, New York: Modern Library, 1924).

10. Samuel Clemens [Mark Twain], *A Connecticut Yankee in King Arthur's Court* (New York: Norton, 1982); H. L. Mencken, *Notes on Democracy* (New York: Knopf, 1926); Sinclair Lewis, *Babbitt* (New York: Modern Library, 1922); Russell Baker, *There's a Country in My Cellar* (New York: Morrow, 1990).

11. Charles Dickens, *Martin Chuzzlewit* (London: Chapman and Hall, 1844). On Hogarth and his drawing, see Francis D. Klingender, ed., *Hogarth and English Caricature* (London: Transatlantic Arts, 1944). On parody generally, see Linda Hutcheon, *A Theory of Parody: The Teachings of Twentieth-Century Art Forms* (New York: Methuen, 1985). On caricature generally, see Feinberg, *Introduction*, pp. 116–119.

12. Feinberg, *Introduction*, pp. 108–112, 180, 184–192, 201–205, 207–210.

13. Northrop Frye, *Anatomy of Criticism: Four Essays* (Princeton: Princeton University Press, 1957), p. 223. A classic example of ironic insincere praise is found in Voltaire, *Candide*, p. 143. (Two opposing generals, after a battle, return to their tents, and each thanks God for their great victory. The statement depicts the generals as pious, but in the next instant, the reader realizes they are vain, self-deluding fools.)

14. *Department of Justice v. Landano*, 61 U.S.L.W. 4485, 4486, 4489 (May 24, 1993).

15. *Tennessee Valley Authority v. Hill*, 437 U.S. 153, 160, 187, 194 (1977).

16. 347 U.S. 483, 494–495 (1954) ("Brown I"); 349 U.S. 294, 300–301 (1955) ("Brown II").

17. E.g., *United States v. Nixon*, 418 U.S. 683, 704 (1974).

18. 274 U.S. 200, 205, 207–208 (1927).

19. 163 U.S. 537, 538–540, 543, 551 (1896).

20. 448 U.S. 371, 374–384, 424, 435 (1980).

21. Id. at 436–437, quoting Samuel Morison, *The Oxford History of the American People* (New York: Oxford University Press, 1965), pp. 539–540.

22. Id. at 435.

23. 497 U.S. 871, 889 (1990).

24. 112 S. Ct. 2130, 2135, 2138, 2139 (1992).

25. Id. at 2154 (Blackmun, J., dissenting).

26. *Merritt v. Faulkner,* 823 F.2d 1150, 1157 (7th Cir.), cert. denied, 464 U.S. 986 (1987); see also McKeever v. Israel, 689 F.2d 1315, 1323 (7th Cir. 1982); Free v. United States, 879 F.2d 1535, 1536 (7th Cir. 1989).

27. 112 S. Ct. 1652, 1653 (1992).

28. Id. at 1654, 1656.

29. 823 F.2d 1073, 1077–1078 (7th Cir. 1987), cert. dismissed, 485 U.S. 901 (1988).

30. Id. at 1078.

31. Id. at 1080.

32. *Harris v. Marsh,* 679 F. Supp. 1204, 1224–1226, 1267 (E.D.N.C. 1978).

33. *Jackson v. Carpenter,* 921 F.2d 68, 69 (5th Cir. 1991).

34. *Metro Broadcasting, Inc. v. F.C.C.,* 497 U.S. 547, 600 (1990).

35. Id. at 616.

36. Id. at 631–638 (Kennedy, J., dissenting), quoting *South Africa and the Rule of Law* 37 (1968) (publication of the South African Government).

37. 468 U.S. 364, 402–403 (1984).

38. 488 U.S. 469, 477–480, 507 (1989).

39. Id. at 541, 555.

40. 498 U.S. 146, 150–153, 155 (1990).

41. William F. King, ed., *Classical and Foreign Quotations* (New York: Thomas Whittaker, 1889), p. 326.

42. Enid Welsford, *The Fool: His Social and Literary History* (Garden City: Doubleday, 1961); John Doran, *History of Court Fools* (1858; reprint, New York: Haskell House, 1966).

43. Feinberg, *Introduction,* p. 254.

44. Id., pp. 168–169.

45. Juvenal, *Satires,* p. 59; Gilbert Highet, *The Anatomy of Satire* (Princeton: Princeton University Press, 1962), p. 39.

46. Robert C. Elliott, *The Power of Satire: Magic, Ritual, Art* (Princeton: Princeton University Press, 1960), p. 85; Feinberg, *Introduction,* p. 216.

47. Lewis, *Babbitt;* Mencken, *Notes;* Aldous Huxley, *Brave New World* (London: Chatto & Windus, 1932); George Orwell, *Nineteen Eighty-Four* (New York: Harcourt Brace & World, 1949), pp. 203, 211.

48. Feinberg, *Introduction,* p. 210.

49. Edward Bloom and Lillian D. Bloom, *Satire's Persuasive Voice* (Ithaca: Cornell University Press, 1979), p. 205.

50. See, e.g., Alexander Bickel, *The Least Dangerous Branch: The Supreme Court at the Bar of Politics* (Indianapolis: Bobbs Merrill, 1962); John Hart Ely, *Democracy and Distrust: A Theory of Judicial Review* (Cambridge: Harvard University Press, 1980); Laurence Tribe, *American Constitutional Law,* 2d ed. (Mineola, NY: The Foundation Press, 1988), pp. 1451–1474.

51. David M. O'Brien, *Storm Center: The Supreme Court in American Politics,* 2d ed. (New York: Norton, 1990), p. 131.

52. *Merritt v. Faulkner,* 823 F.2d 1150, 1157 (7th Cir.), cert. denied, 464 U.S. 986 (1987); see also *McKeever v. Israel,* 689 F.2d 1315, 1323 (7th Cir. 1982); *Free v. United States,* 879 F.2d 1535, 1536 (7th Cir. 1989).

53. 60 U.S. 393, 407, 410, 411 (1856).

54. 83 U.S. 130, 138–139, 140, 142 (1872).

55. 130 U.S. 581, 592–596, 606 (1889).

56. 432 U.S. 464 (1977).

57. 410 U.S. 113 (1973).

58. *The The New Republic,* February 15, 1993, pp. 21, 22, 24 (reviewing Marian W. Edelman, *The Measure of Our Success: A Letter to My Children and Yours*).

59. Linda Chavez, "Just Say Latino," *The New Republic,* March 22, 1993, pp. 18–19.

60. "Bilingualism," *The Economist,* May 22, 1993, p. 32; Abigail M. Thernstrom, "Bilingual Miseducation," *Commentary,* February 1990, p. 44; Michelle Maglalang, "A Day to Remember What it Means to be American," *Boulder Daily Camera,* July 5, 1993, p. 2C, col. 1.

61. "Ways and Means," *Chronicle of Higher Education,* March 17, 1993, p. A23.

62. 488 U.S. 469, 493, 495–501 (1989).

63. 109 U.S. 3, 25 (1883).

64. Midge Decter, "How the Rioters Won," *Commentary,* July 1992, pp. 18–19.

65. "Notebook," *The New Republic,* March 1, 1993, p. 8.

66. Charles Whalen and Barbara Whalen, *The Longest Debate: A Legislative History of the 1964 Civil Rights Act* (Washington: Seven Locks Press, 1985).

67. 438 U.S. 265, 298 (1978).

68. E.g., *Sheet Metal Workers v. EEOC,* 478 U.S. 421, 500 (1986); *Fullilove v. Klutznick,* 448 U.S. 448, 530 n.12 (1980); *Wygant v. Jackson Board of Education,* 476 U.S. 267, 276 (1986).

69. 481 U.S. 279, 285, 297, 315–317, 319 (1987).

70. E.g., Adam Nagourney, "Homophobia; Clinton and Gays," *The New Republic,* January 4 & 11, 1993, p. 16; John Leo, "We Need Not Endorse Everything We Tolerate," *Boulder Daily Camera,* August 10, 1992, p. 7A, col. 1. See also "Editorial, Medical Corrections," *National Review,* March 15, 1983, p. 18.

71. E. g., Editors, "The Immigrants," *The New Republic,* April 19, 1993, p. 7; Peter Brimelow, "Tired? Poor? Huddled? Tempest-Tossed—Rethinking Immigration," *National Review,* June 23, 1992, p. 7.

72. Editors, "Race on Campus," *The New Republic,* February 18, 1991, p. 46; George Will, "'Compassion' on Campus," *Newsweek,* May 31, 1993, p. 24; Robert Lerner and Stanley Rothman, "Newspeak, Feminist Styles," *Commentary,* April 1990, p. 54; Richard Bernstein, "The Rising Hegemony of the Politically Correct," *New York Times,* October 28, 1990, p. A1; Dinesh D'Souza, *Illiberal Education: The Politics of Race and Sex on Campus* (New York: Free Press, 1991), pp. 140–146; Nadine Strossen, "Regulating Racial Speech on Campus: A Modest Proposal?" *Duke Law Journal* 1990 (1990): 484.

73. 448 U.S. 297, 318 (1980).

74. 476 U.S. 267, 274–276 (1986).

75. D'Souza, *Illiberal Education,* pp. 47–51, 56–64, 82–95, 112–118, 157–167, 184–190, 230–242; Dinesh D'Souza, "The New Segregation on Campus," *Commentary,* Winter 1991, p. 22.

76. John Leo, "Attack on White Males Starting to Get Ugly," *Boulder Daily Camera,* April 22, 1993, p. B3, col. 1.

77. Cal Thomas, "After Gay Rights, What?" *Boulder Daily Camera,* April 27, 1993, p. 7B, col. 2.

78. Jack Kisling, "No ... Uh ... Men Need Apply," *Denver Post,* May 4, 1993, p. B9; Christina Hoff Sommers, "Sister Soldiers: Live from a Women's Studies Conference," *The New Republic,* October 5, 1992, p. 29.

79. Derrick Bell, *And We Are Not Saved* (New York: Basic Books, 1987).

80. 494 U.S. 872, 878–882, 888–889 (1990).

81. 488 U.S. 469, 505–506 (1989).

82. 481 U.S. 279, 315–317 (1987).

83. Martin Luther King, Jr., *Why We Can't Wait* (New York: New American Library, 1964).

About the Book and Authors

Forty years after school integration became the law of the land, African-American poverty, isolation, and despair are as deep as ever. Thirty years after the environmental revolution of the 1960s, our environment continues to deteriorate. Why have these and so many other hopeful revolutions failed?

Focusing on the crucial discipline of the law, *Failed Revolutions* casts light on the many forces working against meaningful social change. Through the construction of authority, the marginalization of dissenting views, and institutions designed to replicate established opinion, the legal profession systematically blocks not just the possibility of change but even our ability to imagine it.

In this engaging, learned, and sharply-argued book, Delgado and Stefancic show how we derail even our most sincere reform efforts. They reveal the defenses, brakes, and conservative impulses that work to undermine the realization of revolutionary goals. The result is a theory of social regression but not a counsel of despair. With understanding come tactics for reformers that can still make a difference.

Charged with passionate and lucid eloquence, *Failed Revolutions* will be of particular interest to lawyers and legal scholars, but its wide implications make it valuable reading for any citizen concerned with the possibility of social reform.

Richard Delgado is Charles Inglis Thomson Professor of Law at the University of Colorado. He is the author of many articles on critical race theory and "outsider" law. **Jean Stefancic** is a research associate at the University of Colorado Law School. Delgado, one of the founders of critical race theory, is coauthor of *Words That Wound: Critical Race Theory, Assaultive Speech, and the First Amendment* (Westview, 1993). Stefancic writes on legal scholarship and law reform. Both have won numerous awards and recognitions, including a 1993 Rockefeller Foundation Bellagio grant under which they completed this book.

Index